To TEAL

with Love from

Geoh

Xmas 1993

x

The Daily Telegraph
FLAT RACING
YEARBOOK

The Daily Telegraph
FLAT RACING
YEARBOOK

THE COMPLETE ILLUSTRATED REVIEW OF THE 1991 SEASON AND PREVIEW OF 1992 PROSPECTS

COMPILED BY SEAN MAGEE
PHOTOGRAPHS BY ED BYRNE

HEADLINE

First published in 1991
by HEADLINE BOOK PUBLISHING PLC

10 9 8 7 6 5 4 3 2 1

British Library Cataloguing in Publication Data

Magee, Sean
    The Daily Telegraph flat racing yearbook.
    I. Title
    798.4
    ISBN 0-7472-0485-3

Designed and produced by the Pen & Ink Book Company Ltd,
Huntingdon, Cambridgeshire

Printed and bound in Great Britain by Butler & Tanner Ltd, Frome,
Somerset

HEADLINE BOOK PUBLISHING PLC
Headline House
79 Great Titchfield Street
London W1P 7FN

Frontispiece: **Generous at home.**

CONTENTS

INTRODUCTION

The 1991 Flat season was a memorable one.

Generous, Suave Dancer and, most spectacularly, Arazi gave individual displays which will be remembered for a long time by anyone who saw them. Many of the big races produced wonderful finishes – Mystiko and Lycius in the Two Thousand Guineas, Environment Friend and Stagecraft in the Eclipse, Kooyonga and Shadayid in the Coronation Stakes. Then there were remarkable human achievements from such as Pat Eddery and Darryll Holland, Alan Munro and Lester Piggott, Paul Cole and Jack Berry.

The aim of this book is to record, in words and in Ed Byrne's photographs, the flavour of the racing year in 1991 – not only the big races but also the personalities and some of the issues – and look forward to 1992.

The text describing the main races and meetings (which is by Sean Magee) was written as the season progressed, and it was not possible to make significant alterations subsequently. Those parts of the book thus concentrate on the immediate reaction to the runnings of the big races, and the reader may have fun assessing the validity of connections' post-race comments in the light of subsequent events!

Complete results are provided for Group One races in Britain, along with the Irish Derby and the Prix de l'Arc de Triomphe. For the other major races, the first four places are given. For foreign races, distances are provided in their British equivalents. Breeding details are supplied for winners of the English Classics and the Prix de l'Arc de Triomphe.

Some of the articles in this volume by *The Daily Telegraph* racing writers originally appeared in the newspaper: these are indicated by the date of first publication at the foot of the piece. All other contributions were written specifically for the book.

The Daily Telegraph Flat Racing Yearbook has been produced under great pressure of time in order to make it available as soon as possible after the end of the season, and it is a tribute to the optimism, resilience and good humour of those concerned with its production that the various parties involved are still (at least at the time of writing this) on speaking terms.

Thanks are particularly due to Marilyn Warnick and Lynne Brannan at *The Daily Telegraph*; to Alan Brooke and Celia Kent at Headline; to Tim Peagram and Tony Leonard at Pen & Ink; and to Phillip Jones, who compiled the results boxes and breeding details.

A debt of gratitude is also owed to all the contributors to the book, and especially to Ed Byrne, whose performance was the photographer's equivalent of Arazi in the Breeders' Cup Juvenile.

S.M.

REVIEW OF THE 1991 FLAT SEASON

J.A. McGrath

The 1991 Flat season belonged to Generous, the dual Derby hero who captured the King George VI and Queen Elizabeth Diamond Stakes, right up until the dying stages in November. Then, at the unlikely venue of Churchill Downs, Kentucky, we witnessed a performance that was to overshadow all others throughout a long, eventful racing year.

Arazi is the colt's name, and his staggering effort in overcoming all obstacles in his path to score an exciting, breathtaking win in the Breeders' Cup Juvenile left observers on track with that numbing, spine-tingling feeling, only experienced when watching something quite extraordinary.

If Arazi's backstretch acceleration had been scripted in Hollywood it would have been slung out for the writer having exercised far too much licence. It was not so much *Trainer* as a scene from a Mickey Rooney film. The new Secretariat? Perhaps, but one thing is for certain; Arazi, the French-trained colt, is certain to become the first horse ever to top America's Experimental Handicap and the International Classification.

Remarkably, Arazi proved as dominant on turf against European juveniles as he was superior against America's best when he met them on his first outing on dirt. We have a lot more than Desert Orchid and cups of Wincanton's ox-tail soup to keep us warm this winter; we also have instalments of the Arazi story. Will he go for the American Triple Crown? Will he

tackle the *Durby/Darby* double? And where will he start his campaign?

One of the drawbacks in having voting for Horse of the Year completed in its entirety at the very end of the season is that what is freshest in the mind has the greatest influence. For instance, Shadayid's exciting win in the General Accident One Thousand Guineas and Mystiko's triumph in the Two Thousand Guineas back in early May seem an eternity ago and in an overview the merit of their respective performances on those days may be undervalued.

Generous is another good example. Paul Cole maintained the utmost confidence in the colt throughout the season, training and placing him quite expertly, and yet because of a crushing defeat in the Prix de l'Arc de Triomphe, a series of marvellous efforts at Epsom, The Curragh and Ascot immediately lose a little of their glitter.

There were many highlights; many extraordinary occurrences. For example, who would ever have thought the day would arrive when a colt trained in New York would jet over to lift one of Europe's Classics? Fourstars Allstar, trained by the former jump jockey Leo O'Brien, did – in mid-May – scoring narrowly in the Airlie-Coolmore Irish Two Thousand Guineas at The Curragh under a cool, confident ride from his 25-year-old partner Mike Smith, who hails from Hot Springs, Arkansas. The Atlantic is, all of a sudden, shrinking.

Jet Ski Lady hammered home the point yet again that it is folly to dismiss

any Classic contender from Jim Bolger's stable on the mountain in Co Carlow. Allowed to be sent off at 50-1, Jet Ski Lady proceeded to pulverise her opposition, scoring by ten lengths from Shamshir, with Shadayid clearly failing to stay the trip but an honourable third, nevertheless.

Pat Eddery, first jockey to Saudi Prince Khalid Abdullah, again dominated in the riding ranks, with Willie Carson at times threatening to break the Irishman's firm grip on the title but never quite doing it. The milestones for Eddery were riding his 3,000th winner at Bath in July, and later in the season landing the Coalite St Leger at Doncaster aboard French colt Toulon, who had failed inexplicably in the Derby at Epsom. So, Eddery, 39, takes his place on the honour board alongside Sir Gordon Richards, Lester Piggott, Willie Carson and Doug Smith, the only others to reach the 3,000-winner mark on British tracks.

Eddery, who gladly shuns the limelight and public attention, is deserving of the accolades that come his way. Just ask any punter in the land, and the answer is always the same: I get a run for my money when Pat is aboard. It makes little difference to him whether it is the Derby at Epsom or a seller at Nottingham; in a finish there is the same element of enthusiasm, and at times desperation.

Alan Munro was the other jockey to capture headlines. The first occasion when Munro 'surfaced' was in May at Chester when it was announced that he would ride for Prince Fahd Salman under contract for the remainder of the season. Under the agreement Munro was expected to partner the sixty or so horses Prince Fahd had in training in Britain with Paul Cole, Sir Mark Prescott, Michael Bell, Henry Candy and William Jarvis. Of all those horses, none was to prove as attractive a prospect as Generous, who at that stage of the season had finished fourth in the Two Thousand Guineas and was beginning to shape as a Derby contender of some note.

The man to lose out was Richard Quinn, who only the season before had won the Irish Oaks on Knight's Baroness and the Irish St Leger on Ibn Bey, both for Prince Fahd. Quinn won new popularity with the dignified manner in which he accepted this reverse and in late August gained consolation – of sorts – with big-race wins on Affair Of State in the lucrative Tattersalls Breeders Stakes at The Curragh, and then 24 hours later aboard Snurge in the Grand Prix de Deauville Lancel.

Another 'loser' was Gerald Mosse, the former champion apprentice of France who won the 1990 Prix de l'Arc de Triomphe on Saumarez. Mosse made the rather curious decision during 1991 to accept an offer from Patrick-Louis Biancone to ride as his retained jockey in Hong Kong from September onwards. This meant severing his relationship with Francois Boutin. The timing could scarcely have been worse, as no sooner had Mosse given Biancone his verbal agreement than virtually everything in the Boutin yard started winning – and winning good races to boot.

If Mosse did not have second thoughts the day he landed a lucrative double on Priolo in the Prix du Moulin and Arazi in the Prix de Salamandre, he must certainly have done some soul-searching when the brilliant Arazi cruised home in the Grand Criterium on the eve of the Arc. History records that Pat Valenzuela, from California, had the mount when Arazi blitzed his

rivals in the Breeders' Cup Juvenile at Churchill Downs, and under the new agreement between owners Allen Paulson and Sheikh Mohammed, Steve Cauthen will be in the saddle in Europe. Almost certainly, Mosse would have retained the mount – even in America – if he had remained loyal to Boutin and owner Jean-Luc Lagardere.

Paul Cole, thanks to his expert handling of Generous, Dilum and Culture Vulture, just to mention the obvious stars, spring-boarded to the top of the trainers' table for the first time. He was deserving of every success he enjoyed with his stars, as apart from placing and training them to perfection, he had the happy knack of keeping the public informed via the media, an important ingredient in the recipe of marketing racing to a wider audience.

The winner factories operated by Jack Berry and Richard Hannon showed no signs of slowing down on production, and it really does remain one of the deepest mysteries of the Turf why neither of these highly successful and talented trainers does as yet enjoy the support of one of the more committed Middle Eastern owners.

It is perhaps a comment on the game overall that Sheikh Mohammed was the leading owner despite having by his standards a fairly miserable season, with minimal success in Group One races considering the fact that most of the horses he purchases are bred along Classic lines. Hailsham, trained by Clive Brittain, captured the Derby Italiano for Sheikh Mohammed but it was not until October that Keen Hunter, prepared by John Gosden, carved a second Group One notch on the belt in the Prix de L'Abbaye de Longchamp, followed by Tel Quel in the Champion Stakes at Newmarket for trainer André Fabre.

Sheikh Hamdan Al Maktoum expressed his discontent regarding the finances of racing when interviewed on television late in the season. Sheikh Hamdan called for more help from government – and bookmakers for that matter – in getting more money back

into racing. He announced that he would be increasing the numbers of horses he owns that are sent to France, Australia and America, making the point that no matter how wealthy an owner, he has to have a reasonable chance of covering expenses if he has a decent horse. This is not possible in Britain, although Sheikh Hamdan points out that his small but select band of runners in Australia are self-financing, thanks to that country's healthy racing climate (comparatively, that is).

Nevertheless, Sheikh Hamdan's grey filly Shadayid lived up to the immense promise she displayed at the back end of the previous season, sprinting clear when hitting the rising ground to land the General Accident One Thousand Guineas at Newmarket. There were fears that she would boil over in the parade, but this she survived and went on to score by two lengths from the gutsy Irish filly Kooyonga. This was to be the first of the memorable clashes between these two talented fillies, and the finish featured racing's two galloping grandfathers, Willie Carson and Lester Piggott, fighting an intense battle to the line. It could easily have been the same twenty years ago.

Marju, the half-brother to Sheikh Hamdan's wonder filly of the previous year, Salsabil, was sent off favourite for the General Accident Two Thousand Guineas two days later but this time there was no happy follow-up. Marju failed dismally, and subsequent testing and veterinary examination showed that the colt – brilliant on his day – was suffering from a stifle problem that was to interrupt his entire campaign for the remainder of the season. Marju finished 11th, well behind Clive Brittain's popular winner Mystiko, who staked his claim in the Free Handicap and lived right up to expectations with an exciting victory under Michael Roberts. The fact that Lady Beaverbrook owned the winner was seen as a positive boost to British owning and breeding, and despite the disappointment of her seeing Minster Son injured in the Derby at Epsom previously, Lady B was persuaded to let Mystiko take his chance in the Classic at Epsom. This was also the mission for Generous, the chestnut colt with the flaxen mane who had won the Dewhurst at long odds the previous season and went into the first colts' Classic not fully wound up. The fact that he was doing his best work at the finish of the Guineas was seen by some as a significant pointer to Epsom, especially as he was from the family of the ill-fated and talented Triptych.

One of the many admirable qualities Clive Brittain boasts is confidence in himself and his horses. Call him the supreme optimist, if you like, but genial Clive was uncharacteristically deflated three days before the Ever Ready Derby when it was discovered that Mystiko was lame and consequently doubtful for the big one. Under constant veterinary supervision, Mystiko made it to Epsom but despite bullish reports from both Brittain and Roberts, it was obvious that the grey colt was never going to win. Although the setback at the eleventh hour could not have helped, it was more a case of Mystiko not staying the mile and a half, going out like a light after rounding Tattenham Corner.

As Mystiko was making his exit out the back door, Generous was slipping into top gear, finishing full of running to set up a tidy lead after taking it up over two furlongs out. Powering away, Generous had five lengths to spare at the line from Marju, with Star of Gdansk seven lengths away third. Form students were later to point out that Generous had pulverised rivals, eight of whom were later to record Group wins. The form looked very strong.

As Derbys go, this was a good one, and it was no surprise to see Generous travel to The Curragh at the end of June and record a victory in which he was forced to do it the hard way, taking it up a mile from home and then out-gunning his main opponent, Suave Dancer, in the process. Suave Dancer, with Walter Swinburn replacing the injured Cash Asmussen, did not look fully mature and left the impression that given his chance later in the season, he could go on to better things. He was to get his chance later at Longchamp.

We had become accustomed to expecting something a little special from Generous, whose enthusiastic owner Prince Fahd Salman won growing popularity with his openness about his colt.

As great as expectations were, nothing could really have prepared us for Generous' effort in the King George VI and Queen Elizabeth Diamond Stakes at Ascot in July when he showed incredible acceleration to draw clear for victory by a race-record distance of seven lengths. Sanglamore, the French Derby winner of the previous season, held on to take second, with Rock Hopper third and Terimon fourth. The announcement that there would be one final run before retirement – in the Prix de l'Arc de Triomphe – was regretfully received by racing enthusiasts, but at least there would be one last chance to witness the ways of the new wonder horse. 'There are Derby winners that come and go but Generous just keeps on improving,' was how Cole summed up the colt, who looked the spitting image of Grundy, another memorable King George hero.

The Prix de l'Arc de Triomphe never fails to generate maximum interest, and with Generous to make his swansong on foreign soil, the British presence at Longchamp was strong, even with a recessional chill in the air.

To all intents and purposes, Generous travelled well, looked well, and although drawn wide, the field was not over-large by Arc standards and it did not seem inconceivable that the colt would be able to work over towards the inside rail without undue stress. But those thoughts, although along the right lines for a normal race, did not hold true for the Arc, as competitive and tough a race as we are likely to see on the Flat each season.

Generous did have to work to get a handy position and he was never travelling within himself. The extra gear that he displayed at Ascot could not be found and Suave Dancer, expertly ridden by Cash Asmussen, came from the back of the field, pouncing on the outside two furlongs out and sprinting away for an exciting victory. News that Suave Dancer is to stay in training at four is welcome, and this colt, prepared to the minute by John Hammond, must have excellent prospects of repeating his Arc success. He was stronger at the end of the season than he had been in the summer and why shouldn't he be even stronger in 1992?

Toulon, who ran on powerfully for fourth, is another Classic winner (St Leger) who should be on the short list for the Arc at four; he has all the attributes necessary to make his presence felt at Longchamp in October.

But as we start thinking of the 1992 Flat season, there will always be memories of Generous and Arazi, the two equine stars in a year that was special in many ways.

HIGHLIGHTS
OF 1991

Arazi and Pat Valenzuela after the Breeders' Cup Juvenile.

Horses of the year: Generous (Alan Munro, *above***) and Suave Dancer (Cash
Asmussen).**

Two of the year's best fillies: *above,* **Kooyonga, winner of the Irish One Thousand Guineas and the Coronation Stakes, and** *below,* **Culture Vulture, who won two Group One races within the space of nine days – the Brent Walker Fillies' Mile and the Prix Marcel Boussac.**

Four of the great racing moments of 1991. *Above,* **Generous leaves Marju in his wake in the Derby, and** *below,* **Environment Friend (near side) just gets the better of Stagecraft in the Eclipse Stakes.**

Above, **Marju (near side) and Second Set fight out the finish of the St James's Palace Stakes at Royal Ascot,**
and *below,* **Suave Dancer shoots away from Magic Night and Pistolet Bleu in the Prix de l'Arc de Triomphe.**

Owners. *Above,* **Fahd Salman leads in Generous after the colt's demolition of Suave Dancer in the Irish Derby.**

Below, **Christopher Wright with jockey Richard Quinn and trainer's wife Vanessa Cole after Culture Vulture had won the Prix Marcel Boussac at Longchamp.**

Owner Henri Chalhoub with Cash Asmussen and trainer John Hammond after Suave Dancer's Arc.

Trainers. Jack Berry beat Henry Cecil's 1987 record for the fastest fifty and the fastest century.

Paul Cole was champion trainer for the first time, thanks to the achievements of the likes of Generous, Culture Vulture, Dilum and Magic Ring.

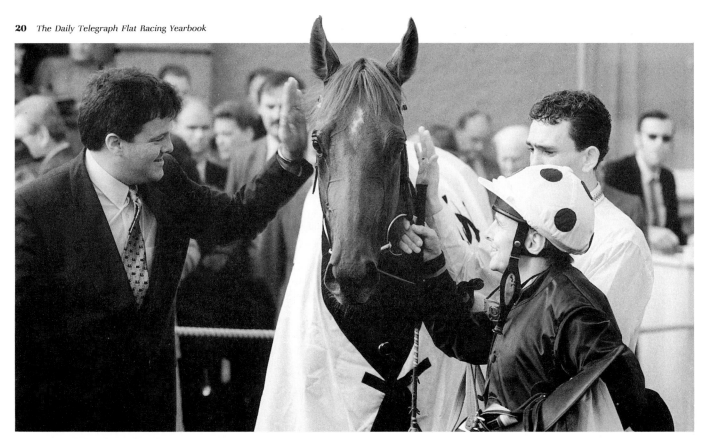

Above: **Peter Chapple-Hyam, the new master of Manton, had a memorable first season as a trainer, winning the Dewhurst Stakes with Dr Devious and the Middle Park with Rodrigo De Triano – seen here (with jockey Willie Carson) after his victory in the Champagne Stakes at Doncaster.**

Below: **Alex Scott (left) with Jim Bolger after his Possessive Dancer had beaten Bolger's Jet Ski Lady in the Irish Oaks to land Scott the then biggest win of his training career. Jet Ski Lady's Epsom victory was Bolger's first English Classic win.**

Lester Piggott with trainer Michael Kauntze after Kooyonga had finished second to Shadayid in the One Thousand Guineas at Newmarket.

Kooyonga's subsequent achievements helped County Meath-based Kauntze – formerly assistant to Vincent O'Brien – to his best ever season.

Pat Eddery riding Morocco to victory in the Tattersalls Maiden Auction Series Qualifier at Bath on 22 July. This was rapturously hailed by racegoers as Eddery's 3,000th victory – until careful consideration of the records suggested that it was his 2,999th. Never mind, the 3,000th – if such it was – came an hour later on Sure Victory.

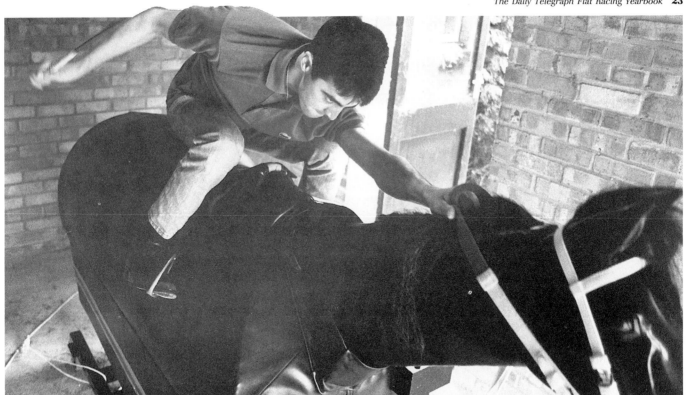

Practice makes perfect. Alan Munro, who was hardly out of the headlines for one reason or another during 1991, hard at work *(above)* **astride the mechanical horse on which he rides regular work in his garage, and** *(below)* **enjoying the fruits of such dedication when, with Paul Cole looking on, he collects his award from Her Majesty The Queen after Generous had won the King George VI and Queen Elizabeth Diamond Stakes at Ascot.**

Alan Munro and Lester Piggott *(above)* **before the Irish Derby at The Curragh. Richard Quinn** *(below)* **lost the job as jockey to Generous's owner** Fahd Salman to Munro in the spring, but remained stoical: 'I am disappointed but you have to go forward.'

Darryll Holland, the Champion Apprentice and the riding find of the season.

One of the season's most promising apprentices was Francis Norton, here winning the Ebor Handicap at York on Deposki.

A SELECTION OF THE LESS OBVIOUS MEMORIES OF 1991

21 March

On the morning of the start of the Flat the racing press points out that the Henry Cecil colt Desert Sun, quoted in some bookmakers' lists at 33–1 for the Derby, is not entered in the race.

23 March

Lester Piggott rides his first all-weather winner in Britain on La Masaas at Lingfield, then doubles his tally on First Stage.

The death is announced of Kingston Town, one of the greatest Australian horses of the century. He was fourteen. Kingston Town won thirty of his forty-one starts, netting A$1,605,790 in prize money.

24 March

Pat Eddery is named Jockey of the Year and Flat Jockey of the Year for 1990 at the Jockeys' Association Awards Ceremony in London.

25 March

Jockeys Alan Munro and Allan Mackay are fined for starting from the wrong stalls in a claiming race at Folkestone.

27 March

Gods Solution wins the Gods Solution Handicap at Catterick. It is the the sixth time that the ten-year-old grey has won the race (first named after him in 1990, when he was third), and his eighth course victory. Successful on eleven of his eighty-three outings, he now retires to stud.

28 March

A front-page 'exclusive' in *The Sun* reports the claim that Shergar is alive and well and living in the Channel Islands. Stephen Chappell, deputy chairman of Lloyds Bloodstock Committee, confirms that Lloyds have been approached by a middle-man looking to negotiate a £365,000 'finder's fee', but pronounces himself 'very sceptical'.

Full Cry at Brighton is Steve Cauthen's first winner under his new retainer with Sheikh Mohammed.

2 April

The death is announced of Royal Palace, put down at the National Stud at the age of 27. The oldest surviving English Classic winner, Jim Joel's horse won the Two Thousand Guineas and Derby in 1967 and was unbeaten as a four-year-old, when his victories included the Coronation Cup, the Eclipse Stakes (in a famous finish with Taj Dewan and Sir Ivor) and the King George VI and Queen Elizabeth Stakes.

5 April

Eddie Maple, the American jockey with over 4,000 winners to his credit, has his first ride in Britain, on Another Bob at Kempton. Now based in Italy, Maple is retained by Antonio Balzarini (owner of the Arc winner Carroll House).

8 April

The runners in the John & Aileen Oswell Westminster Agency Handicap at Newcastle encounter an unusual distraction in running: four deer are grazing on the course five furlongs out, but they scatter as the leading horses bear down on them.

Bill Shoemaker, the American jockey who has ridden more winners than any rider in history, is seriously injured after driving his car off the road in California.

11 April

Trainers in North Yorkshire reveal that they have a problem in disposing of their stable muck heaps, now that Middlebrook Mushrooms in Selby are using a synthetic alternative to naturally produced muck.

12 April

The stewards of the Australian Jockey Club allow the two-year-old Tierce, winner of the A$2 million Golden Slipper Stakes at Rosehill on 23 March, to keep the race despite his post-race dope test showing positive to the prohibited substance lignocaine. Trainer Clarrie Connors is fined A$10,000 for administering the substance in a mouthwash.

18 April

Julie Cecil sends out her first winner as a trainer when Golan Heights, ridden by Lester Piggott, wins the Remy Martin VSOP Cognac Handicap at Newmarket. On the same card, Alfaares provides Major Dick Hern with his first winner from his new Kingwood yard at Lambourn.

19 April

North Wind becomes the first winner to carry the colours of Princess Michael of Kent when taking the Spring Maiden Stakes at Newbury. At the same course strong winds prevent Steve Cauthen's plane landing, and he forfeits all his booked rides.

Julie Cecil's first winner as trainer: Lester Piggott drives Golan Heights (left) clear of Steve Cauthen on Local Derby in the Remy Martin VSOP Cognac Handicap at Newmarket on 18 April.

At Oaklawn Park, USA, Bayakoa fails to set a new world record for earnings by a mare when running unplaced in the Apple Blossom Handicap, her final race before retirement.

25 April

The Jockey Club's annual statistical report reveals that there are 11,109 horses in training, compared with 11,059 in 1990.

The Jockey Club announces the alternative venues for Group One races, should abandonment cause removal from the home track: for instance, should the Derby be abandoned on the first Wednesday in June, it would be run at Epsom on Oaks day or, failing that, the following week at Newbury.

Laz Barrera, who trained Affirmed to win the American Triple Crown in 1978, dies in California, aged 66. Among the many famous horses he handled was J. O. Tobin, who had been trained by Noel Murless at Newmarket and was sent to the USA after a brilliant two-year-old career in 1976.

7 May

A footnote in betting history: the Tote Credit Trophy at Chester marks the launch of the Tote's first new bet for fourteen years, the Trio, in which punters select the first three in the nominated race in any order. The six who correctly nominate Arany, Langtry Lady and Dorset Duke get back £722.90 for a £1 stake.

8 May

The Levy Board announces a £6 million cut in prize money for 1992, following the forecast in March that a cut of £2½ million (plus £500,000 off the Daily Grant scheme) would be necessary. It is anticipated that the Board will fund 1,000 fixtures, compared with 1,136 in 1991. (But see 17 May . . .)

The 1990 Ascot Gold Cup winner Ashal dies of a peritonitis-related illness. Owned by Sheikh Hamdan Al Maktoum and trained by Tom Jones, Ashal won five of his eleven starts.

11 May

Alan Munro's first ride as retained jockey to owner Prince Fahd Salman proves a winning one – Ausherra in the Marley Roof Tile Oaks Trial at Lingfield Park.

16 May

Ladbrokes publish an analysis of the top fifty races in 1990 in terms of betting turnover. The top ten are:

Grand National
Derby
Cheltenham Gold Cup
Two Thousand Guineas
King George VI and Queen Elizabeth
   Diamond Stakes
Champion Hurdle
Lincoln Handicap
One Thousand Guineas
Triumph Hurdle
Oaks

The top fifty contains no two-year-old races at all, and queries the status of some of the traditional 'big betting races' of the season: the Royal Hunt Cup was thirty-first, and the Ebor Handicap forty-sixth.

17 May

The Levy Board revises it financial cutbacks, announcing the need to save almost £8.7 million, £1 million from 1991 prize money and the remainder from savings in 1992, when a proposed 'two-tier' fixture list would come into operation: 836 'criteria' fixtures would be fully funded by the Board, and up to 300 non-criteria fixtures (such as evening and additional Saturday and Bank Holiday meetings) would be partially funded.

18 May

Frankie Durr annnounces that he is to retire from training. A successful Flat jockey for thirty-four years, he had held a trainer's licence since 1979, with the brilliant sprinter Ahonoora his best-known charge.

20 May

Sizzling Saga at Folkestone is trainer Jack Berry's fiftieth winner of the season, breaking by twenty days the record for the fastest half-century set by Henry Cecil in 1987.

Jockeys' riding fees are to be increased from 29 July: Flat jockeys will receive £52.40 per ride (plus VAT if applicable), National Hunt jockeys £71.50.

29 May

Lester Piggott is suspended for two days by the Swiss Jockey Club after being deemed to have failed to ride out Gilt Premium for second place at Dielsdorf the previous Sunday.

30 May

Alex Greaves rides a double on Love Jazz and Mac Kelty at Hamilton Park and becomes the first girl rider on the Flat ever to ride out her claim.

3 June

The death is announced at the age of eighty-five of Freddie Maxwell, trainer of the Ascot Gold Cup winners Pandofell (1961) and Fighting Charlie (1965 and 1966). Other well-known horses he handled included Young Christopher, Merry Madcap and Cawston's Pride.

4 June

A survey of betting trends carried out by Southampton University on behalf of Ladbrokes reveals that women are becoming less intimidated by 'male-dominated' betting shops. A man's average stake in a betting shop is £3.73, a woman's £2.03.

7 June

Wolverhampton racecourse is sold to Ron Muddle, owner of Southwell, for £3.2 million.

14 June

Gary Carter becomes only the second jockey in Britain to ride winners at three different racecourses in one day. He lands the 1.30 at Southwell on Luvly Jubly, the 4.40 at York on Romany Rye, and the 8.15 at Doncaster on Able Susan.

15 June

Peter O'Sullevan, doyen of racing commentators, is awarded a CBE in the Queen's Birthday Honours List. He was already an OBE. John Egginton, Clerk of Works at Sandown Park, Kempton Park and Epsom for twenty years, is awarded the British Empire Medal.

25 June

Ryan Jarvis, trainer of such horses as Constantia, Front Row, the Ebor winner Lomond and the sprinter Absalom, dies at the age of seventy–seven. On the same day the death is announced of another famous trainer, Tony Dickinson.

3 July

The Aga Khan's attempt to have the Jockey Club's disqualification (after a positive dope test) of his 1989 Oaks winner Aliysa fails in the High Court.

8 July

The death is announced of Balidar, champion European sprinter in 1970 and a successful sire. The 1975 Two Thousand Guineas winner Bolkonski came from his first crop, and his daughter Balidaress is the maternal grandam of Shadayid.

9 July

The Home Secretary's response to the Home Affairs Committee's report on racing kills off any chance of Sunday racing in the foreseeable future, the Government maintaining the line that racing cannot take place without betting shops opening.

11 July

Calumet Farm, one of the most famous Thoroughbred studs in the world, files for bankruptcy in Lexington, Kentucky, with liabilities of $118 million.

15 July

Steve Cauthen pays his first visit to the Northern Ireland track Down Royal, where he wins the Ulster Harp Derby on Dowland.

16 July

Japanese golf course magnate Yoshio Asakawa pays $2.6 million for a Nureyev colt at the Keeneland July Select Sale.

17 July

Jack Berry smashes Henry Cecil's record for training the fastest century of winners when Our Fan wins at Hamilton Park. Cecil had taken six days longer to notch up one hundred winners in 1987.

18 July

Details are announced of the new entry scheme for the Derby. A prospective runner can be entered as a yearling by 11 December 1991, or as a three–year–old by 3 March 1993. The cost to run for a yearling entrant will total £5,000, for a three–year–old entrant £14,000.

19 July

Mrs Moss, dam of such horses as Jupiter Island, Precocious, Pushy and Krayyan, is put down at Woburn at the age of twenty–two.

20 July

Jack Berry scores the most valuable win of his career when Paris House wins the £100,000 Newbury Sales Super Sprint Trophy.

22 July

Pat Eddery notches his three thousandth win in Britain when Sure Victory lands the Keynsham Handicap at Bath. His three thousand took him twenty–two years and three months, faster than Gordon Richards (over twenty–four years), Lester Piggott (almost twenty–seven years), Willie Carson (nearly twenty–eight years) and Doug Smith (over thirty–three years).

25 July

Darryll Holland loses his claim when winning the Raggetts Selling Stakes at Brighton on Kirby Opportunity. In the following race, the Brighton Summer Challenge Cup, he notches his first win as a fully fledged jockey, on Corrin Hill.

30 July

The Hull City AFC Handicap at Beverley is declared void after starter John Mangles sends the runners off 1 minute 6 seconds early.

5 August

Gainesway Farm in Kentucky announces the retirement from stud duties of seventeen–year–old Blushing Groom, who had failed to get in foal any of the twenty–three mares he covered in 1991. Among his offspring are Nashwan, Rainbow Quest, Snow Bride and Al Bahathri.

7 August

Calls for the overnight declaration of jockeys are stepped up after Barney Curley–trained Threshfield, without a jockey in the morning papers, wins the Jim Gundill Memorial Handicap at Pontefract – ridden by Lester Piggott.

It is announced that the Aga Khan intends to take the Aliysa case to the Court of Appeal.

9 August

At the fourth annual meeting of Classic Thoroughbreds, chairman Dr Michael Smurfit tells shareholders that the 'noble experiment has failed', and it is decided that the company will cease operations at the end of the season.

10 August

Trainer David Murray Smith and jockey Chris Rutter have their first Pattern victory when Amigo Menor wins the Phoenix Sprint Stakes (Group Three) at Leopardstown.

11 August

Lester Piggott wins his first Derby since returning from retirement – the Swedish version on the German–trained Tao.

12 August

Jim Bolger lands the first five–timer of his training career, winning with all of his five runners at Gowran Park.

17 August

Premier Touch, trained by David Barron and ridden by Alex Greaves, wins the Great St Wilfrid Handicap at Ripon, relieving the ring bookmakers of a reported £80,000 in major bets. But the colt's improved performance compared with his last run leads the local Stewards to refer the change in form to the Jockey Club. (See 24 September.)

30 August

Sir Ivor, winner of the 1968 Two Thousand Guineas and Derby, is retired from stud duties at the age of twenty–six. Among his offspring were Bates Motel, the Arc winner Ivanjica, and two winners of the Irish One Thousand Guineas, Lady Capulet and Godetia.

Zino, winner of the 1982 Two Thousand Guineas, dies at stud in France following an attack of colic.

1 September

The Arlington Million is won by Tight Spot, the 9–5 favourite. Algenib is second and Kartajana, who was trained at Newmarket by Michael Stoute before the removal from Britain of the Aga Khan's horses, third.

5 September

The death is announced of Dan Prenn, owner of such horses as Showdown, Folle Rousse, Balidar, Balliol, Dione and Ballyhot.

8 September

A story in the *Sunday Express* that racehorse owners are to go on strike to further their claims for a better deal are dismissed as 'a dead fag–end' by David Pipe, the Jockey Club's Director of Public Affairs.

The first episode of the new BBC Television series *Trainer* attracts over nine million viewers.

10 September

At the inaugural meeting of the National Association for the Protection of Punters (NAPP), Lord Oaksey is voted president.

19 September

Jockey John Lowe rides his one thousandth winner in Britain when partnering Lobinda to a short–head victory in the Willerby Maiden Fillies' Stakes at Beverley.

20 September

Sarcita, ridden by apprentice Brett Doyle, wins the Ladbroke Ayr Gold Cup easily from Tbab and Dominuet, and thus becomes the first horse to complete the Portland Handicap–Ayr Gold Cup double since Jon George in 1977. She is David Elsworth's first winner at Ayr and Doyle's first ride there, and she breaks the course record for six furlongs, which has stood since 1969.

Trainer Richard Hannon scores his first century of winners when Knight Of Mercy wins the ITB Handicap at Newbury, and . . .

21 September

Richard Hannon passes the £1 million prize money mark for the first time when Showbrook beats Jeune and Dilum in the Rokeby Farms Mill Reef Stakes at Newbury.

23 September

Former champion apprentice Jimmy Bleasdale announces his retirement from the saddle because of continuing side effects of head injuries. He had ridden 414 winners in Britain.

24 September

Trainer Barney Curley announces that he is to refuse to tell the press who is to ride his horses, as part of his effort to win a better deal for racing – 'And if the jockey tells the press, I'll take him off the horse.'

Trainer David Barron and jockey Alex Greaves are fined £600 and £750 respectively over the running of Premier Touch in the Donny Dormouse Handicap at Doncaster on 25 July and the horse's subsequent performance when winning the Great St Wilfrid Handicap at Ripon on 17 August.

26 September

The death is announced of Ravinella, winner of the One Thousand Guineas and the Poule d'Essai des Pouliches (the French One Thousand Guineas) in 1988. The six–year–old mare, who was in foal to Nashwan, suffered an internal haemorrhage of the gutoral pouch.

1 October

Willie Carson rides the first five winners – Aasff, Perjury, Lord Oberon, Subsonic and Najeb – at Newcastle, the course where he rode six in one day in June 1990.

Trainer Richard Hannon passes the £1 million prize money mark for the first time when Willie Carson and Showbrook (near side) take the Rokeby Farms Mill Reef Stakes at Newbury on 21 September. Struggling to keep up with the winner is Dilum, who came third.

4 October

The Tattersalls Highflyer Yearling Sales end with the total takings the lowest in any year since 1978, mainly on account of a severe reduction in the number of lots offered. The average sale is 82,132 guineas, slightly lower than in 1990, and the median of 50,000 guineas likewise shows a small drop. The top price of the Sale is 380,000 guineas, paid by Sheikh Mohammed's Darley Stud Management for a colt by the Arc winner Rainbow Quest out of the Sun Chariot Stakes winner Triple First. This is the lowest top price since 1978.

8 October

The official Jockey Club statistics for the period January to September bolster the notion that racing is in decline. The number of two–year–olds in training is down to 2,964 from 3,398 in the same period in 1990, and the total number of horses in training on the Flat down to 6,114 from 6,578. The number of new owners registered falls from 2,445 to 1,878, nearly a quarter.

Walter Swinburn breaks his left collarbone and left wrist in a fall from Hamanaka almost in the shadow of the winning post at Redcar, and is sidelined for the rest of the season.

20 October

It is confirmed that Dancing Brave, winner of the Two Thousand Guineas, Eclipse Stakes, King George and Arc in 1986, has been sold to continue his stud career in Japan.

Lester Piggott at The Curragh with his daughter Tracy, now a racing presenter for RTE. Piggott is in the colours of Classic Thoroughbreds, the multi-million pound syndicate headed by Vincent O'Brien, John Magnier, **Michael Smurfit and Robert Sangster, which in August announced its intention to cease operations at the end of the season.**

Trials for the Two Thousand Guineas.
Above: **Ganges (Gerard Mosse) beating Lycius (Steve Cauthen, near side) in the Prix Djebel at Maisons-Laffitte.**

Below: **Mystiko and Michael Roberts come home alone in the Ladbroke European Free Handicap at Newmarket.**

Trials for the One Thousand Guineas.
Above: **Crystal Gazing (Lanfranco Dettori) wins the Shadwell Stud Nell Gwyn Stakes at Newmarket from Tetradonna (Steve Cauthen) and Lilian Bayliss (Walter Swinburn).**

Below: **Shadayid (Willie Carson, second left) starts to go clear of Chicarica (Walter Swinburn, left), Lee Artiste (Richard Quinn) and Only Yours (Pat Eddery) in the Gainsborough Stud Fred Darling Stakes at Newbury.**

The Guineas.
Above: **Entering the closing stages of the One Thousand, Willie Carson and Shadayid have flown as Lester Piggott and Kooyonga (in the sheepskin noseband) come to take second place off Crystal Gazing (Lanfranco Dettori).**

Below: **In a pulsating climax to the Two Thousand, Mystiko (Michael Roberts) holds off Lycius (Steve Cauthen) by a head.**

Two sides of the Chester May Meeting. An admonition against adultery, but (*below*) Absolution is at hand as the popular grey sprinter, ridden by David Nicholls, has the inside track in the Grahams Machinery Sales Handicap.

The race went to Breezy Day (Bruce Raymond) in the centre of the picture.

The Irish Guineas.
Above: **History is made in the Two Thousand as the American-trained Fourstars Allstar (Mike Smith, right) comes to collar Star Of Gdansk (Christy Roche).**

Below: **By contrast, Kooyonga is out on her own in the One Thousand.**

Alan Munro and Generous make their mark in the Derby.

The Derby field at Tattenham Corner. Michael Roberts and Mystiko still have the lead, with Arokat (Paul Eddery) trying to keep up and Generous poised behind them, coasting along in front of Hector Protector (Freddie Head, white cap) and Hokusai (Lester Piggott) on the rails. Marju (Willie Carson) is on the inside behind Hokusai and Star Of Gdansk (Christy Roche) on Marju's outside. But even at this stage, there's really only one horse in it.

Owner Fahd Salman leads in Generous after the Derby.

Other Epsom highlights.

Above: **In The Groove (Steve Cauthen) powers home in the Hanson Coronation Cup from Terimon (Michael Roberts, green cap), Rock Hopper (Willie Carson, light blue cap) and Quest For Fame (Pat Eddery, rails).**

Below: **Jet Ski Lady (Christy Roche) going to post for the Gold Seal Oaks in the style of an obvious winner.**

Royal Ascot, the first two days.
Above: **A stirring finish in the St James's Palace Stakes as Marju (Willie Carson, striped cap) heads Second Set (Lanfranco Dettori). Hokusai (Lester Piggott, left) is third.**

Below: **Eurolink The Lad (John Reid, no. 12) lands the Royal Hunt Cup from Operation Wolf (Michael Roberts, no. 10) and 1990 winner Pontenuovo (Willie Carson).**

Royal Ascot, the last two days.
Above: **Polish Patriot (Ray Cochrane, far side) gets up to short-head Chicarica (Willie Carson) in the Cork and Orrery Stakes.**

Below: **With time rapidly running out in the Hardwicke Stakes, Rock Hopper (Pat Eddery) goes for the gap between Spritsail (Willie Carson, rails) and Topanoora (Christy Roche).**

Ladies' days.
Above: **Steve Cauthen and Possessive Dancer edge past Christy Roche and Jet Ski Lady in the Kildangan Stud Irish Oaks at The Curragh.**

Below: **Sweet consolation at Ascot for Lydia Pearce (grey and blue stripes, centre). A year after controversially losing the prestigious Diamond Day ladies' race in the stewards' room, she and Susurration already have the Centenary Diamond Stakes sewn up as the field swings into the straight.**

Led by Robert Latham, Generous leaves the paddock to parade before the King George VI and Queen Elizabeth Diamond Stakes at Ascot.

The King George. At the turn into the straight (*above*) **Saddlers' Hall (Lester Piggott) on the inside, Generous (Alan Munro) and Sanglamore (Pat Eddery)** form the front rank, but the picture of equality is an illusion, and a few seconds later (*below*) Generous comes home in glorious isolation.

**THE COMPLETE ILLUSTRATED REVIEW OF THE
1991 SEASON AND PREVIEW OF 1992 PROSPECTS**

DONCASTER SPRING MEETING

Doncaster, 21–23 March 1991

Amenable (Alex Greaves) sails home in the Lincoln from St Ninian (Mark Birch).

In this age of all-weather racing, the Flat season officially begins on 1 January and ends on 31 December, but the opening of the turf season at Doncaster remains, for all but the most pedantic or sand-loving, 'the start of the Flat'.

The new term began with a 20–1 winner. Margs Girl, ridden by Joe Fanning and trained by Tommy Fairhurst, landed the Raceform Apprentice Handicap on Thursday 21 March by a short head from 10–1 shot Premier Dance. The other placed jockeys – Darren Biggs, Alex Greaves and Darryll Holland – would all make a significant impact in the early stages of the season, and it was only two days later that Alex grabbed the headlines.

The William Hill Lincoln Handicap, traditionally the first big betting race of the season, looked beforehand like being dominated by the draw. Everyone seemed to agree that horses drawn with low numbers – that is, on the far side of Doncaster's straight mile – would have a significant advantage, and Selaah (drawn 4) went off the 5–1 favourite.

But when Michael Stoute's colt having led for the first half of the race weakened rapidly inside the final half mile, the running was taken up by the second favourite, St Ninian. Scarcely had Mark Birch begun to calculate his percentage than Amenable and Alex Greaves, drawn 23 of the 25 runners and starting at 22–1, came steaming up the centre of the track to take the lead inside the final furlong and go on to win by one and a half lengths.

The result was doubly significant. The winner's immediate form before the Lincoln had been on all-weather surfaces, on which his trainer David Barron had made such an impact. Amenable had won five races on the sand since December 1990, including the Zodiac Handicap at Lingfield (then the most valuable all-weather race ever run in Britain). His Lingfield victory brought with it a seven-pound penalty for the Lincoln, without which he would not have had sufficient weight to get into the race. The six-year-old gelding was clearly extremely fit, but his high draw and a general sniffiness about all-weather form caused few punters to rate his chance seriously. His victory at Doncaster had many vowing to take all-weather form that bit more to heart.

But it was Amenable's jockey who made this such a memorable race. The twenty-two-year-old Alex Greaves had been acknowledged as a first-rate all-weather rider: on the day of the Lincoln she led the jockeys' table, and earlier that week had received an award as Most Promising Apprentice. But the Lincoln, for which she had put up three pounds overweight, was different: this was The Real Thing.

In coolly bringing Amenable past his rivals with a perfectly timed run, Alex Greaves not only landed the most valuable prize yet won by a lady jockey in Britain, but went a long way towards erasing the patronising epithet of 'Queen of the Sand'.

The Lincoln was her sixty-ninth winner, of which fifty-one had been on all-weather surfaces. But the significance of Amenable's victory was not lost on the rider: 'I hope that winning the Lincoln will knock on the head the theory that I'm just an all-weather jockey'.

On the day after the Lincoln, Alex Greaves travelled to London to accept the Lady Jockey of the Year Award at the Café Royal. It had been quite a weekend.

Owner Geoff Spink shows his appreciation to Alex Greaves.

William Hill Lincoln Handicap

23 March 1991

1 mile (going: soft)

1st: £45,878; **2nd:** £13,770; **3rd:** £6,635; **4th:** £3,068

1	AMENABLE	Alex Greaves	22–1
2	ST NINIAN	M. Birch	8–1
3	BAND ON THE RUN	L. Dettori	20–1
4	LINPAC WEST	K. Fallon	25–1

25 ran (Selaah 5–1 fav)

distances: 1½ lengths, ¾ length
time: 1 min. 42.75 secs

Winner owned by W. G. Spink, trained by T. D. Barron (Maunby, North Yorkshire), bred by C. A. Moore

Tote: win £24.80; places £5.60, £2.60, £2.90, £4.80; dual forecast £162.90

NEWMARKET
CRAVEN MEETING

Newmarket, 16–18 April 1991

Thanks: Lanfranco Dettori and Crystal Gazing after the Nell Gwyn Stakes.

At the Craven Meeting at Newmarket the season finally bursts into life, and Classic pointers abound – not always in the races where you most expect them.

The fixture opened with an eye-catching performance from Young Buster – in the Moller colours carried to Derby victory by his sire Teenoso. Such was the ease with which the colt stormed away from his rivals in the Constant Security Maiden Stakes that he entered the Derby reckoning, albeit at odds between 33–1 and 50–1.

A more likely Derby candidate emerged from the Museum Maiden Stakes which wound up the first day's card. This was Wakashan, trained by Henry Cecil for Sheikh Mohammed. The colt was immediately quoted at 20–1 to give his owner a first Derby victory.

In the event neither of the two maiden winners made it to Epsom.

But in any case the principal Classic interest on the first day of the Craven Meeting was in the Shadwell Stud Nell Gwyn Stakes, one of the more reliable trials for the One Thousand Guineas. Run over a furlong shorter than the Guineas itself just two weeks later, the Nell Gwyn has in recent years gone to such fillies as Flying Water, One In A Million, Fairy Footsteps, Pebbles and Oh So Sharp *en route* to greater glory in the Classic.

No one seriously thought that the 1991 renewal contained a horse to rank alongside those famous names, and with Shadayid already firmly established as One Thousand Guineas favourite at 11–8, the main interest in the Nell Gwyn centred around Luca Cumani's filly Crystal Gazing, who had been backed from 14–1 to 10–1 for the Guineas in anticipation of a big run in her trial.

Her band of supporters were not disappointed. Although still sporting her woolly winter coat – very sensible of her on a chilly Newmarket afternoon – Crystal Gazing won the race with the minimum of fuss, moving into the lead under a sympathetic ride from Lanfranco Dettori to beat Tetradonna.

Luca Cumani was happy enough – 'The impressive thing is that she came and took the leaders on the bridle' – but the performance was pleasing rather than scintillating, and its effect on the Guineas market was to shorten the favourite Shadayid as well as Crystal Gazing herself.

Dettori was full of praise for the filly: 'She is kind and sweet and perhaps even brilliant'. A fortnight later he would know whether he was right.

> ## "She is kind and sweet and perhaps even brilliant."

Meanwhile the second day of the Craven Meeting belonged to Lady Beaverbrook, Clive Brittain and Michael Roberts. Terimon now has a permanent niche in racing quizzes as the longest-priced horse ever placed in the Derby (500–1 when second to Nashwan), but started to get clear of that 'freak result' tag when winning the Earl of Sefton Stakes under Ray Cochrane in 1990. Now a five-year-old, he repeated the feat in 1991 when Michael Roberts drove him through in the dying strides of a pulsating race to beat Emperor Fountain, Ruby Tiger and Duke Of Paducah. The distances: neck, neck, and neck.

Half an hour later thoughts were on future, not past, Classics as Roberts – still sporting Lady Beaverbrook's beaver brown and maple leaf green colours – powered home in the Ladbroke European Free Handicap astride a strapping grey horse with distinctive rocking-horse markings and a vast voracious stride.

This was Mystiko. The way he galloped on relentlessly to beat David Elsworth's good filly Zigaura made many think that it was not altogether fanciful to imagine his becoming the first horse to win the Free Handicap and the Two Thousand Guineas since Privy Councillor thirty years ago.

> ## "He's so good I can't afford to put other horses in with him."

Certainly the connections would not dissuade such a view. Trainer Clive Brittain admitted: 'We've been very excited about him and I don't see why he shouldn't win the Guineas. Mystiko has to do almost all his work on his own and he is out before the pheasants get up. He's so good I can't afford to put other horses in with him.'

And jockey Michael Roberts reported that the grey had given him the best feel of any colt he had ridden since the brilliant Mtoto.

We can't say we weren't told.

But at the time others seemed to have stronger Guineas claims, and two of them clashed in the Charles Heidsieck Craven Stakes on the final day of the meeting.

Desert Sun was not exactly a talking horse but was not far off. Despite having had only one run in his life – when winning a twenty-two runner Doncaster maiden in October 1990 – the Henry Cecil-trained colt had been backed for the Two Thousand Guineas from 33–1 to 3–1 favourite. (He was also in some ante-post lists for the Derby – for which he was not even entered!)

Marju had likewise had only one run. He had landed a small race at York in the September of his two-year-old career, but so impressive had his victory been that he had scarcely pulled up before long-range backers were rushing for the ante-post slips. On form alone it was impossible to tell how good Marju would turn out to be. On

Willie Carson pushes Marju clear of Hokusai (Lester Piggott) and Desert Sun (Pat Eddery) in the Craven Stakes . . .

breeding it seemed certain that he would be very good indeed: he was a half-brother (by Last Tycoon) to Salsabil, the filly whose deeds had lit up the summer of 1990.

But there was a cloud on Marju's horizon, for trainer John Dunlop had made no secret of the fact that the horse had not been working as well as he would have liked.

"I was full of doubts but now I am full of hope."

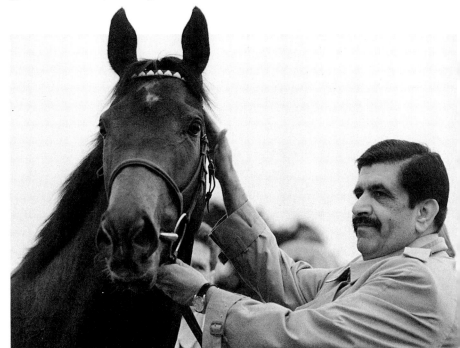

. . . and Sheikh Hamdan Al Maktoum has yet another Classic favourite on his hands.

Talking horses express themselves in different ways. While Desert Sun was supposedly catching pigeons on the gallops, Marju was working sluggishly. The race would give some answers, and they had better be heeded: after all, four of the previous six Craven winners – Shadeed, Dancing Brave, Doyoun and Tirol – had gone on to take the Two Thousand Guineas.

Early on in the race it looked as if John Dunlop's pessimistic prognosis of Marju's chance was about right, as he stayed in the rear. But when inside the final two furlongs Willie Carson asked him for an effort, he responded with such acceleration – despite this being only the second race of his life – that he was instantly installed as the Guineas favourite.

John Dunlop's reaction was that of a man pleased to have been proved wrong: 'I wouldn't have been surprised if he had finished last rather than first after the way he had done some of his work this spring. But he is a lovely horse with a charming character. Yes, I was full of doubts but now I am full of hope.'

That is what these early-season Classic trials do – they leave some connections full of hope, while others have to come to terms with their swans being geese.

Shadwell Stud Nell Gwyn Stakes (Group 3)

16 April 1991

7 furlongs (going: good to firm)

1st: £21,276; **2nd:** £7,878; **3rd:** £3,714; **4th:** £1,542

1	CRYSTAL GAZING	L. Dettori	6–4 fav
2	TETRADONNA	S. Cauthen	5–1
3	LILIAN BAYLISS	W. R. Swinburn	5–2
4	CLOCHE D'OR	M. Roberts	14–1

5 ran

distances: ¾ length, 1 length
time: 1 min 25.29 secs

Winner owned by Mrs A. L. Chapman, trained by L. M. Cumani (Newmarket, Suffolk), bred by Aston House Stud Inc, USA

Tote: win £2.50; places £1.50, £1.90; dual forecast £8.50

Ladbroke European Free Handicap (Listed Race)

17 April 1991

7 furlongs (going: good to firm)

1st: £25,232; **2nd:** £7,556; **3rd:** £3,628; **4th:** £1,664

1	MYSTIKO	M. Roberts	11–1
2	ZIGAURA	C. Asmussen	15–2
3	JUNK BOND	W. R. Swinburn	4–1 jt fav
4	FLYING BRAVE	J. Reid	4–1 jt fav

11 ran

distances: 3½ lengths, neck
time: 1 min 25.72 secs

Winner owned by The Dowager Lady Beaverbrook, trained by C.E.Brittain (Newmarket, Suffolk), bred by Kingston Park Stud Inc, USA

Tote: win £15.20; places £3.10, £2.00, £1.80; dual forecast £89.00

Charles Heidsieck Champagne Craven Stakes (Group 3)

18 April 1991

1 mile (going: good to firm)

1st: £23,193; **2nd:** £8,613; **3rd:** £4,082; **4th:** £1,717

1	MARJU	W. Carson	11–2
2	DESERT SUN	Pat Eddery	6–5 fav
3	HOKUSAI	L. Piggott	8–1
4	HAILSHAM	S. Cauthen	33–1

8 ran

distances: 1½ lengths, head
time: 1 min 36.12 secs

Winner owned by Hamdan Al Maktoum, trained by J. L .Dunlop (Arundel, W. Sussex), bred by Kilcarn Stud, Ireland

Tote: win £5.70; places £2.00, £1.40, £1.70; dual forecast £5.50

NEWBURY
SPRING MEETING

Newbury, 19–20 April 1991

The day after Marju had seemingly solved the Two Thousand Guineas, it was the turn of his illustrious stablemate Shadayid to make her seasonal reappearance. Like Marju before her she was owned by Sheikh Hamdan Al Maktoum, trained by John Dunlop, and ridden by Willie Carson, and her more recent career had borne a strong resemblance to another famous filly with the same connections, Salsabil.

Like Salsabil, Shadayid had set the seal on a fine two-year-old season by winning the Prix Marcel Boussac on Arc day at Longchamp, and was going for Newbury's Gainsborough Stud Fred Darling Stakes as her preliminary for the One Thousand Guineas. Salsabil had won the Fred Darling in 1990 by six lengths, and Shadayid's performance in disposing of her six rivals was only a little less impressive.

Starting the 11–8 on favourite, Shadayid pulled hard early on in the race, but quickened well approaching the final furlong to go away without undue pressure and win by three lengths from Silver Braid, with Chicarica a neck further back in third. 'I could have won by six lengths if I'd really pushed her', said Willie Carson.

One major bookmaker brought Shadayid's odds for the One Thousand Guineas down to 7–4 on, and the first Classic looked as good as over.

Not so the second, for although Marju's Craven Stakes victory had thrust him to Two Thousand Guineas favouritism, Sheikh Hamdan Al Maktoum and Willie Carson had another string to their Classic bow in the shape of Mukaddamah, trained by Peter Walwyn. This colt had been beaten a short head by Peter Davies in the Racing Post Trophy at Doncaster in October 1990, and his reappearance in the Singer & Friedlander Greenham Stakes was keenly awaited – though

Shadayid (Willie Carson) goes clear in the Gainsborough Stud Fred Darling Stakes.

Rock Hopper (Pat Eddery) nips past Warm Feeling (Michael Hills) in the John Porter.

not since Wollow in 1976 had the Greenham winner gone on to take the Two Thousand Guineas.

Like Mukaddamah, Bog Trotter had been runner-up in one of 1990's top two-year-old events, narrowly beaten by Generous in the Dewhurst Stakes. For the Greenham, trainer William Haggas had engaged as jockey his father-in-law Lester Piggott, who had the colt smartly out of the stalls and was never headed. Mukaddamah moved up to challenge with a quarter of a mile to run, but could not peg back the battling Bog Trotter and went under by three quarters of a length.

The proximity in third place of Shalford – a genuine but by no means top-class colt – cast doubt on the value of the form, although the race was memorable enough for its exposition of Piggott's skills. All the wonted strength was evident as he drove Bog Trotter home, and half an hour earlier the Newbury crowd had seen The Long Fellow in a different but no less effective mode when winning the Miller Construction Spring Cup on Lady Murless's St Ninian, who cruised into the lead two furlongs out and won comfortably.

Other highlights of a fascinating afternoon were the victories of the well-bred fillies Umniyatee (by Green Desert out of dual Classic winner Midway Lady) and Ristna (by Kris out of Roussalka) in their respective maiden races, together with a highly promising performance in the Lanes End John Porter Stakes by Rock Hopper. Another superbly bred horse (previously, his dam Cormorant Wood won the Champion Stakes and the Benson and Hedges Gold Cup), Rock Hopper had been favourite for the 1990 Derby after winning the Derby Trial at Lingfield, but had then been sidelined for the rest of the season by a leg injury. The way Pat Eddery pushed him through the gap between Warm Feeling and Rudjig in the final furlong of the John Porter hinted he would be a force to be reckoned with in 1991.

Lester Piggott (black cap) pushes Bog Trotter between Mukaddammah (Willie Carson) and Shalford (Bruce Raymond) to land the Greenham Stakes.

Gainsborough Stud Fred Darling Stakes (Group 3)

19 April 1991

7 furlongs 60 yards (going: good)

1st: £21,315; **2nd:** £7,940; **3rd:** £3,782; **4th:** £1,613

1	SHADAYID	W. Carson	8–11 fav
2	SILVER BRAID	J. Williams	12–1
3	CHICARICA	W. R. Swinburn	5–1
4	LEE ARTISTE	T. Quinn	7–1

7 ran

distances: 3 lengths, neck
time: 1 min 32.18 secs

Winner owned by Hamdan Al Maktoum, trained by J. L. Dunlop (Arundel, W. Sussex), bred by Shadwell Farm Inc, USA

Tote: win £1.60; places £1.30, £4.40; dual forecast £10.00

Singer & Friedlander Greenham Stakes (Group 3)

20 April 1991

7 furlongs (going: good)

1st: £22,134; **2nd:** £8,207; **3rd:** £3,879; **4th:** £1,620

1	BOG TROTTER	L. Piggott	4–1
2	MUKADDAMAH	W. Carson	Evens fav
3	SHALFORD	B. Raymond	20–1
4	SAPIEHA	S. Cauthen	4–1

7 ran

distances: ¾ length, 1½ lengths
time: 1 min 26.49 secs

Winner owned by B. Haggas, trained by W.J. Haggas (Newmarket, Suffolk), bred by Wayside Stable, USA

Tote: win £4.00; places £1.80, £1.30; dual forecast £2.60

SANDOWN PARK
APRIL MEETING

Sandown Park, 26–27 April 1991

All to play for the Trusthouse Forte Mile as Steve Cauthen on In The Groove comes to collar the white-faced Zoman (Richard Quinn) and Aldbourne (Lester Piggott).

The unusually high number of top-class older horses kept in training for 1991 added an extra edge to the early weeks of the season, as familiar names made their reappearances.

The Friday of the Sandown Park April Meeting saw the seasonal bow of In The Groove, David Elsworth's fine, strapping filly who in 1990 had won the Irish One Thousand Guineas, the International Stakes and the Champion Stakes. Somewhat controversially, the 1990 International Classifications had rated her superior to Salsabil, but whatever the rights or wrongs of that decision, her 1991 debut was awaited with a mixture of excitement and

trepidation. Had she trained on? Would she justify the decision to keep her in training?

In The Groove faced four opponents in the Trusthouse Forte Mile, the first Group Two race of the season. Among them was Zoman, who had won the Prix du Rond-Point at Longchamp on Arc day 1990. Prince Fahd Salman's colt took over as favourite for the Mile as In The Groove's price drifted from 5–4 to 15–8.

But that walk in the market seemed so misguided during the race. Steve Cauthen pulled In The Groove to the outside as Zoman made for the line and she got upsides the colt without

apparent effort, then had to be shown the whip as she tired in the closing stages. But it was a highly satisfactory run first time out, and had Cauthen enthusing: 'She's a smasher, and her engine is as good as ever.'

On the same card was the Harvester Graduation Stakes, won in 1990 by the subsequent Prix de l'Arc de Triomphe winner Saumarez. The 1991 running was significant primarily for the seasonal debut of Sheikh Mohammed's Suomi, who had attracted a good deal of interest in the betting market for the Derby on the strength of a single juvenile victory at Newcastle, a welter of Newmarket rumour, and an obvious enthusiasm for his prospects from jockey Lanfranco Dettori. When asked in a radio interview at the beginning of the season which horse he most looked forward to riding, Dettori had plumped for Suomi.

The Sandown race severely deflated such enthusiasm, for Suomi had only momentarily looked a likely winner, before fading to finish fourth of the five runners behind the filly Fife.

As Sandown rang to the sound of ante-post vouchers being ripped up, Suomi's trainer Luca Cumani launched a scathing attack on the Newmarket work-watchers whose glowing reports of the horse's gallops had supposedly precipitated the Derby support:

'Personally I'm not too disappointed because I wasn't expecting too much. It seems to be the reporters who know best and hype up the horses. . . . They start writing up horses as world-beaters just because they have seen them finish in front in a gallop. But I can tell you that it is difficult enough for trainers to interpret home gallops.'

Noble Patriarch (John Reid, right) lands the Gordon Richards Stakes from Stapleford Manor (Lanfranco Dettori, rails) and Karinga Bay (Brian Rouse).

The Thresher Classic Trial: Hailsham (Michael Roberts, left) withstands the challenge of Jaffa Line (Cash Asmussen), with Jahafil (Willie Carson) plugging on in third.

All five runners in the Harvester Graduation Stakes were owned by three of the Maktoum brothers – a sign of the times. Another sign of the times came on the Saturday, when the three-year-old handicap previously known as the Esher Cup was run as the T.G.I. Friday's Stakes. This was of course Whitbread Gold Cup day, and though the controversial finish to the big steeplechase between Cahervillahow and Docklands Express dominated the headlines, there was plenty of good Flat racing.

The CCH Gordon Richards Stakes, a natural early-season target for older middle-distance horses, attracted a lesser field than usual, but still produced a fine performance from Noble Patriarch, who finally collared Stapleford Manor and Karinga Bay in the last furlong and won going away.

The field for the Thresher Classic Trial, previously won by such as Troy, Henbit, Shergar, Shahrastani and Old Vic, also seemed sub-standard. But the race climaxed in a stirring finish between Sheikh Mohammed's colt Hailsham and the filly Jaffa Line, who ran on courageously in the final furlong but failed by a short head.

Hailsham may not have been a Shergar or an Old Vic, but he did go on to win a Derby – the Derby Italiano at Rome in May.

Trusthouse Forte Mile (Group 2)

26 April 1991

I mile (going: good to soft)

Ist: £37,818; **2nd:** £14,034; **3rd:** £6,642; **4th:** £2,786

1	IN THE GROOVE	S. Cauthen	15–8
2	ZOMAN	T. Quinn	7–4 fav
3	ALDBOURNE	L. Piggott	13–2
4	BOLD RUSSIAN	Pat Eddery	100–30

5 ran

distances: I length, 2½ lengths
time: I min 42.45 secs

Winner owned by Brian Cooper, trained by D. R. C. Elsworth (Whitsbury, Hants), bred by Capt. John Macdonald-Buchanan

Tote: win £2.60; places £1.40, £1.30; dual forecast £2.10

CCH Gordon Richard EBF Stakes (Group 3)

27 April 1991

I mile 2 furlongs (going: good)

Ist: £23,550; **2nd:** £8,750; **3rd:** £4,150; **4th:** £1,750

1	NOBLE PATRIARCH	J. Reid	7–1
2	STAPLEFORD MANOR	L. Dettori	2–1 fav
3	KARINGA BAY	B. Rouse	100–30
4	ETON LAD	Pat Eddery	9–1

6 ran

distances: 3 lengths, ¾ length
time: 2 mins 07.33 secs

Winner owned by Peter S. Winfield, trained by J. L. Dunlop (Arundel, W. Sussex), bred by Andrew Bradley
Tote: win £7.30; places £3.10, £1.90; dual forecast £8.10

Thresher Classic Trial (Group 3)

27 April 1991

I mile 2 furlongs (going: good)

Ist: £35,460; **2nd:** £13,177; **3rd:** £6,250; **4th:** £2,637

1	HAILSHAM	M.Roberts	3–1
2	JAFFA LINE	C.Asmussen	6–1
3	JAHAFIL	W.Carson	11–8 fav
4	EVASIVE PRINCE	Pat Eddery	4–1

5 ran

distances: short head, 4 lengths
time: 2 mins 08.30 secs

Winner owned by Sheikh Mohammed, trained by C.E.Brittain (Newmarket, Suffolk), bred by Kingsbrook Farm, Canada
Tote: win £4.10; places £2.00, £2.00; dual forecast £14.70

GENERAL ACCIDENT
ONE THOUSAND GUINEAS

Newmarket, 2 May 1991

The grandfathers who came first and second in the One Thousand Guineas – Willie Carson on Shadayid on the right and Lester Piggott on Kooyonga on the left – return to unsaddle.

Shadayid was the eighth odds-on favourite for the One Thousand Guineas since the war. Of the previous seven, three had been beaten.

Undaunted by the warning in the statistics, punters piled into Shadayid, with only the Nell Gwyn winner Crystal Gazing and Michael Stoute's Dartrey – the winner of one race as a two-year-old and not yet seen out in 1991 – starting at less than 10–1 to beat her. David Elsworth saddled three runners: Zigaura (second to Mystiko in the Free Handicap but still a maiden), Silver Braid (second to Shadayid in the Fred Darling but without any obvious hope of turning the tables), and Tetradonna (second to Crystal Gazing in the Nell Gwyn): Ladbrokes offered 6–1 against Elsworth training the winner. Kooyonga from Ireland (winner in April of the Leopardstown Trial) and Once In My Life from France (most recently a winner of a Listed race at Evry) formed the overseas challenge.

But whichever way you looked at it, Shadayid was the only rational choice on form. One of the few possible chinks in her armour was that she might become upset during the prolonged preliminaries to the race. She was attended by two lads in the paddock but did not get on edge, and she took the parade calmly enough. The chink was being closed up.

The 100–1 outsider Gentle Aria led for the first half mile before rapidly weakening as the race began in earnest and Cloche D'Or took over. Then, with over two furlongs to go, Only Yours took up the running, but it was clearly on sufferance. Willie Carson had kept Shadayid covered up in the early stages before starting to make a forward move with three furlongs to go, and with a quarter of a mile left he launched her challenge. She took the lead over a furlong out and her jockey had to do no more than push her out to secure the prize.

Behind her Kooyonga (who had been backed from 33–1 in the morning to a starting price of 14–1) ran on to take second place and give Lester Piggott a

Shadayid (Willie Carson) storms clear.

slice of the glory on his first ride in an English Classic since Lanfranco in the 1985 St Leger. Piggott's ride gave the 1991 One Thousand Guineas the arcane distinction of having grandfathers riding the first two horses home.

Third place went not to a grandfather but to a teenager: Frankie Dettori made good progress on Crystal Gazing coming to the final furlong, but well though Luca Cumani's filly ran, she had no answer to the acceleration of the favourite.

Shadayid had won the Guineas by two lengths, whereas Salsabil in 1990 had won by just three quarters of a length. Comparisons were clearly in order. Shadayid's had been a supremely efficient win, but respect rather than rapture was the principal reaction. 'Salsabil was more relaxed', said Willie Carson, 'but Shadayid is not stupid. She is hyper. Not a worrier; she's just got plenty of energy.'

The statisticians pronounced. Shadayid was the first grey filly to win the One Thousand Guineas since Nocturnal Spree in 1975. John Dunlop was the first trainer to win the race in successive years since Noel Murless in 1967–8, and Carson the first jockey to do so since Charlie Elliott in 1931–2.

Of more urgent import was the possibility of Shadayid's taking her chance in the Oaks, the major question mark being that about her stamina.

Her sire Shadeed had been a superb miler, winning the Two Thousand Guineas and the Queen Elizabeth II Stakes in 1985 and finishing third behind Cozzene in the Breeders' Cup Mile. Although bred to get middle distances, Shadeed had been very headstrong, and a measure of this trait had apparently been passed on to Shadayid. Her dam Desirable had won the Cheveley Park Stakes in 1983 before the following year finishing third to Pebbles in the One Thousand Guineas, second in the ten-furlong Nassau Stakes and a close-up fourth to Sadler's Wells in the ten-furlong Phoenix Champion Stakes. She had been sold to Sheikh Hamdan's Shadwell Estate Company in 1986 for $1.6 million.

So doubts about Shadayid's getting the mile and a half of the Oaks were at the very least well-founded. Only the race would tell.

Meanwhile the lingering memories of the One Thousand Guineas itself were of the pent-up Shadayid being quietly contained and soothed in the paddock and the parade, and then coming away from her field with a devastating surge to land the Classic with the minimum of fuss. As Willie Carson said, 'When she hit the rising ground, she grabbed hold of it and won well.'

Whatever the future held, she was a brilliant filly that day.

General Accident One Thousand Guineas Stakes (Group I)

2 May 1991

1 mile (going: good)

1st: £109,821; 2nd: £40,539; 3rd: £19,369; 4th: £7,823; 5th: £3,011; 6th: £1,087

1	SHADAYID	W. Carson	4–6 fav
2	KOOYONGA	L. Piggott	14–1
3	CRYSTAL GAZING	L. Dettori	6–1
4	ONCE IN MY LIFE	C. Asmussen	20–1
5	ONLY YOURS	B. Raymond	50–1
6	DARTREY	S. Cauthen	9–1
7	ZIGAURA	R. Cochrane	16–1
8	LEE ARTISTE	T. Quinn	66–1
9	POSITIVE ACCLAIM	D. Nicholls	150–1
10	CLOCHE D'OR	M. Roberts	66–1
11	TETRADONNA	J. Reid	18–1
12	GENTLE ARIA	W. R. Swinburn	100–1
13	SILVER BRAID	J. Williams	20–1
14	MIRANDA JAY	Pat Eddery	33–1

14 ran

distances: 2 lengths, 1 length
time: 1 min 38.18 secs

Winner owned by Hamdan Al Maktoum, trained by J. L. Dunlop (Arundel, W. Sussex), bred by Shadwell Farm Inc, USA

Tote: win £1.70; places £1.20, £1.70, £2.10; dual forecast £9.60

SHADAYID grey filly, born 10 April 1988	Shadeed	Nijinsky	Northern Dancer
			Flaming Page
		Continual	Damascus
			Continuation
	Desirable	Lord Gayle	Sir Gaylord
			Sticky Case
		Balidaress	Balidar
			Innocence

PLEASE SAVE US FROM ALL THE 'MUKS'

John Oaksey

What's in a name? How much, if at all, does it matter that, to a vast majority of the punters whose money she carried to victory in the One Thousand Guineas, Shadayid's name ('Long Strength') is both meaningless and difficult to pronounce?

One answer, of course, is that, within certain limits and regulations (Appendix E to the Rules of Racing), a racehorse's name is strictly its owner's business. Foreigners have always been perfectly entitled to name their own horses in their own language, and I don't suppose that many of those who worshipped 'The Flying Filly' in 1924 knew the meaning or significance of Mumtaz Mahal.

In the same way, names have always been a matter of taste. The historic fact happens to be that remarkably few really good horses have been lumbered with really unattractive or tasteless names.

I, for one, never fancied the sound of 'Pot-8-os', but he won thirty-five races and sired two Derby winners, one of them called Waxy.

Then, last year, Snurge made us all swallow our sneers, bringing nothing but glory to his owner's unglamorous schoolboy nickname.

As a rule, nevertheless, from Diomed to Quest For Fame, Lottery to Golden Miller, racing's rolls of honour have tended to read like poetry.

When the Maktoum brothers decided to name seven of their horses Mukaddamah, Mukddaam, Mudaffar, Mukaafah, Mujtahid, Mujaazif and Mujadil, they no doubt had what seemed to them good literal, linguistic or romantic reasons.

But, in the immortal words of Bertie Wooster: 'There's some rough work done at the font, Jeeves.' However musical and significant they may sound to Arab ears, names like those are, in Britain, the phonetic equivalent of seven-pound penalties. They also seem to ignore at least two of Appendix E's nine 'names not available' rules.

Besides the quarter-of-a-million-plus names that are officially protected, or appearing in the current (biennial) list, 'names that are similar in spelling or pronunciation to those already registered' are not allowed, nor are 'names which would cause confusion in the administration of racing or betting.'

Just ask a few commentators how confusing names can be these days – especially when various 'Muks' and 'Mujs' are distinguished only by sashes or the colour of their riders' caps.

But Rules apart, it seems to me that there are many other good reasons for a respectful suggestion (which is all it can be) that owners in general, and the Sheikhs in particular, might look again at their naming policy. The best names, I believe, should, if possible, derive from – and therefore suggest – the names of the horse's sire and dam.

That does *not* just mean using three letters from one and three from the other. Even if some of the same letters are used, the object should always, as far as possible, be to combine the sense of meaning of the parents' names.

Northern Dancer's dam, Natalma, was a ballerina, and the Northern part came, presumably, and quite justifiably, from the 'Arctic' half of his sire Nearctic's name. In any case, what a

blessing that the twentieth century's most successful stallion should have such a 'creative' name.

Hence, Nijinsky, Nureyev, Sadler's Wells – the names trip off the tongue.

Despite the worldwide success of Northern Dancer's huge numbers of descendants, the rich vein of attractive theatrical and musical names is never likely to run out. But finding a name which sounds good, fits, and stays in the memory ought to be not only the first, but also one of the greatest pleasures of ownership. It certainly was for the late Lord Rosebery. What a joy, for example, to think of Monty, for a colt by Bellicose out of Exhibitionist.

Nowadays, you have to ask permission to use the name of a living person. I wonder if Rosebery asked permission of one particularly flamboyant Indian Maharajah before he gave his name Baroda to a colt by His Highness out of Frantic.

No permission, presumably, was needed, or anyway granted, for the offspring of Blandford and a mare by the name of Lady Southampton. It was simply and memorably called Unlikely.

The naming game can cut both ways, mind you. Just after my father was made Lord Oaksey for presiding over the Nuremberg Trials, Gerry Fielden, who had a colt by Fair Trial out of Loaded Dice, asked permission to call it Oaksey.

My father, a keen chooser of names himself, was delighted. But when, just to make sure, he asked the Lord Chancellor, the answer, perhaps not altogether surprisingly, was an emphatic 'No'.

The Daily Telegraph, 6 May 1991

NEWMARKET SPRING MEETING

Newmarket, 2–4 May 1991

Although dominated by the two Guineas races (pages 45–7 and 50–2), the Newmarket Spring Meeting provided several other memorable contests.

On the Thursday – One Thousand Guineas day – the proceedings started with a power failure, so that the opening Hintlesham Hall May Stakes was run without any racecourse commentary and without photo-finish. The latter would have been needed if functioning, for the race produced a stirring climax, with Lester Piggott getting Lord Weinstock's Saddlers' Hall home by a neck. Two races later the Pretty Polly Stakes went to Michael Roberts on the Clive Brittain-trained Gussy Marlowe.

Friday's feature was the General Accident Jockey Club Stakes, which brought together a good-class field. But the race was completely dominated by Rock Hopper, who confirmed the promise of his comeback race at Newbury (page 41) with a superb turn of foot. At the line he beat Mountain Kingdom by only a neck, but there was never any doubt about his superiority. The big middle-distance prizes of the summer beckoned. The Friday also saw the racecourse debut of Marling, a two-year-old filly by the flying sprinter Marwell: she won the EBF Wilbraham Maiden Fillies' Stakes so comfortably that already her name was being noted as a live prospect for the Queen Mary Stakes at Royal Ascot.

The five-furlong Palace House Stakes (Group Three) was the principal event supporting the Two Thousand Guineas on the final day of the Spring Meeting, and saw a pulsating finish, with Peter Makin's much improved Elbio beating Sir Harry Hardman by a neck. This was the season's first win for his trainer, whose immediate reaction also looked towards Royal Ascot: 'I'd love to run

him in the King's Stand'. And just to show that in racing and breeding nothing is predictable, it was reported that the dam of Elbio, the best sprinter yet seen in 1991, had won over hurdles!

Jack Berry's Paris House (John Carroll) short-heads Branston Abby (Pat Eddery, right) in the Arlington Auction Stakes at Newmarket on the middle day of the Guineas meeting.

General Accident Jockey Club Stakes (Group 2)

3 May 1991

1 mile 4 furlongs (going: good)

1st: £39,186; 2nd: £14,559; 3rd: £6,904; 4th: £2,911

1	ROCK HOPPER	Pat Eddery	8–11 fav
2	MOUNTAIN KINGDOM	S. Cauthen	25–1
3	KARINGA BAY	B. Rouse	13–2
4	SESAME	W. R. Swinburn	25–1

8 ran

distances: neck, 1½ lengths

time: 2 mins 34.48 secs

Winner owned by Maktoum Al Maktoum, trained by M. R. Stoute (Newmarket, Suffolk), bred by Gainsborough Stud Management Ltd

Tote: win £1.50; places £1.10, £3.40, £1.80; dual forecast £13.60

GENERAL ACCIDENT
TWO THOUSAND GUINEAS

Newmarket, 4 May 1991

Mystiko (Michael Roberts, rails) just gets the better of Lycius (Steve Cauthen) in the Two Thousand Guineas.
Running into fourth place on the extreme left is Generous (Richard Quinn).

If the One Thousand Guineas had seen a virtuoso individual performance from Shadayid, the General Accident Two Thousand Guineas brought into the minds of some Newmarket observers the words of George Lambton in his classic book *Men and Horses I have Known*:

'About the best thing in racing is when two very good horses single themselves out from the rest of the field and have a long-drawn-out struggle.'

Maybe the two involved in the Guineas finish were no Ard Patrick and Sceptre, never mind Grundy and Bustino, but the last-furlong battle between Mystiko and Lycius was none the less a stirring sight.

It was also, in its way, an unexpected one, for the build-up to the Two Thousand Guineas had been clearly dominated by Marju. Since his brilliant victory in the Craven Stakes (pages 37–9), Sheikh Hamdan Al Maktoum's colt had been all the rage in the ante-post market, and in many quarters victory was considered a formality, and with it a piece of history: the same owner-trainer-jockey combination had not won both Guineas races since King George VI, Fred Darling and Gordon Richards with Sun Chariot and Big Game in 1942, and before that you had to go back to 1879 to find the same achievement.

Marju started 6–4 favourite, with only the Free Handicap winner Mystiko (13–2) and Craven runner-up Desert Sun (7–1) also starting at less than 10–1. Late interest in the two French challengers was significant. The front pages of both the *Sporting Life* and the *Racing Post* proclaimed the name of Freddie Head's mount Ganges, and some canny early-morning Ladbrokes punters snapped up 40–1 against the 1990 Middle Park Stakes winner Lycius, who opened on the course at 20–1 and started four points shorter.

In the parade most of the field looked as Classic runners should, and Mystiko, on the very brink of boiling

over, was taken to the start with extreme caution by Michael Roberts.

He came back rather faster, breaking smartly from the stalls and making the running on the stands rail while Lester Piggott on the Greenham winner Bog Trotter led the main group of runners towards the centre of the course. Some noticed that Marju left the stalls awkwardly and was at no point travelling well, but as the leaders passed the Bushes all eyes were on Mystiko, whose raking stride was maintaining a furious pace up the rail.

As they came inside the final furlong Mystiko was beginning to pull clear of his rivals, but then the maroon and white colours of Steve Cauthen on Sheikh Mohammed's Lycius broke clear of the pack in the middle of the course and set off in fierce pursuit of the leader. In the Dip it seemed as if Lycius's momentum would carry him to the front, but Mystiko was not stopping, and on meeting the rising ground the grey rallied. Lycius continued his charge despite edging noticeably towards the stands and his rival, but Mystiko showed great courage to hold on by a head.

Ganges ran on to take third place, six lengths behind his compatriot Lycius, and Generous, without the benefit of a previous run this season, stayed on well to be fourth over a trip probably too short for him. Marju, who seemed to have knocked himself leaving the stalls and sustained a leg injury, was eleventh.

Although the favourite had been comprehensively beaten, Mystiko's was an immensely popular victory, for his owner, trainer and jockey each have special claims on the affections of racegoers. Lady Beaverbrook had been a great supporter of racing for decades, Clive Brittain's infectious enthusiasm for his calling and his charges has long endeared him to the racing public, and Michael Roberts has now established himself as one of the most likeable Flat jockeys currently riding.

All the connections enthused about

the horse himself, whom they had long regarded as something special. In order to keep the lid on the grey's potentially explosive energy, Brittain and Roberts had been working the horse on Newmarket Heath at the crack of dawn, gradually persuading him to relax. Their care and patience worked triumphantly during the Guineas preliminaries in keeping the colt just short of the level of tension where steam would come out of his ears. 'He's not stupid', said Roberts after the race, 'and I kept talking to him and on the way down to the start I sat down in the saddle and let him flow gently on his own. When we got to the start he was fine and almost fell asleep in the stalls.' Roberts summed up his reaction: 'Mystiko makes my bones tingle.'

Clive Brittain reported that after a less than perfect piece of work on the Monday before the race, Mystiko had been swimming on the Tuesday and Wednesday – 'and I can tell you it was bloody cold and Mystiko was glad to get back into his box.' Two days before the Guineas the horse worked again: 'Mystiko was spot on: you could tell from the smile in Michael's eye.'

The Guineas win was one of the high spots of Lady Beaverbrook's long career as an owner, and she turned in a virtuoso performance as the journalists badgered her about the Derby prospects of her colt, sounding a word of warning: 'I am not really looking forward to the Derby because it is a rough race, and my lovely horse Minster Son was injured in the race.' But it was widely accepted that Mystiko would go for Epsom, and as the general hubbub in a joyous Newmarket unsaddling enclosure died down talk concentrated on the chances of the volatile grey colt who had kept on so resolutely to win the Guineas.

As with Shadayid's Oaks prospects, a key issue seemed to be whether Mystiko would remain calm enough during the Derby preliminaries to perform to his best, and whether his style of racing gave sufficient cause for hope that he would last home over twelve furlongs.

His breeding certainly offered encouraging signs. His sire Secreto had won the 1984 Derby etched in the memory as the sensational short-head defeat of El Gran Senor, though his dam Caracciola had an undistinguished racing career. Mystiko had been bought for $150,000 at the Keeneland Selected Yearling Sales in Kentucky in 1989. Sold at the same auction had been Guineas runner-up Lycius ($500,000) and the unplaced Mujaazif ($1 million) and Mukaddamah ($375,000). By this token Lady Beaverbrook had quite a bargain.

Mystiko was the third Free Handicap winner to go on and land the Two Thousand Guineas, after Pay Up (1936)

and Privy Councillor (1962), and the first grey to win the race since Palestine in 1950 (which was the last year when both Guineas were won by greys). He was Clive Brittain's third Classic winner, following Julio Mariner (1978 St Leger) and Pebbles (1984 One Thousand Guineas).

Amid all the debate about how the Guineas winner would act at Epsom, some felt that if the Derby winner had been in the field, it was not necessarily Mystiko. Mike Dillon of Ladbrokes, for instance, thought that 'the best Derby trial in the Newmarket Guineas was run by the fourth horse, Generous, who seemed to have everything against him in the race and will be better over a mile and a half.'

Hmmmm . . .

General Accident Two Thousand Guineas Stakes (Group 1)

4 May 1991

1 mile (going: good)

1st: £107,994; **2nd:** £39,846; **3rd:** £19,023; **4th:** £7,665; **5th:** £2,932; **6th:** £1,039

1	MYSTIKO	M. Roberts	13–2
2	LYCIUS	S. Cauthen	16–1
3	GANGES	F. Head	16–1
4	GENEROUS	T. Quinn	11–1
5	MUKADDAMAH	L. Dettori	14–1
6	DESERT SUN	Pat Eddery	7–1
7	FLYING BRAVE	J. Reid	66–1
8	HOKUSAI	M. Kinane	16–1
9	MALVERNICO	C. Roche	66–1
10	SHALFORD	B. Raymond	100–1
11	MARJU	W. Carson	6–4 fav
12	BOG TROTTER	L. Piggott	11–1
13	MUJAAZIF	W. R. Swinburn	20–1
14	JUNK BOND	E. Maple	100–1

14 ran

distances: head, 6 lengths

time: 1 min 37. 83 secs

Winner owned by The Dowager Lady Beaverbrook, trained by C. E. Brittain (Newmarket, Suffolk), bred by Kingston Park Stud Inc, USA

Tote: win £6.60; places £2.10, £3.50, £2.70; dual forecast £42.70

			Nearctic
		Northern Dancer	Natalma
	Secreto		Secretariat
MYSTIKO		Betty's Secret	Betty Loraine
grey colt,			Grey Sovereign
born 22 February 1988		Zeddaan	Vareta
	Caracciola		Charlottesville
		Cendres Bleues	Aigue-Vive

POULE D'ESSAI DES POULAINS

Longchamp, 5 May 1991

In advance the Dubai Poule d'Essai des Poulains – the French Two Thousand Guineas – looked to be a true one-horse race, and although that one horse duly won, the manner in which he did so was far from as anticipated.

Hector Protector had been unbeaten in a six-race two-year-old campaign which had taken in some of France's top juvenile races (three of them Group One), and on his first outing as a three-year-old had easily landed the Prix de Fontainebleau over the course and distance of the first French Classic. Victory would be a formality, and only five opposed him: they included his pacemaker Mousquetaire, Acteur Francais, who had been beaten by Hector Protector in the Fontainebleau, and a solitary foreign challenger in the shape of Sapieha, trained by James Fanshawe at Newmarket and who had finished fourth to Bog Trotter in the Greenham Stakes at Newbury.

Hector Protector stood on a nail and damaged his near-fore hoof while being loaded into the horsebox for his trip to Longchamp, and for a while withdrawal was a real possibility. But he was deemed fit to race, and little seemed amiss in the early stages. Entering the straight Hector Protector was fourth. Acteur Francais took up the running approaching the final furlong but Hector Protector was soon in hot pursuit. The expected easy sweep to victory did not materialise, however, and only in the shadow of the post did the hard-ridden favourite force his nose in front to win by a head. Sapieha was a highly honourable third.

So Hector Protector maintained his unbeaten record and took his Group One haul to four, but even allowing for his pre-race injury, this had been a scrambled, unsatisfactory triumph. The Derby was still on the agenda, but his Longchamp performance would not have the ante-post punters battering down the bookies' doors first thing Monday morning.

Hector Protector (Freddie Head, near side) just gets up to beat Acteur Francais (Alain Lequeux) in the Poule d'Essai des Poulains.

Dubai Poule d'Essai des Poulains (Group 1)

5 May 1991

I mile (going: soft)

1st: £101,833; **2nd:** £40,733; **3rd:** £20,367; **4th:** £10,183

1	HECTOR PROTECTOR	F. Head	1–10 fav
2	ACTEUR FRANCAIS	A. Lequeux	8–1
3	SAPIEHA	W. R. Swinburn	12–1
4	ORAGE NOIR	T. Jarnet	14–1

6 ran

distances: head, 4 lengths
time: 1 min 37. 6 secs

Winner owned by S. Niarchos, trained by F. Boutin, bred by Flaxman Holdings Ltd, USA

Pari-Mutuel: win FF1. 10 (coupled with Mousquetaire); places – stakes returned; straight forecast FF2. 00

CHESTER
MAY MEETING

The three-day Chester May Meeting is traditionally a fixture expected to throw up clues for the Epsom Classics, now just a month away, but the special atmosphere at the meeting owes less to reading the entrails of the results than to the unique nature of the course. Crammed in between a bend in the River Dee and the old Roman walls of the city, the track is just over a mile in circumference and has a home straight of little more than a furlong.

If this all makes for great viewing, such a tight and tricky course can cause problems in running. Just five runners went to post on the opening day for the Dalham Chester Vase (the race which provided Shergar with his pre-Epsom prep ten years ago), but the size of the field did not prevent them from getting into a rare old tangle. The early pace was slow, but as the quintet made for the straight the lead was

being disputed by Sheikh Mohammed's Peking Opera (11–8 on favourite on the strength of a ten-length win at Kempton and joint-favourite for the Derby) and the 25–1 outsider Luchiroverte. Behind them, going best of all, was Pat Eddery on Khalid Abdullah's Toulon, trained in France by André Fabre.

Eddery was sitting with a double handful on Toulon as Luchiroverte and Peking Opera led round the home turn, then tried to go for a narrow gap between the leaders, at which point Steve Cauthen on the favourite shut the door on him to such effect that the French horse had to be pulled back and switched to the outside. With Chester having such a short run to the winning post, this did not leave much time for Eddery to gather his horse and mount a fresh challenge, but the acceleration which Toulon found to sprint past his

rivals (allowing his jockey the leisure to make some suitable comment to Cauthen as he swept past) landed him not only the race by one and a half lengths, but soon the dubious privilege of heading the Derby market.

> ## "We wanted to learn about him and we wanted him to learn about racing. We felt he would learn a lot from racing around here."

Toulon (Pat Eddery) sprints to Derby favouritism past Luchiroverte (Alan Munro, far side) and Peking Opera (Steve Cauthen) in the Chester Vase.

Toulon was the first French-trained winner at Chester for thirty-nine years, and Grant Pritchard-Gordon, racing manager to Khalid Abdullah, reported afterwards that the purpose of the colt's trip had been education, for horse and connections: 'We wanted to learn about him and we wanted him to learn about racing. We felt he would learn a lot from racing around here.' Many ante-post backers – who never learn – thought Toulon's final sprint the key to the Derby, and by the day's end the colt had been backed from 10–1 offered immediately after the race to 4–1.

At least punters who took those odds had a few weeks to wait before knowing their fate. Not so the fellow who watched the desperately close finish to Chester's opening race, the Lily Agnes Stakes, and was so convinced that Jack Berry's Tino Tere had got the verdict over Chadleigh House that he

Star Player (Lanfranco Dettori, centre) takes command in the Chester Cup.

The Dee Stakes: Hundra (Bruce Raymond, left) beats Half A Tick (Richard Quinn).

raced around the betting ring taking the odds on the outcome of the photo-finish – an absolute certainty. He staked £2000 to win £100 and £1000 to win £50 (both 20–1 on), then £1000 to win £100 (10–1 on) and a few smaller bets. Within a couple of minutes he had to face the awful truth that he was wrong: Chadleigh House was the winner by a short head.

The main betting race of the meeting, the Ladbroke Chester Cup, looked an open affair, with One For The Pot going off market leader at 4–1. But it was second favourite Star Player, trained in Devon by John Baker, who dominated the race, taking the lead with a furlong to go and winning easily from Nomadic Way.

Having landed the Chester Vase with Toulon, Khalid Abdullah took the main three-year-old fillies' event, the Shadwell Stud Cheshire Oaks, with Peplum, who earned a 16–1 quote for the real thing at Epsom (where she started at 12–1 and finished eighth of nine behind Jet Ski Lady).

It was the turn of the older horses to take centre stage on the final day, when the Ormonde EBF Stakes brought a popular victory for Per Quod and a treble in consecutive races for jockey Bruce Raymond (following Hundra in the Dee Stakes and Breezy Day in the sprint) on the eve of his forty-eighth birthday. Per Quod's task was made easier by the withdrawal of Henry Cecil's River God, found to be lame on arrival at the start, but he still had a formidable opponent in the favourite Warm Feeling, who seemed to have the race sewn up on the final bend before a typically game run from Per Quod got the six-year-old gelding home by a length. Third was Indian Queen, of whom we'd be hearing more.

Dalham Chester Vase (Group 3)

7 May 1991

1 mile 4 furlongs 65 yards (going: good to soft)

1st: £29,268; **2nd:** £10,849; **3rd:** £5,125; **4th:** £2,138

1	TOULON	Pat Eddery	9–4
2	LUCHIROVERTE	A. Munro	25–1
3	PEKING OPERA	S. Cauthen	8–11 fav
4	WIDYAN	T. Quinn	11–2

5 ran

distances: 1½ lengths, ¾ length
time: 2 mins 45.69 secs

Winner owned by K. Abdullah, trained by A. Fabre (France), bred by Juddmonte Farms

Tote: win £3.00; places £1.40, £3.50; dual forecast £40.20

Ladbroke Chester Cup (Handicap)

8 May 1991

2 miles 2 furlongs 97 yards (going: good)

1st: £18,925; **2nd:** £5,650; **3rd:** £2,700; **4th:** £1,225

1	STAR PLAYER	L. Dettori	9–2
2	NOMADIC WAY	Pat Eddery	8–1
3	TAROUDANT	J. Lowe	9–1
4	GO SOUTH	N. Carlisle	25–1

16 ran

distances: 1½ lengths, neck
time: 4 mins 13.41 secs

Winner owned by Paul Smith, trained by J. H. Baker (Stoodleigh, Devon), bred by Baronrath Stud Ltd

Tote: win £6.20; places £1.70, £1.60, £1.80, £4.60; dual forecast £20.00

Ormonde EBF Stakes (Group 3)

9 May 1991

1 mile 5 furlongs 88 yards (going: good)

1st: £29,394; **2nd:** £10,944; **3rd:** £5,209; **4th:** £2,218

1	PER QUOD	B. Raymond	5–1
2	WARM FEELING	M. Hills	11–8 fav
3	INDIAN QUEEN	W. Carson	8–1
4	PIER DAMIANI	M. Roberts	25–1

7 ran

distances: 1 length, 4 lengths
time: 2 mins 55.68 secs

Winner owned by H. Turney McKnight, trained by B. Hanbury (Newmarket, Suffolk), bred by H. Turney McKnight and June H. McKnight, USA

Tote: win £5.80; places £2.50, £1.60; dual forecast £4.20

POULE D'ESSAI DES POULICHES

Longchamp, 12 May 1991

The French One Thousand Guineas seemed not much less of a foregone conclusion for Danseuse Du Soir than the French Two Thousand had been for Hector Protector. Winner of two races as a two-year-old (including the Prix Robert Papin) and of the Group Three Prix de la Grotte at Longchamp in April, she was justifiably a hot favourite at 5–2 on (coupled with her pacemaker Isenay) to beat eight rivals, of which Richard Hannon's One Thousand Guineas fifth Only Yours was the sole foreign raider.

When the stalls opened Danseuse Du Soir's mind was elsewhere, and she was slowly into her stride, but Dominique Boeuf was in no hurry to make up the lost ground. Gradually she made her way forward to a challenging position, avoiding an incident in which Lester Piggott's mount Caerlina was nearly brought down. Danseuse Du Soir took the lead from Sha Ta over a furlong out, and despite tiring a little towards the end Daniel Wildenstein's filly won comfortably by two lengths to score a first Classic victory for trainer Elie Lellouche.

Only Yours, never seen with a chance, finished eighth but was placed seventh after La Carene, who had caused the interference early in the race, was disqualified and placed last.

Danseuse du Soir (Dominique Boeuf) skips away from Sha Ta (Steve Cauthen) to land the Poule d'Essai des Pouliches.

Dubai Poule d'Essai des Pouliches (Group 1)

12 May 1991

1 mile (going: soft)

1st: £101,833; 2nd: £40,733; 3rd: £20,367; 4th: £10,183

1	DANSEUSE DU SOIR	D. Boeuf	2–5 fav
2	SHA TA	S. Cauthen	19–2
3	CAERLINA	L. Piggott	77–10

9 ran

distances: 2 lengths, short head
time: 1 min 38.6 secs

Winner owned by D. Wildenstein, trained by E. Lellouche, bred by Ridgecourt Stud

Pari-Mutuel: win FF1.40 (coupled with Isenay); places FF1.10, FF1.60, FF1.70; dual forecast FF7.70

THE NEW RETAINERS

*Many of the top Flat jockeys are now retained by owners
rather than by stables, and such arrangements are
affecting the traditional trainer-jockey relationship.*
RICHARD ONSLOW *examines the trend.*

**Alan Munro's first ride — and first winner — as retained jockey for Fahd Salman: Ausherra wins the Marley
Roof Tile Oaks Trial at Lingfield Park from Gai Bulga (Gary Carter).**

One of the most discernible changes in the pattern of British racing, as we come to the end of the century, is to be seen in the way in which the top jockeys are retained. Instead of having a contract from a trainer, whose owners paid a share of the retaining fee proportionate to the number of horses they had in the stable, first claims on top riders are being taken by the wealthy owners from the Middle East, who have their many horses spread amongst a large number of stables, running into double figures in at least one case.

Of course, jockeys have been retained by owners, as opposed to public stables, from time immemorial. During the present century Harry Wragg, Doug Smith, Willie Carson and others have ridden for the Earls of Derby. The shipping magnate Lord Glanely had first call on Gordon Richards, the late Aga Khan on Charlie Smirke, Major L.B. Holliday on Stan Clayton *inter alia*, and Mr Jim Joel on Eph Smith. All those owners had private stables, except the Aga Khan, though in England he had horses only with Dick Dawson, then Frank Butters and finally Marcus Marsh. Mr Joel did have horses in other yards, besides Sefton Lodge, Newmarket, but Eph Smith's retainer applied only to the Sefton Lodge horses. Thus when Mr Joel won the Eclipse Stakes with Henry The Seventh, Bill Elsey's stable jockey Eddie Hide had the mount.

Surely one of the most significant announcements of the 1991 season was made on 9 May, when we learned that twenty-four-year-old Alan Munro had been appointed first jockey to Mr Fahd Salman, who has horses with Paul Cole, his principal trainer, as well as with Michael Bell, Henry Candy, William Jarvis and Sir Mark Prescott. Munro described it as 'a chance of a lifetime' and took it with both hands. Within a month he had won the Derby for Mr Salman on Generous, from Paul Cole's Whatcombe Stable, then completed a scintillating treble with success on the same colt in the Irish Derby and the King George VI and Queen Elizabeth Diamond Stakes. While Munro was admired for making the best of his opportunities, much sympathy was felt for Paul Cole's stable jockey Richard Quinn, a thoroughly reliable and most effective rider, who had won the Dewhurst Stakes on Generous in 1990.

Riding in the American style, with the low crouch that reduces the wind resistance to the minimum, Alan Munro had been regarded as an obvious candidate for a top job in the near future as he had finished eighth in the jockeys' list with 89 winners in 1990, a significant increase on his 37 successes of the previous season.

Brought up in Hertfordshire, where he still lives, Munro was originally apprenticed to Barry Hills, had his indentures transferred to Mel Brittain in Yorkshire, and rode his first winner on Sentimental Roses at Yarmouth in 1985. He acquired his neat, economical style that keeps horses so beautifully balanced on a busman's holiday in the United States, where he had no mounts in public, and was somewhat forcibly told that he could not even ride exercise unless he adapted himself to the American way of riding.

Making a good start to his new job, Munro won the Oaks Trial Stakes with Ausherra at Lingfield on the first occasion that he wore Mr Salman's dark green colours, but very nearly missed the ride on Generous at Epsom. After being disqualified for trying to go through too narrow a gap on Magic Ring at Goodwood in May, his mount was relegated to last place and he was suspended from 1 to 4 June inclusive, resuming on Derby Day itself. Back in the limelight at Royal Ascot, Munro completed a two-year-old treble for Mr Salman and Paul Cole by winning the Coventry Stakes on Dilum, the Norfolk Stakes on Magic Ring and the Chesham Stakes on Fair Cop.

Alan Munro became the fourth jockey to be retained by a leading Arab owner. Since coming to the end of his successful association with Vincent O'Brien at the finish of the 1986 season, Pat Eddery has ridden for Mr Khalid Abdullah. Having previously won the Two Thousand Guineas and Derby on Nashwan for Sheikh Hamdan Al Maktoum in 1989, Willie Carson became

contract rider for that owner, and in October 1990 it was announced that Sheikh Mohammed had taken first claim on Steve Cauthen.

Khalid Abdullah came into racing in 1978. He has horses with Henry Cecil and John Gosden at Newmarket, Guy Harwood in Sussex, Roger Charlton at Beckhampton, and Barry Hills at Lambourn.

'It is only logical for an owner to spread his horses amongst several stables', says a spokesman for Mr Abdullah's racing operation, 'as it ensures the limitation of risks.' If one stable is out of form, Mr Abdullah can rely on the others for winners.

"It is only logical for an owner to spread his horses amongst several stables . . .

Having injected a great deal of money into bloodstock, it is also no more than logical to protect that investment by ensuring that one of the best jockeys in the world is on hand to ride the horses. Pat Eddery is the key member of Mr Abdullah's formidable team. On the Wednesday of each week racing manager Grant Pritchard-Gordon obtains information from the trainers with regards to runners in the coming week. He then confers with Eddery's agent Terry Ellis, with whom he maintains constant liaison, and riding plans begin to be formulated. Eddery's retainer is fully comprehensive, and irrespective of any there may be for

horses in other ownership in the stables patronised by Mr Abdullah. In addition Eddery rides for the owner in France, where he won the Prix de Hedouville on Glorify, trained by André Fabre, at Longchamp in April.

'The arrangements work very well,' says Barry Hills. 'We know that Mr Abdullah likes to see Pat Eddery on his horses, so we do our best to send his runners to meetings where his jockey is riding.'

Having a jockey of the calibre of Eddery available proved of particularly great value to Mr Abdullah last year, when Quest For Fame won the Derby and Sanglamore beat Epervier Bleu by half a length in the French Derby. Both were trained by Roger Charlton, who was in his first season after taking over Beckhampton from Jeremy Tree. After Eddery rode Mr Abdullah's Toulon (trained by André Fabre) to win the Chester Vase in May there seemed a strong possibility that they might share another Derby victory. Toulon however was constantly changing his legs at Epsom, ran well below his form and finished unplaced, but the partnership subsequently won the St Leger.

Second claim on Pat Eddery's services are held by Sheikh Maktoum Al Maktoum, who has horses with Tom Jones, Michael Stoute and other trainers. Notable among the horses Eddery rode for Sheikh Maktoum in 1991 was the four-year-old Rock Hopper, on whom he won the John Porter Stakes, the Jockey Club Stakes and the Princess of Wales's Stakes for Michael Stoute's stable. Eddery also rode the colt when he was awarded the Hardwicke Stakes at Royal Ascot.

Having the services of Willie Carson has proved an important ingredient in the success of Sheikh Hamdan Al Maktoum, so that the run of Classic successes begun by Nashwan has been continued. Last year Carson won for the Sheikh the One Thousand Guineas, Oaks and Irish Derby on Salsabil, trained by John Dunlop, and this year another One Thousand Guineas on

Shadayid, also from the Dunlop stable. Carson was in all but invincible form when riding the Sheikh's horses at the Newmarket Spring Meeting. On the first day he brought off a treble for his principal employer, for after the One Thousand Guineas he won the Rex Cohen Memorial Stakes on Lahib, yet another saddled by Dunlop, and the Microsoft Stakes on Sariah, trained by Major Dick Hern. The following day Carson won the Mayer Parry Handicap on Sheikh Hamdan's Takaddum, trained by Peter Walwyn.

Riding for Sheikh Mohammed, on whose marvellous filly Oh So Sharp he won the One Thousand Guineas, Oaks and St Leger in 1985, involves Steve Cauthen in a heavy commitment. The leading owner in five of the last six seasons, Sheikh Mohammed has more than 300 horses in training in England in fifteen stables, ranging in number from 100 with John Gosden at Stanley House, his private yard at Newmarket, to three with James Fanshawe, also based at Newmarket.

To a very large extent, Steve Cauthen has a free hand in choosing which mounts he will take and where he rides, Anthony Stroud, the Sheikh's racing manager, having the authority to require him for certain horses. That authority is rarely exercised, though occasionally the manager will make the decision on riding arrangements in a big race, or want Cauthen for a particular horse. All the entries will be faxed to Cauthen's agent John Hanmer, the well-known commentator and broadcaster, from the Darley Stud Management, Sheikh Mohammed's racing headquarters in Duchess Drive, Newmarket. John Hanmer always knows the programme of the better horses, and will also be aware of the immediate objectives of some of the others, even though the engagements are yet to be made under the five-day entry scheme.

By Wednesday Hanmer will have a firm idea of what runners the Sheikh will have the following week, and

Cauthen can start to pick his mounts. He has the choice of all the Sheikh's horses except those trained by Paul Cole and Luca Cumani, which are ridden by Richard Quinn and Frankie Dettori respectively. In addition to riding for thirteen of the English stables, Steve Cauthen is required for the Group races on the Continent. In April he went to France to win the Prix d'Harcourt at Longchamp for the Sheikh on Panoramic, and the following month returned to that course to land the Prix du Muguet on Colour Chart, both horses coming from André Fabre's stable. It was also in May that Cauthen won the Italian Derby, worth £138,739,

"...as it ensures the limitation of risks."

for the Sheikh on Clive Brittain-trained Hailsham. The most important successes that Cauthen obtained for Sheikh Mohammed in England during the first half of 1991 were at Royal Ascot, where he won the Prince of Wales's Stakes on Stagecraft, the Jersey Stakes on Satin Flower and the Queen's Vase on Jendali.

As a result of the leading owners having their own jockeys, relatively few of the leading trainers still retain riders. This was only to be anticipated as there would not be many horses for the stable jockey to ride. Moreover, the smaller owners would have to share the retaining fee, and having their own jockey would to no small extent

preclude the use of the services of the likes of Pat Eddery or Steve Cauthen when they were available.

The tradition of mutual trust and co-operation between trainer and stable jockey, often lasting over a large number of years, as was so well exemplified by Captain Boyd-Rochfort and Harry Carr, is no longer one of the cornerstones of British racing. The advent of the new system, by which the owners retain jockeys for horses spread among a number of stables, was inevitable for the very good reason that the leading owners of the present time take an immensely greater stake in racing than did their counterparts of earlier times. For instance, the late Lord Derby, who was a very wealthy man indeed, had about thirty-five horses in Newmarket's Stanley House stable in 1939, whereas Sheikh Mohammed, as already noted, has ten times that number of horses today. If it was only to be expected that Lord Derby would have his own rider, it is still more natural that Sheikh Mohammed should retain a jockey, even if his string is too big to be contained in one stable as was that of Lord Derby.

For eleven years between the wars the late Lord Derby, his stable jockey Tommy Weston and private trainer the Hon. George Lambton were the great triumvirate of British racing. At the outset of that period they won the Derby with Sansovino in 1924 and at the end of it another Derby with Hyperion in 1933.

Lord Derby had a less happy relationship with an earlier stable jockey in Steve Donoghue, who had an abundance of talent and charm, but absolutely no sense of responsibility. He could not understand that a large retaining fee imposed responsibilities on him, and certainly not when it came to choosing his mount in the Derby. In 1921 Lord Derby reluctantly released him from Glorioso so that he could win the Derby on Humorist. Two years later first claim on his services was held by Lord Woolavington, whom he wheedled into letting him off riding Knockando in the Derby in order to win on Papyrus. In the end owners gave up retaining Donoghue, and he lost the jockeys' championship to the very much more businesslike Gordon Richards.

Charlie Smirke first rode for the Aga Khan as an apprentice in 1926 and the association endured until he won the One Thousand Guineas on Rose Royale II in 1957, the year of the Aga's death. Unfortunately there was no affinity at all between the ebullient Smirke and Frank Butters, a somewhat straitlaced trainer of the old school. Although Smirke was

first jockey, Butters made the riding arrangements if the Aga had more than one runner in a race. In the Derby of 1936 Butters insisted Gordon Richards should ride the strongly fancied Taj Akbar and grudgingly agreed to Smirke's riding the Guineas runner-up Mahmoud, who was not expected to stay, rather than the outsider of the Aga's trio Bala Hissar. Smirke had the last laugh as Mahmoud won from Taj Akbar in record time.

The most notable partnership of the post-war era was between Joe Mercer and the West Ilsley Stable – first under

Jack Colling then Major Dick Hern – which lasted from 1953 to 1976. Outstanding among all the good horses Mercer rode in those twenty four years was Mrs John Hislop's Brigadier Gerard, on whom he won the Two Thousand Guineas of 1971 and sixteen out of seventeen other races.

While the stable jockey seems assured his place on the racing scene, those at the top of the profession are finding new roles as contract riders to owners who are racing on a totally unprecedented scale.

Steve Cauthen brings home yet another winner for Sheikh Mohammed – Stagecraft in the Prince Of Wales's Stakes at Royal Ascot.

YORK
MAY MEETING

The Musidora Stakes: Gussy Marlowe (Michael Roberts) hugs the rail.

Classic clues for Epsom – positive, negative or irrelevant, depending on your point of view – continued to pile up during the May Meeting at York.

On the first day the centre of attention was a small but select field for the Tattersalls Musidora Stakes, often a good guide to the Oaks: Diminuendo won at Epsom after landing the Musidora in 1988, and the 1989 winner Snow Bride's name is also in the record books as an Oaks winner – though it took the long-drawn-out process of disqualifying Aliysa to put it there. The 1987 Musidora had gone to Indian Skimmer, the 1990 to In The Groove. Would the 1991 field contain one to mention in the same breath as those?

There were five runners. Joint favourites were Shamshir, winner of the Brent Walker Fillies' Mile at Ascot as a two-year-old, and Dartrey, winner on her only outing as a juvenile and an encouraging sixth behind Shadayid in the One Thousand Guineas. Jaffa Line, a narrowly beaten second in the Thresher Classic Trial at Sandown Park, and Ristna, a daughter of Roussalka and winner of her only previous outing at Newbury in April, were both well supported. Gussy Marlowe, a Newmarket winner at the beginning of the month, was the outsider of the quintet, but turned in a magnificently gutsy performance by leading throughout and simply refusing to give in as her more fancied rivals tried to collar her in the closing stages. Dartrey, Shamshir and Ristna each looked about to wrench the lead from Clive Brittain's game filly, and each was repelled as Gussy Marlowe doggedly maintained her gallop to the line. But the value of the race as an Oaks trial was limited: the winner was not engaged in the Classic.

Environment Friend (George Duffield) is out on his own at the end of the Dante Stakes, with Hailsham (Steve Cauthen) and Perpendicular (Willie Ryan) beaten off.

The following day's William Hill Dante Stakes produced a typical field of Epsom hopefuls for this traditional Derby trial, though the sponsors had announced that it would be the last running of the race with their support. Favourite was the 1990 Racing Post Trophy winner Peter Davies, ridden by Lester Piggott. His seven rivals included Hailsham, winner of the Thresher Classic Trial, Bravefoot, making his first appearance since his Doncaster doping in September 1990, and Perpendicular, an impressive winner of the White Rose Stakes at Ascot. Not for the last time, punters seemed to have forgotten the grey Environment Friend, a good two-year-old but seemingly out of his depth in such company. Not so. After a slow start, Environment Friend came storming through approaching the final furlong and showed a fine turn of foot to sweep past the others and record an easy five-length victory over Hailsham. Peter Davies and Bravefoot both weakened rapidly once the heat was turned on, and yet again the Derby picture took on a fresh hue.

This Group Two success was the most important win so far notched up by second-season trainer James Fanshawe, previously assistant to Michael Stoute. Owner Bill Gredley reported that Steve Cauthen had ridden Environment Friend as a two-year-old and advised patience: 'He said he was as weak as spaghetti, but the potential was there and he could be anything.' The immediate question was whether he could be a Derby winner,

"He was as weak as spaghetti, but the potential was there and he could be anything."

Cruachan (Ray Cochrane) makes the Glasgow Stakes a one-horse race.

and the grey's odds plummeted from 50–1 to 10–1 in the ante-post lists.

Less than twenty-four hours later another previously little known colt had leap-frogged the Dante winner in the Derby betting. Such was the impression that Cruachan made in winning the Glasgow Stakes by six lengths from Saddlers' Hall that Guy Harwood's charge – who cost a mere $12,000 as a yearling – instantly became fourth favourite for the Classic. Lester Piggott, who had a distant view of Cruachan's rear end at the finish of the

Tattersalls Musidora Stakes (Group 3)

14 May 1991

1 mile 2 furlongs 110 yards (going: good to firm)

1st: £25,710; 2nd: £9,532; 3rd: £4,503; 4th: £1,880

1	GUSSY MARLOWE	M. Roberts	7–1
2	DARTREY	S. Cauthen	11–4 jt fav
3	SHAMSHIR	L. Dettori	11–4 jt fav
4	RISTNA	W. R. Swinburn	4–1

5 ran

distances: head, 1 length
time: 2 mins 12. 23 secs

Winner owned by Mrs John Van Geest, trained by C. E. Brittain (Newmarket, Suffolk), bred by Mrs John Van Geest

Tote: win £7. 60; places £1. 90, £1. 60; dual forecast £10. 70

York race, assured the press that he still did not know what he would ride in the Derby, 'But that'll probably win it.' The Epsom price of 'that' – Cruachan – tumbled to 8–1.

The grey Arzanni announced himself a major contender for the season's big staying races with a smooth victory in the Polo Mints Yorkshire Cup, taking the lead from Shambo a furlong out and running on sturdily to come home well clear. The final day's other Group race, the Duke of York Stakes, produced a much tighter finish. Green Line Express, running for the first time over six furlongs after many heroic efforts at seven furlongs and one mile, beat the other joint favourite Nicholas by a neck, with La Grange Music another neck behind in third.

William Hill Dante Stakes (Group 2)

15 May 1991

1 mile 2 furlongs 110 yards (going: good to firm)

1st: £69,426; **2nd:** £25,966; **3rd:** £12,458; **4th:** £5,410

I	ENVIRONMENT FRIEND	G. Duffield	20–1
2	HAILSHAM	S. Cauthen	9–2
3	PERPENDICULAR	W. Ryan	11–4
4	COMMENDABLE	Pat Eddery	15–2

8 ran (Peter Davies 5–2 fav)

distances: 5 lengths, head
time: 2 mins 12.42 secs

Winner owned by W. J. Gredley, trained by J. R. Fanshawe (Newmarket, Suffolk), bred by Stetchworth Park Stud Ltd

Tote: win £20.80; places £2.60, £1.80, £1.50; dual forecast £32.00

Polo Mints Yorkshire Cup (Group 2)

16 May 1991

1 mile 6 furlongs (going: good to firm)

1st: £49,251; **2nd:** £18,325; **3rd:** £8,712; **4th:** £3,697

I	ARZANNI	L. Dettori	5–1
2	SHAMBO	M. Roberts	11–1
3	TEAMSTER	L. Piggott	11–4 fav
4	PER QUOD	B. Raymond	5–1

7 ran

distances: 3½ lengths, 2½ lengths
time: 2 mins 57.94 secs

Winner owned by David Thompson, trained by L. M. Cumani (Newmarket, Suffolk), bred by H. H. Aga Khan

Tote: win £6.40; places £2.90, £3.60; dual forecast £39.40

Duke of York Stakes (Group 3)

16 May 1991

6 furlongs (going: good to firm)

1st: £27,216; **2nd:** £10,109; **3rd:** £4,792; **4th:** £2,018

I	GREEN LINE EXPRESS	A. S. Cruz	7–2 jt fav
2	NICHOLAS	L. Piggott	7–2 jt fav
3	LA GRANGE MUSIC	W. R. Swinburn	6–1
4	SIR HARRY HARDMAN	Dean McKeown	13–2

11 ran

distances: neck, neck
time: 1 min 11. 33 secs

Winner owned by Ecurie Fustok, trained by M. Moubarak (Newmarket, Suffolk), bred by Buckram Oak Farm, USA

Tote: win £3.90; places £1.80, £1.80, £2.10; dual forecast £6.30

AIRLIE-COOLMORE IRISH TWO THOUSAND GUINEAS

The Curragh, 18 May 1991

History was made in the Irish Two Thousand Guineas when Fourstars Allstar became the first US-based horse to win a Classic in Ireland. Trained at Belmont Park, New York, by Irish-born Leo O'Brien (brother of Michael O'Brien, trainer of the 1980 Mackeson and Hennessy winner Bright Highway), Fourstars Allstar was the first ever American-trained challenger for any of the Irish Classics, but the novelty did not prevent his going off a well-backed 9–1 third favourite.

The two preferred to the American colt in the betting were the French raiders Lycius, beaten a head by Mystiko in the Two Thousand Guineas, and Ganges, six lengths further back when third in that race.

American jockey Mike Smith soon had Fourstars Allstar making the pace, and the only rival to mount a serious challenge was Jim Bolger's Star Of Gdansk, who joined issue within the final quarter mile and headed the American on the inside. Neither Fourstars Allstar nor Smith had previously raced over a course such as the almost straight Curragh mile, but connections were confident that the colt would find extra reserves of stamina once he hit the rising ground approaching the winning post, and so it proved. Fourstars Allstar responded gamely once he had been passed by Star Of Gdansk, rallied and regained the initiative close home, winning by a head.

Neither Lycius (third, six lengths adrift of Star Of Gdansk) nor Ganges (fourth) did much to advertise the quality of the English equivalent race, but on this occasion the niceties of form took second place to admiration for an adventurous bid from the other side of the Atlantic which paid off gloriously.

As Christy Roche, rider of the runner-up, put it: 'Good luck to them. The winner is a very good horse and the jockey is something else as well.'

"I've been hanging around racetracks since I was ten and had my first bet when I was five."

Owner Richard Bomze – 'I've been hanging around racetracks since I was ten and I had my first bet when I was five' – with Fourstars Allstar after the Irish Two Thousand.

Airlie–Coolmore Irish Two Thousand Guineas (Group 1)

18 May 1991

1 mile (going: good)

1st: IR£134,400; 2nd: IR£43,200; 3rd: IR£21,200; 4th: IR£8,000; 5th: IR£5,800; 6th: IR£3,600

1	FOURSTARS ALLSTAR	M. Smith	9–1
2	STAR OF GDANSK	C. Roche	16–1
3	LYCIUS	S. Cauthen	Evens fav
4	GANGES	F. Head	6–1

12 ran

distances: head, 6 lengths
time: 1 min 38.6 secs

Winner owned by Richard Bomze, trained by L. O'Brien (USA), bred by Richard Bomze, USA

Tote: win IR£9.00; places IR£2.30, IR£2.70, IR£1.30; dual forecast IR£53.70

GOFFS IRISH ONE THOUSAND GUINEAS

The Curragh, 25 May 1991

No filly since the War has won the One Thousand Guineas at Newmarket and the Irish One Thousand Guineas, though two horses who finished in the first three on the Rowley Mile in recent years went on to obtain handsome compensation at The Curragh: Al Bahathri (1985) and Sonic Lady (1986). Kooyonga, second to Shadayid at Newmarket, joined this select band with a convincing win under twenty-two-year-old Warren O'Connor on his first Classic ride and only his second mount in a Group One event.

The riding arrangements for

Kooyonga and Warren O'Connor sweep clear of Julie La Rousse (white face) and Umniyatee in the Irish One Thousand Guineas.

Kooyonga received almost as much attention as the race. She had been partnered at Newmarket by Lester Piggott, but for the Irish Guineas he elected to desert her in favour of Rua d'Oro, trained by his old comrade-in-arms Vincent O'Brien. This left Kooyonga's trainer Michael Kauntze looking for a replacement, and it was only on the eve of the race that he convinced the filly's Japanese owner Mitsuo Haga (who had bought her between the Newmarket and Curragh races) that young O'Connor was the man for the job.

Despite her Classic form, Kooyonga did not start favourite, the punters siding with Piggott and sending off Rua d'Oro, unbeaten in her previous two races, at 2–1. Three British-trained fillies were in the line-up – Umniyatee (a daughter of Midway Lady and winner of her only two previous outings), Himiko and Pastorale, while Irish Linnet was seeking to pull off an extraordinary double for the New York-based trainer Leo O'Brien, who had won the Irish Two Thousand with Fourstars Allstar a week earlier.

Umniyatee led for most of the way until, a quarter of a mile out, Kooyonga burst through a gap on the rails and quickened away to win by three lengths from Julie La Rousse. Just what Lester Piggott felt, rowing away fruitlessly on Rua d'Oro as Kooyonga made for the horizon, can only be imagined. Not so the feelings of delighted trainer Kauntze, at one time assistant to Vincent O'Brien and now notching his first Classic win: 'I'm now only forty-three Classic winners behind Vincent!'

"I'm now only forty-three Classic winners behind Vincent!"

Goffs Irish One Thousand Guineas (Group 1)

25 May 1991

1 mile (going: good)

1st: IR£131,475; **2nd:** IR£39,475; **3rd:** IR£19,475; **4th:** IR£7,475

1	KOOYONGA	W. J. O'Connor	4–1
2	JULIE LA ROUSSE	J. P. Murtagh	16–1
3	UMNIYATEE	W. Carson	6–1
4	BLUE DAISY	R. J. Griffiths	25–1

12 ran (Rua d'Oro 2–1 fav)

distances: 3 lengths, 1½ lengths

time: 1 min 37.2 secs

Winner owned by Mitsuo Haga, trained by M. Kauntze (Ireland), bred by Ovidstown Bloodstock Ltd, Ireland

Tote: win IR£4.10; places IR£1.90, IR£5.20, IR£2.10; dual forecast IR£54.90

PRIX DU
JOCKEY-CLUB LANCIA

Chantilly, 2 June 1991

With acceleration which the sponsors would appreciate, Suave Dancer and Cash Asmussen leave their rivals behind in the Prix du Jockey-Club Lancia.

Run three days before the real thing at Epsom, the French Derby – as the Prix du Jockey-Club is commonly termed in Britain – has little in common with its English equivalent except timing conditions and distance. Chantilly is right-handed and fairly flat, quite the opposite of Epsom. Unlike the popular pandemonium of Derby Day, the first Sunday in June at Chantilly is the epitome of quiet elegance. And in 1991 the mood before the respective races contrasted starkly.

If the final few days before the Ever Ready Derby involved a frantic searching for clues from a mass of inconclusive evidence, the possible outcomes to the Prix du Jockey-Club Lancia seemed mercifully few. Probably the race would fall to Daniel Wildenstein's colt Pistolet Bleu, unbeaten in five outings, most recently the Prix Hocquart over the full mile and a half. The claim made (by some) that his chief danger Suave Dancer was the new Sea Bird II after a brilliant victory in the Prix Greffulhe (which Sea Bird had won) was somewhat dented when he could finish only second to Cudas in the Prix Lupin. This was by no means the sort of performance expected of a 10–1 on favourite, and Suave Dancer had some rehabilitation to undertake if he was to give his English-born trainer John Hammond his first Group One success. Prix Lupin victor Cudas reopposed in the Jockey-Club, but both would find Pistolet Bleu a difficult nut to crack. Only Luchiroverte, sent over from Newmarket by the ever-optimistic Clive Brittain after finishing second in the Chester Vase, mounted an overseas effort.

Sadly Pistolet Bleu injured a hock on the day before the race and could not take part, so in a field of seven Suave Dancer was sent off the 5–3 on favourite. Ridden by Cash Asmussen (whose family had bought the horse on behalf of owner Mr Chalhoub in the USA), Suave Dancer was known to possess a remarkable turn of foot and would delay his effort until late, so it was no surprise that as the field came past the incomparable backdrop of the Grands Ecuries – the chateau stable block – Asmussen was content to hold back. At the entrance to the straight Suave Dancer was fifth as Luchiroverte and Justice made for home, then Cudas took over with a quarter of a mile to go. It was clearly on sufferance, though, and suddenly those rash comparisons with Sea Bird II did not look quite so dumb as, with over a furlong to go, Asmussen asked the question. Coming up the centre of the course, Suave Dancer cut down the leader and shot clear of his field with a brilliant burst of acceleration. It was all over, but Suave Dancer made the final few seconds interesting by swerving to the right once safely out of range of his rivals –

"I've never ridden a better horse."

the nearest of whom was Subotica, who finished four lengths behind, with Cudas third and Luchiroverte a one-paced fourth.

For a few days – until Generous turned in a no less impressive display at Epsom – this was hailed as the benchmark performance of the season, and by any standards the change of gear which Suave Dancer showed to leave the other runners trailing in his wake was remarkable. The cry of 'What did he beat?' was partly stilled when Subotica went on to win the Grand Prix de Paris three weeks later, but such testing of the form – and indeed of Suave Dancer himself – lay in the future. On that sunny Sunday at Chantilly, the feeling among many of the crowd was that they might just have seen a colt who would take his place among the greats. Cash Asmussen certainly thought so: 'I've never ridden a better horse.'

Prix du Jockey–Club Lancia (Group 1)

2 June 1991

1 mile 4 furlongs (going: good to firm)

1st: £254,582; 2nd: £101,833; 3rd: £50,916; 4th: £25,458

1	SUAVE DANCER	C. Asmussen	3–5 fav
2	SUBOTICA	T. Jarnet	62–10
3	CUDAS	F. Head	27–10
4	LUCHIROVERTE	M. Roberts	10–1

7 ran

distances: 4 lengths, 1½ lengths
time: 2 mins 27.4 secs

Winner owned by H. Chalhoub, trained by J. Hammond, bred by Lillie F. Webb, USA.

Pari–Mutuel: win FF1.60; places FF1.40, FF2.50; straight forecast FF6.70

EVER READY DERBY

Epsom, 5 June 1991

Beforehand the 1991 Ever Ready Derby looked an open race, and though several pundits considered the field 'substandard' (some always do), there could be little complaining about the line-up. The Derby field can only contain the best available, and most of those were to take their part.

As in 1990, the race seemed to lack an obvious star – a Nashwan or a Reference Point – and the ante-post market produced a succession of hotly fancied horses who then fell by the wayside. Suomi, Hip To Time and Polish King made the mistake of putting Derby claims on the line by actually running in a race and exposing how thin their credentials were. Wakashan won a Newmarket maiden in April but went wrong soon afterwards and missed Epsom. Michael Stoute's Opera House, heavily supported for the Derby in the spring on the strength of a ten-length victory at Leicester on his only outing as a two-year-old, was announced a non-runner in April after a fetlock injury.

Cruachan, keenly fancied after his graduation race win at York, sustained a serious leg injury on the Thursday before the race, but most of the other colts who had run prominently in the Derby trials were in the parade as it left the paddock on a cold and wet Derby Day.

At the off the joint favourites on 4-1 were Toulon, whose spectacular burst of speed in the Chester Vase had plenty of punters looking no further for the Derby winner, and Corrupt. Trained by Neville Callaghan and ridden by Cash Asmussen (fresh from landing the French Derby on Suave Dancer), Corrupt had beaten Selkirk at Kempton in March before winning the Maxims Club Derby Trial at Lingfield Park, thereby demolishing the Derby aspirations of the runner-up Young Buster.

Two Thousand Guineas winner Mystiko was next in the betting at 5-1. His Newmarket victory had been highly regarded despite the failure of Lycius to frank the form in the Irish Two Thousand, and the main questions were whether he would stay the extra half mile of the Derby and whether his temperament would get the better of this volatile colt during the drawn-out preliminaries. Three days before the race he was found to be lame and had a corn removed from his near-fore foot. It was touch and go whether he would take his chance at Epsom, and although he coped well enough with the parade, he was fairly easy in the betting, despite being the medium of the largest on-course wager struck – £100,000 to £20,000.

Four horses who had finished behind Mystiko in the Two Thousand Guineas reopposed at Epsom. Mujaazif, winner of the Royal Lodge Stakes at Ascot in 1990, had been second last at Newmarket and was not expected to do much better at Epsom. Hokusai's presence in the field, difficult to justify on form, at least gave an answer to the traditional question about who Lester Piggott would ride. Marju had been hot favourite at Newmarket but finished lame in eleventh place, since when speculation about his participation in the Derby had caused an unseemly row between his connections on the one hand and some bookmakers and press-men on the other. Never mind, he would take his chance.

The other Guineas runner reappearing in the Derby was Generous. This handsome colt, chestnut with flaxen mane and tail, had enjoyed an unfashionable two-year-old career. His first outing was on 2 May 1990 and he ran six times in all as a juvenile, his season culminating in a hard-fought victory over Bog Trotter in the Three Chimneys Dewhurst Stakes, for which he started at 50-1. He was clearly a tough, honest horse, but apparently short of the highest class, and Timeform's *Racehorses* of 1990 was simply being realistic when it wrote that 'enterprising placement might be necessary if he's to win more good races'. In the Two Thousand Guineas, his 1991 debut, Generous started at 11-1 and finished fourth, beaten just over eight and a half lengths by Mystiko, but the Guineas trip was probably too sharp for him, and he was a live candidate for the Derby. It was a close call, though, for jockey Alan Munro: Derby Day was his first day back in the saddle after a four-day suspension for careless riding at Goodwood on 23 May.

The unbeaten Hector Protector joined Toulon in the French challenge: he had not run since scrambling home in the Poule d'Essai des Poulains, and there were grave doubts about his stamina. Hailsham, winner of the Thresher Classic Trial, was not seriously expected to join Troy, Henbit, Shergar and Shahrastani by adding the Derby to Sandown success, but he came to Epsom fresh from landing the Italian Derby at Rome. Environment Friend, winner of the Dante Stakes, was quietly fancied to become the first grey to win the Derby since Airborne in 1946, and Star Of Gdansk had run a brave second to Fourstars Allstar in the Irish Two Thousand Guineas. Hundra had won the Dee Stakes at Chester but seemed out of his depth here – as, beyond question, was Toulon's pacemaker, 250-1 chance Arokat.

So into the stalls for the Ever Ready Derby went the winners in 1991 of the Two Thousand Guineas, the French Two Thousand Guineas, the Italian Derby, the Dante Stakes, the Classic Trial, the Craven Stakes, the Lingfield Derby Trial and the Chester Vase. Most pundits agreed that they were not *too* substandard a bunch.

Arokat may have been in the field as Toulon's pacemaker, but it was Mystiko who led from the start, and as the runners made the uphill climb to the gradual right-handed bend, the Guineas winner and the rank outsider went clear of the others, led by Hokusai and Generous. At the top of the hill Mystiko and Arokat were still going hell for leather, but Generous was a clear third and the remainder were close behind him. Backers of Toulon and Environment Friend were already down in the dumps, for both were clearly struggling, but as the field came hammering down the hill towards Tattenham Corner it was obvious that none was going better than Generous. Mystiko led into the straight but his tank was running dry, and as he capitulated over two furlongs out Alan Munro shot Generous into the lead.

With one spurt the Derby was over. Storming clear of his rivals, none of whom had a prayer of catching him, Generous made a wondrous sight. For a moment Hector Protector struggled to stay in touch, but lack of stamina was making inevitable the first defeat of his life. Then Marju detached himself from the pursuing posse and tried to mount

Alan Munro celebrates as Generous passes the Derby winning post . . .

a challenge, but he could never get in a blow at the leader. At the line he was an honourable second, five lengths adrift. It was a further seven lengths back to the Irish challenger Star Of Gdansk, and another half length to Hector Protector. Deprived of fourth place (and the £28,000 that went with it) by a mere short head was 66-1 outsider Hundra. Corrupt could only run on at one pace into sixth, and the other joint-favourite Toulon was a bitterly disappointing eleventh: 'He was just never going', reported Pat Eddery. Mystiko, who had not stayed, was tenth. Photos of every Derby finish always seem to include one runner who is no more than a distant speck on the horizon, and this time that role was filled by Mujaazif, tailed off thirty lengths behind Arokat.

But never mind the also-rans. This was a Derby dominated by a superb individual performance, and all of a sudden a star was born. Or perhaps two stars, for the sight of Alan Munro crouched low over Generous's neck, his whip held upright like a guardsman's sword, then punching the air in triumph as the post was passed, was an integral part of the Derby glory. And although in his euphoria Munro raised a few hackles at the post-race press conference, it was a minor smudge on a memorable Derby. 'This is fabulous', said the jockey, 'The best thing that has happened to me in my life.' Munro revealed that the previous day he had analysed several past runnings of the Derby with Lester Piggott's father Keith, to reduce the risks inherent in riding this trickiest of tracks. But alongside the admiration for Munro's achievement went a large measure of sympathy for Richard Quinn, who had ridden Generous in all but one of his previous

"This is fabulous... the best thing that has happened to me in my life."

. . . and has a word of thanks for his partner.

races and who had been replaced as retained jockey to owner Fahd Salman less than a month before the Derby. Quinn rode at the Beverley evening meeting on Derby Day, winning on Generous's stable-mate Zonda and stating stoically: 'You've got to keep working.'

The result of the 1991 Derby brought satisfaction to many quarters. It was especially pleasing for those who had expressed alarm at the way in which prospective middle-distance Classic colts are not subjected to a full campaign as two-year-olds, thus devaluing the top juvenile races. It was good to see Fahd Salman and Paul Cole, both of whom had been knocking at the door of the biggest of the big time for several years, finally coming up with a true champion. Most of all, it thrilled all racing enthusiasts to see the premier Classic won in such dazzling style and then to learn that the winner would be aimed at the two other big midsummer mile and a half races, the Irish Derby and the King George VI and Queen Elizabeth Diamond Stakes. We knew Generous to be tough and consistent. Now that we also knew him to be brilliant, the expectation of great races to come – especially of a promised clash with Suave Dancer at The Curragh – tingled.

The Derby was a triumph for Irish bloodstock. Bred at the Barronstown Stud in County Wicklow, Generous is from the fourth crop of Caerleon, a son of Nijinsky who was trained by Vincent O'Brien to win four races, including the Prix du Jockey-Club and the Benson and Hedges Gold Cup in 1983. His dam Doff The Derby, who never raced, is from one of the best middle-distance families: her dam Margarethen is the dam of the great French mare Trillion, herself dam of the even greater Triptych. No wonder Generous turned out so tough and consistent. He was sold as a foal at Kill for IR80,000 guineas to 'pinhooker' Hamish Alexander, then sold on as a yearling (again at Kill) to Fahd Salman for IR200,000 guineas. The Derby brought his career earnings to over £500,000. Nice work all round.

Less than eight weeks after Derby Day the experts would be locked into discussions about where Generous stood in the pantheon of great middle-distance horses. Can he be considered better than Dancing Brave? Perhaps. Would he have beaten Nashwan? Perhaps.

But on Derby Day what mattered was simply his performance. On an afternoon beset by bad weather, a course which was in part still a building site, the lowest paying attendance for many years (just 26,300) and a curious absence of atmosphere, the burst of acceleration with which Generous won the Derby glowed like a rainbow.

Ever Ready Derby (Group 1)

5 June 1991

1 mile 4 furlongs (going: good to firm)

1st: £355,000; 2nd: £133,000; 3rd: £64,000; 4th: £28,000

1	GENEROUS	A. Munro	9–1
2	MARJU	W. Carson	14–1
3	STAR OF GDANSK	C. Roche	14–1
4	HECTOR PROTECTOR	F. Head	6–1
5	HUNDRA	B. Raymond	66–1
6	CORRUPT	C. Asmussen	4–1 jt fav
7	HOKUSAI	L. Piggott	25–1
8	HAILSHAM	S. Cauthen	28–1
9	TOULON	Pat Eddery	4–1 jt fav
10	MYSTIKO	M. Roberts	5–1
11	ENVIRONMENT FRIEND	G. Duffield	11–1
12	AROKAT	Paul Eddery	250–1
13	MUJAAZIF	W. R. Swinburn	33–1

13 ran

distances: 5 lengths, 7 lengths
time: 2 mins 34.00 secs

Winner owned by Fahd Salman, trained by P. F. I. Cole (Whatcombe, Oxon), bred by Barronstown Stud, Ireland

Tote: win £11.20; places £3.70, £3.30, £2.20; dual forecast £77.70; trio £326.70

GENEROUS chestnut colt, born 8 February 1988	Caerleon	Nijinsky	Northern Dancer
			Flaming Page
		Foreseer	Round Table
			Regal Gleam
	Doff The Derby	Master Derby	Dust Commander
			Madam Jerry
		Margarethen	Tulyar
			Russ-Marie

HANSON
CORONATION CUP

Epsom, 6 June 1991

In The Groove (Steve Cauthen) asserts her authority in the Coronation Cup.

In advance, one of the most pleasing features of the 1991 Flat season was the number of top-class older horses kept in training, and several of these turned out for the Coronation Cup, the first Group One opportunity for horses older than three. A field of seven runners – several of whom had already done sufficient to justify their being still in action – offered a fascinating race.

Favourite was Rock Hopper, winner of the John Porter Stakes at Newbury (page 41) and the Jockey Club Stakes at Newmarket (page 49): Willie Carson had the mount in the Coronation Cup as regular partner Pat Eddery was claimed for Khalid Abdullah's Quest For Fame. Scarcely twenty-four hours after Generous had passed the post at Epsom, hard evidence of the advantages (or otherwise) of keeping Derby winners in training was about to be provided. Though an impressive winner of the 1990 Derby, Quest For Fame had seemed to beat a substandard field in the Classic, and his only subsequent performance – injured when unplaced behind Salsabil in the Irish Derby – told us little about his true ability. No nonsense about this Derby winner having 'nothing to prove': Quest For Fame had plenty to prove, but without a run for nearly a year there was inevitably a question mark over his fitness.

No such doubts surrounded In The Groove. Since winning the Trusthouse Forte Mile (page 42) she had been surprisingly beaten when 2–1 on favourite for Newbury's Lockinge Stakes, outsprinted by Polar Falcon at the end of a falsely run race. Most pundits were prepared to overlook that setback, but she was weak in the market, drifting from 5–2 to a starting price a point longer. The five-year-old Terimon had won the Earl of Sefton Stakes (page 37), Karinga Bay had been third to Rock Hopper at Newmarket and third in the Gordon Richards Stakes, and Spritsail had recently won in good style at Goodwood.

Quest For Fame made the early running and led the field into the straight, where Pat Eddery quickened the pace and tried to get clear of his rivals. But inside the final quarter mile it was clear that, well though the Derby winner had run on his first outing for so long, he was leading only on sufferance. In The Groove, who had steadily improved her position throughout the last half mile, was the first to attack. The undulations and cambers of Epsom are far from ideal for this large filly (she had flopped there in the 1990 Oaks), but Steve Cauthen brought her through with a beautifully balanced run, and

once in front she managed to repel the frantic challenges of Rock Hopper – who edged over to the inside rail in the final furlong - and Terimon, who plugged on gamely up the stands side to deprive Rock Hopper of second place by a neck.

It was In The Groove's first victory over twelve furlongs, and illustrated her great versatility as well as her class: this was her fourth Group One success. Immediate plans for the filly pointed to the Eclipse and perhaps the King George, but whatever the future held, the decision to keep her in training had been thoroughly vindicated.

Hanson Coronation Cup (Group 1)

6 June 1991
1 mile 4 furlongs (going: good)
1st: £82,542; 2nd: £30,624; 3rd: £14,487; 4th: £6,068

1	IN THE GROOVE	S. Cauthen	7–2
2	TERIMON	M. Roberts	12–1
3	ROCK HOPPER	W. Carson	15–8 fav
4	QUEST FOR FAME	Pat Eddery	11–4
5	KARINGA BAY	B. Rouse	33–1
6	SPRITSAIL	L. Piggott	6–1
7	SAPIENCE	W. R. Swinburn	33–1

7 ran

distances: ½ length, neck
time: 2 mins 36.32 secs

Winner owned by Brian Cooper, trained by D. R. C. Elsworth (Whitsbury, Hants), bred by Capt. John Macdonald–Buchanan

Tote: win £4.50; places £2.00, £2.50; dual forecast £9.90

A LIFETIME IN RACING

The **nom de plume** *'Hotspur' has been used in the* **Daily Telegraph** *since the nineteenth century. Here* **PETER SCOTT***, who held the position for twenty-six years until his retirement in 1991, reviews the highlights of a lengthy career.*

Best Horses of 1943, a birthday present sent to my boarding school, fired my ambition to become a racing journalist. This book, largely written by Phil Bull, was beautifully produced by wartime standards and well illustrated. National daily paper racing coverage had austerity restrictions and Bull took me into a new world.

He analysed the champions of that year – Straight Deal, Nasrullah, Herringbone, Ribbon and Persian Gulf – with incisive essays still fascinating to read. There were no video replays to help Bull, but the accuracy of his race-reading was underlined years later when I taped an old newsreel of Straight Deal's Derby and played it over several times with the aid of a racecard.

Wartime Derbys were run on the Summer course at Newmarket, and barely two lengths covered the first six home in a twenty-three-horse field.

Although Bull was a substantial backer in those days and must have been drawn to certain horses, he missed nothing of note. His summary of the temperamental Nasrullah, third in that Derby, ended with a forecast of stud success which time fully justified.

The 1943 Flat season – National Hunt racing was not permitted at that stage of the war – comprised 471 races on six tracks. Only horses trained north of the Trent could run at Pontefract or Stockton; Ascot, Salisbury and Windsor were also operational. Newmarket staged the top sixteen races and these alone were open to horses trained elsewhere.

Straight Deal's Derby earned Miss Dorothy Paget £4,388. Gordon Richards was champion jockey with 65 wins from 281 rides. Cecil Boyd-Rochfort, Fred Darling and Joe Lawson all trained fewer than twenty-five horses. Jack

Jarvis and Walter Earl both had teams of about thirty and Frank Butters forty. The biggest string, approximately fifty, was with Walter Nightingall at Epsom. He trained Straight Deal and the champion two-year-old Orestes. Two-year-olds were allowed to race un-named, in the names of their dams, until 1946. Orestes and Happy Landing, the second best juvenile, first ran as the Orison colt and the Happy Morn colt.

Best Horses of 1943 covered 450 of about 1,500 horses which ran that year. It followed a much slimmer little paperback, *Best Horses of 1942*, written under the name William K. Temple. Bull, later to found the Timeform organisation continuing the *Racehorses* annuals, was then a schoolmaster and deemed a pseudonym advisable.

Racing's first major post-war changes included the photo-finish camera, introduced at the 1947 Epsom

April meeting, and Hamilton Park pioneering an evening fixture that July. Sir John Crocker Bulteel headed a new breed of imaginative promoters, transforming Ascot with a string of fresh summer and autumn big races. Ascot, pre-war, had simply staged the four-day Royal meeting.

Helped by a recommendation from Peter O'Sullevan, I entered racing journalism as a sub-editor on the Press Association news agency in 1950. This chance followed months of despair, with unanswered applications to the humblest tipping sheets and some fruitless journeys.

One took me from London to the Leeds offices of the long defunct *Sporting Pink*. This was at the editor's invitation, but I arrived to be told he was 'too busy' to see me. The junior reporter sent downstairs to turn me away was Jim Stanford, later such a success on the *Daily Mail*. Jim and I often recalled our first meeting.

Press rooms in the 1950s were supposed to be unfriendly towards newcomers, but I never found them so. Particular kindness was shown by Geoffrey Hamlyn, who returned starting prices for so many years, Norman Pegg (Gimcrack of the *Daily Sketch*) and the Gilbey brothers, Geoffrey and Quinny. Geoffrey used to attack ignorant and lazy local stewards in rhyming verse: 'The stewards lunch till half past three, When they commence to have their tea', is a well-remembered broadside.

Stewards are often criticised in the press nowadays, but it was not so then. Norman Pegg and Clive Graham (The Scout) were both had up for outspoken comments. I was also 'interviewed' for attacking the Jockey Club's deplorable PR when a post-race dope test threatened to deprive Relko of the 1963 Derby. No official statement was made until the Jockey Club's hand had been forced by a newspaper leak.

Quinny Gilbey, Kettledrum of the *Sporting Chronicle*, and Peter O'Sullevan both made a close study of racing in France. I was proud to be their

disciple. We were regarded as eccentrics, although French horses won so many big English races. Peter's fame as a television commentator now overshadows the tremendous impact he made as a journalist when joining the *Daily Express* in 1950. He and Clive Graham were a formidable team, giving the opposition as much trouble as Lindwall and Miller gave the English batsmen.

Trainers and jockeys were not then so accessible to questioning. Trainers often took the 'none of your business' line over big race plans. One of my colleagues, seeking a quote from a jockey who had been second in an early post-war Derby, was met with a 'You saw the race didn't you?' rebuff. I wonder how that jockey and some of his contemporaries would have reacted to television interviews.

"You saw the race didn't you?"

Lester Piggott might well have wished to be part of the old era. His mistrust of the media took many years to overcome. His early impact as a teenager made such attention inevitable and it was heightened by brushes with the stewards who considered his methods too rough. Lester was still only eighteen when his riding of Never Say Die at Royal Ascot in 1954 caused him to be suspended for the rest of that season. Officialdom proved incapable of understanding public interest. Journalists, crowded outside the weighing room, were told to 'wait for the verdict in next week's *Racing Calendar*'.

I was still then a racecourse reporter

for The Press Association and its problems included the delay in introducing overnight declared runners until 1961. The PA supplied newspapers with 'probable' runners and jockeys. Certain trainers, seeking a better price for some fancied horse, would tell the PA it was a non-starter. This meant it carried little or no off-course money. I was among the reporters who made late-evening checks at racecourse stables to ensure that every horse there was in the probables, but such precautions were not foolproof.

In 1956 I joined the *Sporting Life*, sub-editing copy often sent from the racecourses by telegram, and became a columnist the following year when signed up by the *Evening Standard* to succeed Richard Baerlein who was temporarily disillusioned with racing journalism. He came back to join the *Observer* in 1963 and took over at the *Guardian* in 1968, when that paper finally decided to give racing regular coverage. Richard has never been one to mince words and I recall one of his comments during the run up to Kelling's 1950 Cambridgeshire. 'Spots' were given as the reason for Kelling being announced a doubtful runner, but his price shortened again and caused Baerlein to write that 'the spots have gone and so has the 33–1.' Kelling was eventually backed down to less than half those odds.

Work on the *Evening Standard* required 7 a.m. copy for the Midday edition, a different story for the country editions, which then sold as far afield as Cornwall, and updated afternoon race reports until 4.30 p.m.

Betting shops, with their immediate results that hit evening papers sales so hard, did not become legalised until shortly before the Levy Board's 1961 introduction. Evening papers previously enjoyed a clear run. Punters often bought several editions to keep up to date with their luck.

Televised racing was also a rarity and the *Evening Standard* course reports had a wide readership. The 1962 Derby provided my most difficult one. As usual, there was an open line to the office and copy was expected to flow as the runners were pulling up. Larkspur's win was overshadowed by seven of his rivals – including the favourite Hethersett – galloping riderless past the post. The incident which caused this took place at the one stage invisible from my viewpoint and it took some time to establish what had happened.

In January 1965 I succeeded Bill Curling as Hotspur and was privileged to hold that position for a record twenty-six years. It has been a *nom de plume* on the *Daily Telegraph* since the middle of the last century.

The spring of my first Hotspur season included Arkle's second Cheltenham Gold Cup victory over Mill House and the Lincoln Handicap's transfer to Doncaster after Lincoln had closed. A few months later came, at Newmarket, the first English race started from stalls. It was won by Lester Piggott on Track Spare. Women trainers first received official licence recognition the following year.

A betting tax was introduced – by Chancellor James Callaghan – in 1966. Seven years later came computer-assisted centralised handicapping. Until then, racecourses had employed different handicappers and trainers would study to see where their horses were 'best in'. Run-of-the-mill races closed about three weeks beforehand. The five-day entry system was not introduced until 1989. Lingfield staged the first 'All Weather' track fixture on 30 October that year. Brigadier Gerard died the day before. Seldom has a changing era been so sharply symbolised.

Back in the 1950s live Press Association work was anonymous, and I waited six years for my name to be attached to a column. This took place in July 1956, when the *Sporting Life* sent me to Ascot for Ribot's last gallop before the King George VI and Queen Elizabeth Stakes, staged only two days prior to the race. Ribot covered the full distance in

what turned out to be faster time than he took when winning the King George by five lengths.

His second Prix de l'Arc de Triomphe victory that autumn provided the finest exhibition of Thoroughbred class I have ever seen. Six lengths was the official margin, but reliable photographs show it nearer to nine. Ribot then retired unbeaten in sixteen races, between five and fifteen furlongs, spread over three seasons. I was at San Siro, Milan, for his vociferously cheered exhibition gallop two weeks later.

I dined that evening with Ugo Penco, who trained Ribot and was head lad to Sr Federico Tesio when that owner's other unbeaten international star, Nearco, swept all before him in 1938. Penco assured me that Ribot was much superior, although Nearco easily beat

No race excites me as much as the Derby.

the Derby winner Bois Roussel in their Grand Prix de Paris clash and also accomplished the rare feat of winning a Classic (the Italian Derby) by a distance. The Ribot line is second only to Northern Dancer's as an influence on present-day pedigrees.

Tantieme, another dual Arc winner (1950–51) is my pick of many French-trained post-war champions. He also raced at a variety of distances over three seasons and won big races in England, but his stable made the disastrous decision to fly him over on the morning of the 1951 King George: bad weather made it a wretched trip, and the drained Tantieme could finish only third.

Longchamp was a different world in

the days of Ribot and Tantieme, with no proper parade ring. The runners virtually walked round through the crowds. To find out the latest Pari Mutuel odds, one had to buy slips of paper from touts.

The English press is now bombarded with revised big race odds after every trial, but bookmakers used to hold their hands until the periodic 'Call Over' of odds at their Victoria Club. One notable exception was William Hill, and few would dispute Geoffrey Hamlyn's assessment of Hill as the most powerful post-war racecourse bookmaker. I often stood near Hill's pitch as he bet in tens of thousands. He made his own big race prices without waiting for Call Overs.

No race excites me as much as The Derby and Gordon Richards' 1953 win on Pinza remains my greatest racing thrill. Running it close was Nashwan's 1989 triumph, when trainer Dick Hern was under notice to quit his beloved West Ilsley stable.

Nijinsky and Mill Reef are the best of forty-six Derby winners that I have seen: their successes were achieved in consecutive years (1970/71). Grundy and Troy later helped make the 1970s a vintage decade for Epsom heroes.

Tudor Minstrel and Brigadier Gerard were specially brilliant in the Two Thousand Guineas. Tudor Minstrel coasted home the eight-lengths winner in 1947, with Gordon Richards patting his neck. Dayjur's tremendous early speed reminded me of Tudor Minstrel.

Alycidon and Sagaro will always be associated with the Ascot Gold Cup. Both were superb long-distance performers. Alycidon, assisted by two pacemakers, outstayed Black Tarquin at Ascot in 1949. Black Tarquin, who had beaten him in the previous season's St Leger, also won the six-furlong Gimcrack Stakes as a two-year-old.

Dick Hern, Henry Cecil and John Dunlop are among the present-day English trainers every bit as good as the giants of bygone times. Noel Murless, who began as a pre-war steeplechase rider, controlled a small stable in

Yorkshire before succeeding Fred Darling at Beckhampton, but Noel's greatest successes came after his 1952 move to Newmarket. Vincent O'Brien's record, first with jumpers more than forty years ago and then with flat racers, is unrivalled for versatility. He is still going strong. Irish racing was small time when Vincent started, and early champions had to make their marks in England after sea voyages or air travel far less speedy and comfortable than nowadays.

Lester Piggott, riding for O'Brien again, and also associated with many of the Murless stars, must rank with Gordon Richards and Fred Archer as the three greatest English jockeys of all time.

I did not see much of that wily tactician Harry Wragg, who retired in 1946, but superb big-race rides by Charlie Elliott and Charlie Smirke are well remembered. Eph and Doug Smith had excellent day-to-day consistency. Manny and Joe Mercer were also brothers. Joe had classical style. Manny's trump card was instinctive flair. His death – thrown going down to the start at Ascot in September 1959 – occurred long before compulsory crash helmets and body protectors.

Pat Eddery, Steve Cauthen and Willie Carson, whose every move is analysed by video replays, maintain exceptional standards despite the pressure of evening racing and Sunday demands on the Continent.

My brief is not to dwell much on National Hunt racing, but who could review the post-war era without paying tribute to the incomparable Arkle? He was foaled in 1957, the year that Whitbread and Hennessy launched steeplechases to be the forerunners of modern-day sponsorship. Freebooter, Roimond, Persian War, Bula and National Spirit have been my other jumping favourites: National Spirit gained lengths in the air with spectacular hurdling.

The 1990s, in their turn, will be remembered by some as the good old days when racing delights new generations. Phil Bull made a rare misjudgement when he described the sport as 'the great triviality'. Relaxation is essential to life's enjoyment and racing will continue to play its part.

GOLD SEAL OAKS

Before the Oaks, Jet Ski Lady (Christy Roche) hardly looks the part of the complete outsider . . .

The 1991 Oaks was the one thousandth Classic race run in Great Britain, completing a millenium which stretched back to 24 September 1776, the day of the first running of the St Leger.

Appropriately, the thousandth Classic produced its share of records, with the winner's starting price equalling the longest odds ever returned in the Oaks as well as her margin of victory matching the second longest winning distance.

As is so often the case, the Oaks seemed beforehand to hinge on whether the One Thousand Guineas winner would stay the extra half mile at Epsom. Shadayid had won the Guineas handily enough, and expert opinion differed as to whether she would be more or less suited by the longer distance. The day before the race the pessimists seemed to be holding sway as her odds drifted from evens to 5–4 against, and although she opened in the course betting at that price and touched 11–8, weight of money brought her in to 11–10 on before settling at a starting price of evens. Oblivious to these market moves, the grey filly herself had to undergo the parade, which some thought might cause her to fret away her chance. In the event she remained laudably calm, unlike one of her main rivals Shamshir. Second favourite at 6–1, Shamshir became very worked up during the preliminaries, but was marginally preferred in the betting to Sheikh Mohammed's other runner Dartrey. The Sheikh's pair had finished second and third in the Musidora Stakes (page 64), and both were quietly fancied.

Of the other runners, Ausherra had won the Lingfield Oaks Trial and had the connections of the moment – Fahd Salman, Paul Cole and Alan Munro; Khalid Abdullah's Peplum was unbeaten but very inexperienced, the Oaks being just the third race of her life; Jaffa Line had been last in the

. . . and by Tattenham Corner her rivals are already toiling in her wake. Immediately behind her are Willie Carson on Shadayid (rails) and Steve Cauthen on Dartrey.

Musidora; Paul Mellon's Fragrant Hill had won the Lupe Stakes at Goodwood impressively but was something of an unknown quantity; Magnificent Star had won her last race at Newbury; and Jet Ski Lady looked to have a forlorn hope of becoming the fifth Irish-trained Oaks winner.

Maktoum Al Maktoum's imposing chestnut filly hardly boasted form to suggest she was capable of overturning the likes of Shadayid, but after closer inspection of her past performances an each-way nibble might have beckoned. She had won three of her six races, and had been beaten only four lengths by Shadayid when seventh in the Prix Marcel Boussac at Longchamp on Arc day 1990. Her last victory had been over ten furlongs at The Curragh in April, after which she had run fourth to Runyon at Leopardstown the following month. But there was an excuse for that defeat: she had lost both her hind shoes during the race and had cut herself badly. By Vaguely Noble out of a Nijinsky mare, she clearly had no stamina worries, and might improve significantly when moved up from ten furlongs to twelve.

Jet Ski Lady's trainer Jim Bolger and jockey Christy Roche walked the course before racing to assess the effect of overnight rain and plot their race. 'The plan was to quicken it up from the six-furlong marker and stretch them from there', said Bolger, but in the event at the six-furlong marker the one thousandth Classic was already beginning to look a bit of a one-horse race.

Jet Ski Lady broke quickly from the stalls and proceeded to make every inch of the running. She maintained a tremendous gallop, turned on the heat coming down the hill, and once in the straight simply went further and further away, her giant stride powering her relentlessly home.

In her wake her more fancied rivals had tried in vain to get anywhere near her. Shadayid had pulled hard in the early stages, but it was a very obvious lack of stamina which found her out after she had made a valiant attempt to get to the leader two furlongs out. As the One Thousand Guineas winner weakened, she was passed close home by Shamshir. Jaffa Line stayed on at one pace to be fourth.

It's one thing for a horse like Noblesse – another ten-length winner of the Oaks – to power home in glorious isolation. In 1963 that great Irish filly was confirming her status, and the crowd rose to her. The 1991 situation was somewhat different. Few in the paying crowd of just 6,312 had ever heard of Jet Ski Lady before the day of the race, let alone backed her, and the reception to which she returned was decidedly muted.

One group of people who were cheering the filly home was the bookies, for many of whom Jet Ski Lady had been a 'skinner'. William Hill's Don Payne reported that 'today has been embarrassing . . . we took virtually no money for her at all'. Less happy were those who had backed her on the Tote, which paid a dividend of just £16.50 (15½–1) for a winner whose returned starting price was 50–1.

Jet Ski Lady's connections did not share the general surprise. 'On a scale of 0 to 10, I'd say 3 for how surprised I am', said trainer Jim Bolger.

Others put their surprise higher up the scale, but once the sense of shock had evaporated, there was no disputing that this was a true Classic

Just a furlong between Jet Ski Lady and Oaks glory

"On a scale of 0 to 10, I'd say 3 for how surprised I am."

performance by a filly of remarkable toughness and stamina. Subsequent performances would show Jet Ski Lady to be a real battler and a racehorse of some class, and the manner in which she strode right away from her more vaunted rivals in the Oaks remains one of the great sights of the 1991 season.

JET SKI LADY (USA) chestnut filly, born 20 February 1988	Vaguely Noble	Vienna	Aureole
			Turkish Blood
		Noble Lassie	Nearco
			Belle Sauvage
	Bemissed	Nijinsky	Northern Dancer
			Flaming Page
		Bemis Heights	Herbager
			Orissa

Gold Seal Oaks (Group 1)

8 June 1991

1 mile 4 furlongs (going: good)

1st: £147,500; **2nd:** £55,000; **3rd:** £26,250; **4th:** £11,250

1	JET SKI LADY	C. Roche	50–1
2	SHAMSHIR	L. Dettori	6–1
3	SHADAYID	W. Carson	Evens fav
4	JAFFA LINE	M. Roberts	14–1
5	MAGNIFICENT STAR	A. S. Cruz	16–1
6	DARTREY	S. Cauthen	7–1
7	AUSHERRA	A. Munro	12–1
8	PEPLUM	Pat Eddery	12–1
9	FRAGRANT HILL	R. Cochrane	20–1

9 ran

distances: 10 lengths, ¾ length
time: 2 mins 37.30 secs

Winner owned by Maktoum Al Maktoum, trained by J. S. Bolger (Ireland), bred by Ryehill Farm, USA

Tote: win £16.50; places £3.70, £2.00, £1.30; dual forecast £112.40

U.S. TRIPLE CROWN

Strike The Gold and Hansel made 1991 a memorable year for the Triple Crown, producing one of the most captivating sequences of Kentucky Derby, Preakness Stakes and Belmont Stakes for some time.

For the first leg, the ten-furlong Kentucky Derby at Churchill Downs on 4 May, Hansel – winner of his last two races – was sent off the 5–2 favourite. Second choice for the punters was Fly So Free, winner of the Breeders' Cup Juvenile at Belmont Park in 1990. This year he had won the Florida Derby from Strike The Gold and then been beaten three lengths by that colt in the Blue Grass Stakes at Keeneland. Strike The Gold started at a shade under 5–1 for the Derby, slightly shorter than Best Pal, trained in California by Englishman Ian Jory: he had been the best two-year-old in the West, and had run second to Fly So Free in the Breeders' Cup.

It looked a hot race on paper, but it was won conclusively by Strike The Gold, who after staying towards the rear in the early stages started to pick off his rivals going into the home turn. Jockey Chris Antley was careful to keep his mount towards the outside as his most prominent rivals were stretched out across the track, and once he asked Strike The Gold to quicken away the Alydar colt responded well, despite veering towards the stands. Best Pal made his bid on the other side of the track and made rapid progress once he was clear of traffic problems, but never looked like catching the winner. Mane Minister was third and Hansel faded in the straight to finish tenth of the sixteen runners.

The first three in the Kentucky Derby joined the also-rans Corporate Report (ninth) and Hansel in an eight-runner line-up for the Preakness Stakes (1 mile 1½ furlongs) at Pimlico, Baltimore, just two weeks later. Hansel had worked encouragingly during the week before the Preakness, but his bafflingly poor display in the Derby had undermined his supporters' faith, and he started at just over 9–1. Predictably, the Derby winner Strike The Gold was favourite, but one rival strongly fancied to demolish his Triple Crown aspirations was Olympio, winner of the Arkansas Derby.

This time it was Strike The Gold's turn to flop as Hansel showed his Kentucky Derby running to be all wrong, powering home seven lengths clear of Corporate Report after being in the thick of things throughout. Mane Minister was again third, and Strike The Gold a deeply disappointing sixth.

Although there would be no Triple Crown winner in 1991 – the last was Affirmed in 1978 – both the first two legs had produced a fine winning performance and a major disappointment, and the hope that both Hansel and Strike The Gold would run a true race in the third leg, the Belmont Stakes over twelve furlongs at Belmont Park on 8 June, cranked up the sense of anticipation.

At the off Strike The Gold was favourite, with Hansel almost double his odds at a shade over 4–1: of the two flops in the earlier legs, Strike The Gold's was apparently the easier to forgive. Among their opponents in an eleven-runner field were Mane Minister again, Green Alligator, who had not run since finishing fourth in the Kentucky Derby, and Smooth Performance, trained in Ireland by Dermot Weld and ridden by Michael Kinane, looking to repeat their historic Belmont victory with Go And Go a year before.

It was a race to savour, and for once both the principals ran up to their form. Hansel took up the running with a half a mile to go and once in the home stretch kept to the inside rails as he made for the wire. Strike The Gold made up ground in the stretch and was closing with every stride as the line approached, but could not quite peg back Hansel and was beaten a head. Mane Minister was third and thus pulled off an unusual Triple Crown of his own, having been third in the first two legs as well. Smooth Performance was a disappointing eighth.

Hansel tore a tendon when going down to a head defeat by Corporate Report in the Travers Stakes at Saratoga (with Fly So Free third and the favourite Strike The Gold fifth), and this injury was to abbreviate his season. But his victories in the Preakness and Belmont made all the more galling his lapse in the Kentucky Derby. No matter: his Belmont victory showed him a horse of great courage, and trainer Frank Brothers did not mince words that day: 'This is the greatest moment of my career. The good Lord is on my side!'

> **"This is the greatest moment of my career. The good Lord is on my side!"**

Kentucky Derby (Grade 1)

Churchill Downs, 4 May 1991

1 mile 2 furlongs (Dirt)

1st: £339,792; **2nd:** £75,130; **3rd:** £36,269; **4th:** £18,135

1	STRIKE THE GOLD	C. Antley	48–10
2	BEST PAL	G. Stevens	52–10
3	MANE MINISTER	A. Solis	87–1
4	GREEN ALLIGATOR	C. Nakatani	16–1

16 ran (Hansel 5–2 fav)

distances: 1¾ lengths, 1¾ lengths
time: 2 mins 3 secs
Winner owned by B. G. Brophy & Partners, trained by N. Zito, bred by Calumet Farm
Pari–mutuel: win (including $2 stake) $11.60; places (1–2) $6.20, $6.40; show (1–2–3) $5.40, $5.40, $25.60; exacta (SF) $73.40

Preakness Stakes (Grade 1)

Pimlico, 18 May 1991

1 mile 1 furlong 110 yards (Dirt)

1st: £224,233; **2nd:** £68,995; **3rd:** £34,497; **4th:** £17,249

1	HANSEL	J. Bailey	91–10
2	CORPORATE REPORT	P. Day	11–1
3	MANE MINISTER	A. Solis	19–1
4	OLYMPIO	E. Delahoussaye	24–10

8 ran (Strike The Gold 18–10 fav)

distances: 7 lengths, 2¾ lengths
time: 1 min 54.0 secs
Winner owned by Lazy Lane Farms, trained by F. Brothers, bred by Marvin Little jr
Pari–mutuel: win (including $2 stake) $20.20; places (1–2) $10.80, $11.00; show (1–2–3) $8.00, $6.40, $5.80; exacta (SF) $212.20

Belmont Stakes (Grade 1)

Belmont Park, 8 June 1991

1 mile 4 furlongs (Dirt)

1st: £417,480; **2nd:** £79,314; **3rd:** £43,262; **4th:** £21, 631

1	HANSEL	J. Bailey	41–10
2	STRIKE THE GOLD	C. Antley	22–10 fav
3	MANE MINISTER	A. Solis	18–1
4	CORPORATE REPORT	P. Day	82–10

11 ran

distances: head, 3 lengths
time: 2 mins 28.0 secs
Winner owned by Lazy Lane Farms, trained by F. Brothers, bred by Marvin Little jr
Pari–mutuel: win (including $ stake) $10.20; places (1–2) $6.40, $5.00; show (1–2–3) $5.00, $4.00, $4.40; exacta (SF) $39.20

PRIX DE DIANE HERMES

Chantilly, 9 June 199

With the Prix de Diane Hermes, the French equivalent of the Oaks, being run the day after the real thing at Epsom, it is unsurprising that there was a very slight English challenge - though had the home team had any prescience of what Jet Ski Lady would do to them, they might have thought Chantilly the softer option! The sole English challenger was Kazoo, trained in Richmond by Bill Watts for Sheikh Mohammed and coupled in the betting with the Sheikh's more fancied other runner Sha Ta.

Treble, trained by Criquette Head and an impressive winner of the Prix Saint-Alary, was coupled at the head of the market with her stable companions Brooklyn's Dance and Ring Beaune, and Caerlina was well supported after her third in the Poule d'Essai des Pouliches. (In 1990 she had been runner-up to Shadayid in the Prix Marcel Boussac on Arc day.) Many had thought Caerlina unlucky in the Pouliches after she had been severely hampered in the early stages – not least her owner Kaichi Nitta. Mr Nitta was apparently so superstitious about the ill fortune which had attended his filly that he decided to replace her jockey that day – Lester Piggott – with Eric Legrix, and went so far as to refuse to watch the race in person lest his presence contribute to his horse's bad fortune.

Who is to mock the owner's superstition? Caerlina joined issue with the leaders halfway up the Chantilly straight and sprinted clear to hold the late challenge of 45–1 outsider Magic Night by three quarters of a length.

The Prix de Diane was the first Group One victory for Caerlina's trainer Jean de Roualle, and brought another Classic success for the sire of the moment Caerleon within a few days of Generous's Derby victory.

Magic Night would get her revenge in the Prix Vermeille in September, but there was no denying that the turn of foot which took Caerlina clear in the Diane was a true Classic burst of speed – and one which must have had Lester Piggott musing on what might have been.

Caerlina holds off Magic Night (near side) and Louve Romaine.

Prix de Diane Hermes (Group 1)

9 June 1991

1 mile 2 furlongs 110 yards (going: soft)

1st: £142,566; **2nd:** £57,027; **3rd:** £28,514; **4th:** £14,257

1	CAERLINA	E. Legrix	132–10
2	MAGIC NIGHT	A. Badel	45–1
3	LOUVE ROMAINE	D. Boeuf	10–1
4	MASSLAMA	W. Mongil	21–10

13 ran

distances: ¾ length, neck (Brooklyn's Dance, Ring Beauve and Treble 7–5 coupled favourites)
time: 2 mins 10.5 secs

Winner owned by K. Nitta, trained by J. de Roualle, bred by R. M. Aubert

Pari–mutuel: win FF14.20; places FF4.40, FF9.30, FF3.80; dual forecast FF220.90

ROYAL
ASCOT

Willie Carson is a popular fellow after winning the St James's Palace Stakes on Marju.

Filthy weather may have caused most of the fashion highlights of the first day of Royal Ascot to be new lines in raincoats, but the racing had excitement enough to match the occasion.

The traditional opener, the Queen Anne Stakes, set the mood for a week of pulsating finishes. Clive Brittain's Sikeston had won six pattern races in Italy (including four Group One), all on heavy ground, and with the Ascot going officially good and his opponents including Bold Russian and Candy Glen (Lester Piggott's first ride at Royal Ascot since winning the 1985 King's Stand Stakes on Never So Bold), his starting price of 9–1 seemed a reasonable reflection of his chance.

Keeping close to the massed ranks of umbrellas along the stands rail, Sikeston took the lead with about a quarter of a mile to go and stayed on resolutely as Willie Carson detached Rami from the pursuing pack. The two crossed the line together, and although Michael Roberts had no doubt that he had won on Sikeston, trainer Clive Brittain was less sure – and performed a little jig as the announcement was made that his charge had won by a head.

There was no doubt whatever about the result of the Prince Of Wales's Stakes, which attracted a high-class field including Zoman, Terimon and Karinga Bay, once the hot favourite Stagecraft had set sail for home over a furlong out to win in the manner of a very good horse. The winner of the Brigadier Gerard Stakes at Sandown Park on his only previous outing in 1991, Stagecraft is out of Bella Colora, beaten two short heads by Oh So Sharp and Al Bahathri in the 1985 One Thousand Guineas, and had set Sheikh Mohammed back 520,000 guineas as a yearling. After the colt's performance at Ascot, that money looked well spent.

Likewise the 160,000 guineas paid for Second Set as a yearling. This Luca Cumani-trained colt may not quite have won the St James's Palace Stakes, the feature event of the opening day, but his

effort in going under by a head to Marju on only the third outing of his life proclaimed Second Set a colt of exceptional promise – which he fulfilled on his next outing when landing the Sussex Stakes at Goodwood.

Marju was a strong favourite for the St James's Palace Stakes, but his appearance in the race was a little surprising, for the Ascot engagement came less than two weeks after his excellent effort in finishing second to Generous in the Derby over a distance

"That wasn't very good for my nerves"

clearly too long for him. Brought back to a mile, he should have been in his element, but thirteen days was not long to recover from his Epsom exertions, and he faced some strong opposition. Second favourite was Acteur Francais, touched off by Hector Protector in the Poule d'Essai des Poulains (page 53). Second Set had won his only two races but was very inexperienced, and Hokusai, third in the Craven Stakes, had found the Derby trip beyond him.

It was a wonderful race. Second Set and Hokusai made the early running, while Willie Carson and Marju lurked at the back. Once in the straight, Marju was brought to the outside of the field and swept to the front with an electric spurt, but Second Set soon joined issue, and the two produced a stirring battle

all the way to the line. For a moment it looked as if Marju had come too soon, and that Second Set would worry him out of it, but hard though Lanfranco Dettori tried, Marju rallied close home and just held on. 'That wasn't very good for my nerves', said trainer John Dunlop.

After such excitement it was time for the appearance of what for many Ascot punters was the banker bet of the week, Fahd Salman's imposing colt Dilum in the Coventry Stakes. An emphatic winner at Goodwood and somewhat inadvertently beaten by Dr Devious (also in the Coventry) at Newbury on his debut, Dilum was reported to be held in the highest regard by his connections, and attracted a massive amount of money in the ring. He drifted from 11–10 on to 5–4 against before hardening to 11–10 at the off, and removed a third of a million pounds from the ring when taking over the running in the last three furlongs and powering home by three lengths from Dr Devious. Dilum thus went one better than his distinguished stable companion Generous, second in the Coventry in 1990, and had the ante-post bookmakers offering 16–1 against his winning the 1992 Two Thousand Guineas.

At Royal Ascot 1990 you could have named any price against Lester Piggott riding a winner there in 1991, yet here he was in the King Edward VII Stakes giving Saddlers' Hall one of his magical tactical rides. Piggott made most of the running on this half brother to Sun Princess, and kicked on in the straight to win impressively by six lengths from Secret Haunt. Corrupt, who had started co-favourite for the Derby, and Peking Opera, one time ante-post market leader for that Classic, were well in arrears.

After five pattern races, the first day's programme ended with the Ascot Stakes. This was won with a fine sense of occasion by Cabochon, owned by the Queen's Representative at Ascot Colonel Sir Piers Bengough.

Dilum in all his mid-season glory as Alan Munro steers him to victory in the Coventry Stakes.

Cabochon was trainer David Morley's first Royal Ascot winner, and Satin Flower, who took the opener on Wednesday, the Jersey Stakes, only the second at the Royal fixture for John Gosden. The filly came right away in the final furlong to win by six lengths from Dawson Place and Two Thousand Guineas disappointment Desert Sun, who had been backed from 6–4 to 11–10, including one bet of £22,000 to £20,000.

There was another bet of £20,000 in the Queen Mary Stakes, this time to win £50,000 on the brilliantly speedy Marling, a daughter of the great sprinter Marwell (who had won the King's Stand Stakes at the meeting ten years ago). Marling took the lead a furlong out and quickened in the manner of a good filly to beat Culture Vulture by a length. The rider of the runner-up, Richard Quinn, lodged an objection after a bout of interference, but this was hastily overruled.

Kooyonga (far side) holds off the sustained challenge of Willie Carson on Shadayid in a thrilling Coronation Stakes.

The Queen Mary Stakes: Marling (Gary Carter) wins from Culture Vulture (Richard Quinn, left) and Central City (Bruce Raymond, centre) . . .

The spotlight stayed on the females for the next race, which promised to be the event of the week. The Coronation Stakes, the only Group One contest on the second day of the meeting, brought together the winners of the One Thousand Guineas races in all three of the major European racing countries. Since her victory at Newmarket Shadayid had patently failed to stay when third to Jet Ski Lady in the Oaks – just eleven days before the Coronation Stakes. Although she would undoubtedly benefit from a return to a mile, she had endured a tough race at Epsom and might still be feeling the effects. Kooyonga, second to Shadayid at Newmarket, had won the Irish One Thousand (pages 69–70) in brilliant fashion and seemed to be improving. Danseuse du Soir had won the French One Thousand Guineas, the Poule d'Essai des Pouliches, from Sha Ta and Caerlina and was clearly a filly of the highest class. For good measure there was a fourth One Thousand heroine in the shape of Arranvanna, winner of the

. . . and seems suitably unconcerned afterwards.

The Queen's Vase: Jendali (Steve Cauthen, right) beats Silver Rainbow (Pat Eddery) by a neck. Le Corsaire (Lanfranco Dettori) is third.

The Gold Cup: at the final turn, Trainglot (Willie Carson) leads from Retouch (Richard Quinn), with the blinkered Indian Queen (Walter Swinburn, quartered cap) poised to launch her effort.

Italian equivalent in Rome in April. Add the likes of Crystal Gazing (winner of the Nell Gwyn and third in the One Thousand) and Gussy Marlowe (winner of the Musidora Stakes), and this was a race to slaver over.

It certainly lived up to its billing. Shadayid started favourite after some hefty support in the ring, with Kooyonga second best and Danseuse du Soir drifting from an opening price of 2–1 to 7–2 before coming in to 100–30.

Gussy Marlowe took up the running from the start, up out of Swinley Bottom and round into the straight, where Kooyonga made her move and cruised into the lead on the far rail. Almost immediately Shadayid was at her, Willie Carson bringing the grey filly to challenge on the stands side. Warren O'Connor, having his first ride at Ascot, went for his whip, and Kooyonga responded with great guts, sticking her head out and refusing to give in as Carson roused Shadayid to greater effort. For a moment it looked as if it could go either way, but Shadayid was the first to weaken, and Kooyonga kept up her gallop to land the verdict by three quarters of a length. Gussy Marlowe was third, just in front of the disappointing Danseuse du Soir.

It was the first victory for an Irish-trained horse at Royal Ascot since 1988, and a first winner at the Royal meeting for Michael Kauntze, who paid tribute to the runner-up – 'Shadayid ran a fantastic race' – while revelling in the triumph of his filly. Well he might, for Kooyonga was now the best filly miler in Europe. She had been bought by her owner Mitsuo Haga before the Irish One Thousand Guineas, with part of the deal stipulating that Kauntze would train her until Royal Ascot, and not necessarily beyond. 'I don't know if I'm still in charge of her', joked the trainer after race, but no one doubted that he was.

Shadayid had lost nothing in defeat – 'She got beat, that's all there is to it', said Willie Carson – and as the dust settled it

John Reid pushes 20–1 shot Third Watch home in the Ribblesdale Stakes.

was widely felt that in terms of sheer excitement at the highest level of racing, the Coronation Stakes was the finest race of the season so far.

The Royal Hunt Cup, traditionally the big betting race of the meeting, went to 25–1 chance Eurolink The Lad, who held off by a neck the late challenge of Operation Wolf, with 1990 winner Pontenuovo turning in a sterling effort to run third carrying twenty-two pounds more than the previous year. Eurolink The Lad, trained for the Flat by John Dunlop, had won over hurdles during the winter while in the care of Martin Pipe.

Each of the two races which rounded off the second day of the meeting was also won by a neck, Jendali getting up close home to snatch the Queen's Vase from Silver Rainbow, and Rinja getting the better of Local Derby, First Victory and Hateel in a blanket finish for the Bessborough Stakes. The distances for that one: neck, neck, neck.

Ladies' Day opened with another handicap, Torchon taking the King George V Stakes with ease. Then Polish Patriot pipped Chicarica by a short head in a desperate finish to the Cork and Orrery Stakes.

The Gold Cup had long been the subject of controversy. Should its distance be shortened from two and a half miles to two miles in order to attract a better class of horse? The arguments raged passionately on both sides, but were suspended as usual for the running of the race itself and resumed immediately afterwards.

The field in 1991 could not with a straight face be considered Group One status. The hot favourite was the four-year-old Arzanni, an impressive winner of the Yorkshire Cup and just the sort of stayer with a touch of class which the Royal Ascot showpiece required. Trainglot had won the Cesarewitch in 1990 and had announced his well-being earlier in June with an easy win at Beverley. The popular mare Double Dutch had also won the Cesarewitch, but was surely out of her depth in a Gold Cup. Warm Feeling was a classy performer (just beaten by Rock Hopper in the John Porter at Newbury), Teamster had won the Sagaro Stakes at Ascot in May, Top Of The World had sprung a major surprise when taking the Henry II Stakes at Sandown Park, Per Quod had won the Ormonde Stakes. Then there was Indian Queen, a 25–1 chance for the Gold Cup but, if you looked a little deeper than her immediate form figures of '253' in three runs this season, boasting high-class form. She had dead-heated with Braashee in the Prix Royal-Oak (Group One) at Longchamp in October 1990, and had won Pattern races in Ireland and Italy.

The runners came past the stands on the first circuit with the pace being set by Top Of The World and Crack, who weakened with half a mile to go, and as the field came into the home straight Trainglot took over and made for the line. Then the distinctive head of Indian Queen – sporting black blinkers and a large sheepskin noseband – appeared on the scene. With Walter Swinburn plumbing the depths of her stamina and courage, the six-year-old mare took up the running and fended off a whirlwind finish from Arzanni, whom Lanfranco Dettori had brought wide round his rivals. Arzanni got to the mare but could never quite get past, and Indian Queen won by a neck.

She was the first mare to win the Gold Cup since Gladness in 1958, and her success was a wonderful achievement for owner-breeder Sir Gordon Brunton, who had bought the dam Taj Princess for just 540 guineas as a yearling. When winning the Gold Cup – the decision to run in which was taken only two days before the race – Indian Queen herself was in foal to Night Shift (sire of In The Groove).

Ironically, the mare's trainer Lord Huntingdon (formerly William Hastings-Bass) had been one of those who supported the idea of reducing the Gold Cup distance to two miles, but the pros and cons were forgotten in the unsaddling enclosure in the afterglow of a great race. Sir Gordon Brunton was asked what had inclined him to keep Indian Queen in training after her fine record as a five-year-old: 'Fun. We race our horses for fun and we have fun.'

In that spirit, the intention was to aim Indian Queen at the Irish St Leger and the Prix Royal-Oak, but she met a setback and was retired.

A complete contrast to the Gold Cup was the Norfolk Stakes, a five-furlong sprint for two-year-olds. This attracted a good field, and the biggest individual bet of the week. An Irish punter asked rails bookmaker Stephen Little for £200,000 to £100,000 about Magic Ring at 2–1, and was laid half that amount.

That punter duly collected after Magic Ring – with the Generous and Dilum connections of Fahd Salman, Paul Cole and Alan Munro – had won in a time which set a new track record for a two-year-old. But Jack Berry's brilliantly speedy Paris House ran on well once headed by the winner, and offered promise of greater deeds to come.

There were no £50,000 bets on the winner of the Ribblesdale Stakes. Third Watch, trained by John Dunlop, had seemed to lose her way after such a promising debut as a two-year-old that she had been strongly fancied for the 1991 Oaks. She was favourite for the Brent Walker Fillies' Mile, but finished a remote twelfth behind Shamshir (now favourite for the Ribblesdale after finishing second in the Oaks). One outing as a three-year-old had produced a sixth to Fife at Goodwood, so Third Watch's Ascot starting price of 20–1 was hardly a steal. But she won by a facile seven lengths from Finance Dancer and Sought Out and brought this memorable utterance from John Dunlop: 'They really are extraordinary things, horses. They never cease to surprise me.'

No great surprise in the last on Ladies' Day, joint favourite Fair Cop winning easily from Governor's Imp to give the Salman-Cole-Munro team their

third juvenile winner of the meeting.

Friday had one of the weirdest Royal Ascot stories ever – the appearance of a Cheltenham Gold Cup winner. That was in the Royal fixture's finale, the Queen Alexandra Stakes, but beforehand came plenty to set the place buzzing. The Windsor Castle Stakes went to Isdar, described by his trainer Tom Jones as 'about the fattest horse that has ever won at Ascot'.

The Hardwicke Stakes looked a good thing for Rock Hopper, just over two weeks after his good effort when third in the Coronation Cup (page 79), and he started the only odds-on favourite of the meeting: several bets of £20,000 at even money were seen in the ring.

"Fun. We race our horses for fun and we have fun."

Rock Hopper needed to be held up until the last possible instant and then produced right on the line, and his supporters must have had palpitations as Pat Eddery went to such lengths to cover him up that he encountered severe traffic problems when trying to get clear at the right moment. About two furlongs out Rock Hopper was still being held in the pack as Spritsail took the lead. Christy Roche on the Irish challenger Topanoora, moving out to launch his challenge, slightly came across Rock Hopper, though the favourite had yet to make his own move. Topanoora made for home at full stretch with Spritsail clinging on grimly, and well inside the final furlong the time was right for Rock Hopper. Pat

Eddery asked him to make his challenge between Spritsail on the inner and Topanoora on the outer, but Spritsail edged out and Rock Hopper found himself badly squeezed. In the time it took Eddery to check, then gather his mount and call for a fresh thrust, Topanoora was gone, and though Rock Hopper was flying again once he had got balanced and Spritsail had fallen away, it was too late. Rock Hopper hammered for the line but Topanoora got there a short head sooner.

There was some surprise when the announcement came that Pat Eddery had objected to the winner 'for taking my ground in the last furlong': although it had been a rough race, there had seemed to be no serious interference between Rock Hopper and Topanoora. Then came word of a Stewards' Enquiry, and eventually the finishing order was reversed, the race going to Rock Hopper and Topanoora being demoted to second. It subsequently transpired that the stewards' decision was based not on any incident inside the final furlong but on the manoeuvring earlier in the straight when Topanoora began his move. Pat Eddery had seemed to stop riding for a few strides, but the bone of contention for aggrieved supporters of Topanoora was that *at that stage* Eddery did not want to push his horse forwards, and that if anything the interference actually helped him. It was the later squeezing by Spritsail which lost him the race.

The stewards' secretary Peter Steveney explained: 'We felt that Eddery and Rock Hopper had to check for about five strides and that this cost Rock Hopper the short head by which he was beaten. The stewards gave Roche the benefit of the doubt and said that it was accidental, but they felt that they had to amend the placings.'

Although disqualified, Topanoora maintained his admirable record of never having been out of the first two in ten races. But this was scant consolation for having been so controversially robbed of one of the main races at Royal Ascot, and the debate about the wisdom or otherwise of the stewards' decision raged on for weeks. The immediate reaction of Topanoora's trainer Jim Bolger was that the connections would not make an appeal, but clearly the matter rankled: 'It was a strange decision. Pat didn't use the first incident in his objection because he wasn't going there. He should have got the stewards to write his objection out for him.'

One curious footnote to a contentious race concerns the optimistic punter who staked £1,000 at 8–1 about Rock Hopper getting the photo-finish verdict. On the evidence of the naked eye he seemed highly unlikely to collect, and so it proved when Topanoora was given as the winner – but bets on the photo are settled not on the judge's actual decision but on the official weighed-in result, so the 'losing' punter got his £8,000!

Amigo Menor won the Wokingham Stakes, that manic six-furlong handicap, handily from Local Lass, Cantoris and Notley. He had been narrowly beaten in the race by Knight of Mercy in 1990 but gained a deserved success after taking up the running approaching the final furlong.

The King's Stand Stakes, the top sprint of the meeting, was won in 1990 by Dayjur, and though there was nothing remotely of his calibre in the 1991 field, Paul Makin's improving four-year-old Elbio looked a reasonable bet to take over the sprinting crown after winning the Palace House Stakes at Newmarket and the Temple Stakes at Sandown. Sent off the 13–8 favourite, Elbio positively streaked in at Ascot, making rapid progress to scythe through the field coming towards the last furlong and keeping going to beat the French challenger Irish Shoal by three lengths. Archway, trained by Vincent O'Brien and ridden by Lester Piggott, was third.

Prince Of Wales's Stakes (Group 2)

18 June 1991

1 mile 2 furlongs (going: good)

1st: £58,776; **2nd:** £21,976; **3rd:** £10,538; **4th:** £4,570

1	STAGECRAFT	S. Cauthen	6–4 fav
2	ZOMAN	A. Munro	5–2
3	TERIMON	M. Roberts	5–2
4	KARINGA BAY	B. Rouse	16–1

6 ran

distances: 3 lengths, short head
time: 2 mins 07.58 secs

Winner owned by Sheikh Mohammed, trained by M. R. Stoute (Newmarket, Suffolk), bred by Meon Valley Stud

Tote: win £2.40; places £1.50, £1.90; dual forecast £3.70

St James's Palace Stakes (Group 1)

18 June 1991

Old mile (going: good)

1st: £121,905; **2nd:** £45,435; **3rd:** £21,668; **4th:** £9,267

1	MARJU	W. Carson	7–4 fav
2	SECOND SET	L. Dettori	4–1
3	HOKUSAI	L. Piggott	9–1
4	ACTEUR FRANCAIS	S. Cauthen	3–1
5	SAPIEHA	W.R. Swinburn	20–1
6	MAJLOOD	Pat Eddery	9–1
7	SOLEIL DANCER	J. Reid	33–1

7 ran

distances: head, 2 lengths
time: 1 min 41.97 secs

Winner owned by Hamdan Al Maktoum, trained by J. L. Dunlop (Arundel, W. Sussex), bred by Kilcarn Stud, Ireland

Tote: win £2.30; places £1.70, £2.30; dual forecast £4.80

Coventry Stakes (Group 3)

18 June 1991

6 furlongs (going: good)

1st: £27,648; **2nd:** £10,321; **3rd:** £4,935; **4th:** £2,126

1	DILUM	A. Munro	11–10 fav
2	DR DEVIOUS	Pat Eddery	9–2
3	CASTEDDU	A.S. Cruz	40–1
4	COMPUTER KID	K. Fallon	66–1

14 ran

distances: 3 lengths, 1½ lengths
time: 1 min 15.99 secs

Winner owned by Fahd Salman, trained by P. F. I. Cole (Whatcombe, Oxon), bred by Ron Con Ltd 1, USA

Tote: win £2.30; places £1.30, £1.40, £10.80; dual forecast £3.70

King Edward VII Stakes (Group 2)

18 June 1991

1 mile 4 furlongs (going: good)

1st: £56,673; 2nd: £21,169; 3rd: £10,134; 4th: £4,377

1	SADDLERS' HALL	L. Piggott	7–1
2	SECRET HAUNT	L. Dettori	6–1
3	MARCUS THORPE	B. Raymond	20–1
4	MALMSEY	S. Cauthen	7–1

9 ran (Corrupt 2–1 fav)

distances: 6 lengths, 1 length
time: 2 mins 31.63 secs

Winner owned by Lord Weinstock, trained by M. R. Stoute (Newmarket, Suffolk), bred by Ballymacoll Stud Farm Ltd, Ireland

Tote: win £8.40; places £1.90, £2.20, £4.80; dual forecast £25.10

Coronation Stakes (Group 1)

19 June 1991

Old mile (going: good)

1st: £117,367; 2nd: £43,788; 3rd: £20,919; 4th: £8,987

1	KOOYONGA	W.J. O'Connor	3–1
2	SHADAYID	W. Carson	9–4 fav
3	GUSSY MARLOWE	M. Roberts	10–1
4	DANSEUSE DU SOIR	D. Boeuf	100–30
5	CRYSTAL GAZING	L. Dettori	6–1
6	ARRANVANNA	A. Munro	25–1
7	SUMONDA	G. Carter	100–1
8	SILVER BRAID	J. Williams	66–1

8 ran

distances: ¾ length, 1½ lengths
time: 1 min 42.54 secs

Winner owned by Mitsuo Haga, trained by M.Kauntze (Ireland), bred by Ovidstown Bloodstock Ltd, Ireland

Tote: win £3.90; places £1.30, £1.20, £2.00; dual forecast £3.20

Ribblesdale Stakes (Group 2)

20 June 1991

1 mile 4 furlongs (going: good)

1st: £63,099; 2nd: £23,633; 3rd: £11,366; 4th: £4,967

1	THIRD WATCH	J. Reid	20–1
2	FINANCE DANCER	M. Roberts	9–1
3	SOUGHT OUT	L. Piggott	14–1
4	GAI BULGA	G. Carter	20–1

14 ran (Shamshir 7–2 fav)

distances: 7 lengths, short head
time: 2 mins 32.45 secs

Winner owned by P.G. Goulandris, trained by J. L. Dunlop (Arundel, W. Sussex), bred by Hesmonds Stud Ltd

Tote: win £40.80; places £8.60, £3.00, £4.10; dual forecast £191.00

Ajaad won the Britannia Stakes, supposedly a competitive handicap, by five lengths from Rapid Coracle, and then it was time for the last race of the Royal meeting and the longest race run on the Flat in Britain, the Queen Alexandra Stakes.

More to the point, it was time for the Gold Cup winner whose date with destiny had been not at Ascot but at Cheltenham. The achievements of Norton's Coin were already so unlikely that they had entered racing legend. Owned and trained by a Welsh dairy farmer and housed in a converted milking shed, this lanky chestnut gelding had provided modern racing with one of its most gloriously daft results when taking the 1990 Cheltenham Gold Cup at 100–1 from Toby Tobias and Desert Orchid. Norton's Coin had never run on the Flat, but when earlier in the season his

The King's Stand Stakes: Steve Cauthen and Elbio have matters well under control. The white-faced Irish Shoal (John Reid) is second and Archway (Lester Piggott) third.

indefatigable handler Sirrell Griffiths announced that he would like the horse to run at Royal Ascot, the plan caught the imagination of the racing world. And the subsequent news that the Gold Cup winner would be ridden in the Queen Alexandra by Lester Piggott was icing on the cake.

The complete fairytale ending of victory in the race would have been too much to hope for even by Norton's Coin standards, and in the event the gelding finished eighth behind Easy To Please, who brought Jim Bolger some consolation for his setback with Topanoora earlier in the afternoon. But Norton's Coin far from disgraced himself, and Sirrell Griffiths had the right attitude: 'It's been a wonderful day. I've enjoyed every minute of it.'

It had, indeed, been a wonderful meeting.

Ascot Gold Cup (Group 1)

20 June 1991

2 miles 4 furlongs (going: good)

1st: £108,108; **2nd:** £40,146; **3rd:** £19,023; **4th:** £8,002

1	INDIAN QUEEN	W. R. Swinburn	25–1
2	ARZANNI	L. Dettori	13–8 fav
3	WARM FEELING	M. Hills	8–1
4	TRAINGLOT	W. Carson	5–1
5	TEAMSTER	Pat Eddery	7–1
6	RETOUCH	T. Quinn	25–1
7	DOUBLE DUTCH	W. Newnes	25–1
8	ETHAN FROME	A Lequeux	66–1
9	SHAMBO	M. Roberts	14–1
10	TOP OF THE WORLD	A. Munro	16–1
11	PER QUOD	B. Raymond	14–1
12	CRACK	S. Cauthen	12–1

12 ran

distances: neck, 3½ lengths
time: 4 mins 24.90 secs
Winner owned by Sir Gordon Brunton, trained by Lord Huntingdon (West Ilsley, Berks), bred by Sir Gordon Brunton

Tote: win £37.40; places £7.20, £1.50, £2.20; dual forecast £54.40

Hardwicke Stakes (Group 2)

21 June 1991

1 mile 4 furlongs (going: good)

1st: £58,299; **2nd:** £21,700; **3rd:** £10,325; **4th:** £4,390

1	ROCK HOPPER	Pat Eddery	5–6 fav
2	TOPANOORA	C. Roche	8–1
3	SPRITSAIL	W. Carson	7–1
4	DUKE OF PADUCAH	R. Cochrane	25–1

9 ran

First and second places were reversed following a stewards' enquiry and an objection by the runner–up to the winner, Topanoora

distances: short head, 1½ lengths
time: 2 mins 30.20 secs
Winner owned by Maktoum Al Maktoum, trained by M. R. Stoute (Newmarket, Suffolk), bred by Gainsborough Stud Management Ltd

Tote: win £1.80; places £1.20, £1.90, £1.60; dual forecast £5.70

King's Stand Stakes (Group 2)

21 June 1991

5 furlongs (going: good)

1st: £57,101; **2nd:** £21,241; **3rd:** £10,096; **4th:** £4,281

1	ELBIO	S. Cauthen	13–8 fav
2	IRISH SHOAL	J. Reid	16–1
3	ARCHWAY	L. Piggott	11–4
4	FURAJET	Pat Eddery	16–1

10 ran

distances: 3 lengths, ½ length
time: 1 min 01.40 secs
Winner owned by Brian Brackpool, trained by P. J. Makin (Ogbourne Maisey, Wilts), bred by D. W. Samuel

Tote: win £2.50; places £1.30, £5.00, £1.60; dual forecast £36.20

BUDWEISER IRISH DERBY

The Curragh, 30 June 1991

Going to post. Generous (Alan Munro) . . .

For the second year running the Budweiser Irish Derby really quickened the pulse of the racing world. In 1990 the late decision to pitch the brilliant Oaks heroine Salsabil in against the Derby winner Quest For Fame had packed the Curragh stands, and 1991 promised something even better.

Generous and Suave Dancer had each proved themselves outstanding colts with brilliant Derby victories,

Generous pulverising his Epsom rivals to win the Ever Ready Derby by five lengths (pages 73–7) and Suave Dancer three days earlier showing superb acceleration to land the Prix du Jockey-Club Lancia at Chantilly by four lengths (pages 71–2). The *Racing Post* headline on the morning of the Irish Derby proclaimed this the 'Moment of Truth', and no one thought that an exaggeration. This was a true

showdown between the two aspirants to the crown of the best three-year-old in Europe.

The pair faced just four other runners, of whom only two had even remotely realistic claims of causing an upset. Star Of Gdansk had run third to Generous at Epsom after being narrowly beaten by Fourstars Allstar in the Irish Two Thousand Guineas, and Sportsworld – trained by Vincent

. . . Suave Dancer (Walter Swinburn).

O'Brien and ridden by Lester Piggott – was unbeaten in three races, all at The Curragh: though clearly a colt of great promise, the level of his previous form offered no obvious evidence that he was ready to make his mark in the big time. Nordic Admirer was the pacemaker for Star Of Gdansk, and the maiden Barry's Run was a genuine no-hoper: he had been available at 1,000–1 during the week before the race, but his enterprising trainer Luke Comer knew that he would pick up a useful IR£9,000 just for coming sixth of the six starters. (One Ladbrokes punter had £1,000 to win Barry's Run at 1,000–1. The fact that the bet was struck with tax paid on suggests that he actually harboured illusions of the horse winning and catapulting his fearless supporter into the ranks of the millionaires. Truly, there is one born every minute.)

But never mind the also-rans. The 1991 Irish Derby was one of those rare racing occasions which boiled down to a simple head-to-head between two horses for whom defeat would be well nigh unthinkable, and it had the added attraction of the champions of two different countries meeting on neutral ground.

As the race approached and speculation and analysis gave way to putting the money where the mouths were, it became clear that Generous was expected to prove himself the king. His odds the day before the race hovered around even money, with shades of odds-on and odds-against, but at the off he was a strong even-money favourite, with Suave Dancer drifting from his pre-race price to start at 9–4.

With a small field and the two principals each possessing a devastating finish, one to be delivered early and one late, it looked certain to be a fascinating tactical race, and so it proved – though not in the way that many had anticipated. The outsiders

Barry's Run and Nordic Admirer made the early running, but the pace was not a fierce one, and with over a mile to run Alan Munro on Generous decided to take matters into his own hands, pushing the Derby winner into the lead and quickening the tempo. This was a risky move, for Suave Dancer seemed to have a more powerful burst of acceleration than Generous and Walter Swinburn – deputising for the injured Cash Asmussen – would wait before challenging on Suave Dancer.

With five furlongs to run Lester Piggott moved Sportsworld into second as Generous continued to power along in front, but once the field reached the straight it was clear that the race lay between the two main contenders.

They came inside the final quarter mile with Generous keeping up his lead, but Suave Dancer had now moved into second with ominous ease and looked poised to take the leader whenever Walter Swinburn chose. The French horse got to Generous's quarters and for a few seconds this looked like being one of those unforgettable races in which two horses draw away from their rivals and fight out a duel to the line.

Instead it turned out memorable in another way. When Suave Dancer came to collar Generous on his outside, Munro asked for a renewed effort, and suddenly it was all over. Generous pulled away from his rival inside the final furlong and maintained a relentless gallop to the line, where he

The moment of truth.

was three lengths clear of Suave Dancer. It was a further eight lengths back to Star Of Gdansk – again third in a Derby – and another two to Sportsworld. Nordic Admirer was tailed off, and Barry's Run finished the best part of a furlong behind the winner.

If his win at Epsom had suggested that Generous was an outstanding horse, this performance suggested that he might just be a great one. But a three-year-old earns that tag only by beating his elders, and plans were announced to take on the older horses in the King George at Ascot. Meanwhile it was time to take stock of what Generous had achieved so far. The eleventh horse to add the Irish Derby to victory at Epsom, he was, in the opinion of his connections, a better horse at The Curragh than on Derby Day. For Alan Munro, 'That was a better effort than Epsom. He had to do most of it himself today.' Paul Cole paid tribute to his charge's soundness, and to his jockey's quick thinking: 'Tactically he rode the perfect race. We were afraid the others would want to slow it down to try and beat us, and when there was no pace on he had the intelligence to go on.'

The Irish Derby was without doubt one of the great races of 1991. Truly run and brilliantly won, it made a superstar of Generous and provided anticipation of sustained excitement for the rest of the season. Although there were no specific excuses for Suave Dancer, many felt that under different circumstances the French colt would not necessarily give best to his Curragh conqueror. Come the Arc, there might be another result.

And as a footnote to a great race, let's not forget the horse who finished last but still landed his owner IR£9,000. Kevin Manning, who as the jockey on Barry's Run had had a distant view of Generous's flaxen tail making for the horizon, said: 'I wish you got that sort of money for finishing last every day.'

Fahd Salman leads his hero in.

Budweiser Irish Derby (Group 1)

30 June 1991

1 mile 4 furlongs (going: yielding)

1st: IR£366,500; 2nd: IR£117,000; 3rd: IR£57,000; 4th: IR£21,000; 5th: IR£15,000; 6th: IR£9,000

1	GENEROUS	A. Munro	Evens fav
2	SUAVE DANCER	W. R. Swinburn	9–4
3	STAR OF GDANSK	C. Roche	12–1
4	SPORTSWORLD	L. Piggott	100–30
5	NORDIC ADMIRER	W. J. Supple	150–1
6	BARRY'S RUN	K. J. Manning	300–1

6 ran

distances: 3 lengths, 8 lengths

time: 2 mins 33.3 secs

Winner owned by Fahd Salman, trained by P. F. I. Cole (Whatcombe, Oxon), bred by Barronstown Stud, Ireland

Tote: win IR£2.60; places IR£1.60, IR£2.20; dual forecast IR£2.90

CORAL-ECLIPSE STAKES

Sandown Park, 6 July 1991

With the running of the Eclipse Stakes, the season moves up another gear. The first Group One middle-distance race of the term in which three-year-olds take on their elders and thus the first major opportunity for the cream of one crop to meet the cream of another, it usually produces a fascinating contest.

It certainly delivered the goods in 1991, when seven runners represented top-class form from three generations.

Of the three-year olds, Marju had won the St James's Palace Stakes at Royal Ascot (page 99) over one mile following his game effort when second in the Derby. In terms of distance he was the splitting the difference between those two races by moving up to ten furlongs. Environment Friend had won the Dante Stakes impressively (page 67) but flopped comprehensively behind Generous at Epsom. The third three-year-old was Green's Ferneley, recently acquired by Khalid Abdullah to act as a pacemaker to his colt Sanglamore. Winner of the Prix du Jockey-Club at Chantilly in 1990,

The grey Environment Friend (George Duffield) and Stagecraft (Steve Cauthen) battle it out.

Sanglamore had not raced again as a three-year-old, and – like his stable companion Quest For Fame – was considered something of an unknown quantity. But his first appearance at four had proclaimed him a true force to be reckoned with: in the nine-furlong Prix d'Ispahan at Chantilly he had made all the running to beat Priolo and Zoman.

The other four-year-olds were In The Groove – fresh from her battling success in the Coronation Cup (page 78) and returning to the scene of her victory in the Trusthouse Forte Mile (page 44) – and Stagecraft, whose performance in the Prince of Wales's Stakes at Ascot had made him one of the stars of the season.

Completing the field was good old Terimon, second to Elmaamul in the 1990 Eclipse, and most recently third to Stagecraft at Ascot and second to In The Groove at Epsom. Now five, he represented solid form and was running at his best distance.

Stagecraft was a solid favourite, backed from 5–2 to 2–1. Marju and In The Groove shared second slot in the betting at 3–1, Sanglamore was 5–2. Terimon attracted little support, going off at 14–1, while a couple of punters looking for an outsider nibbled at Environment Friend: bets of £15,000 to £600 and £5,000 to £200 were recorded, and the grey started at 28–1. The pacemaker Green's Ferneley was unconsidered at 500–1.

A crowd of 14,000 packed the Esher slopes – ten per cent more than on Eclipse day 1990 – and were rewarded with a memorable race. Green Ferneley fulfilled his role for the first seven furlongs by leading at a good pace. Sanglamore was second early in the straight and with three furlongs to go took up the running. A top-class field really getting down to work at the far end of the Sandown straight is a glorious sight, which for favourite backers became more glorious by the moment as Steve Cauthen wound Stagecraft up and pushed him into the lead with a quarter of a mile to go.

A huge roar was sent up from the stands as it became apparent that Stagecraft had detached himself from his rivals, but Environment Friend was not privy to the market moves, and, under hard riding from George Duffield, joined Stagecraft as the two came further and further clear. Sanlamore was back-pedalling, In The Groove ran on at one pace, Marju was not firing at all, Terimon was going nowhere.

Even at that stage the outcome was obvious. Stagecraft would win and Environment Friend would be a gallant second. But Stagecraft started to idle in front and Environment Friend rallied. The two came up the hill hammer and tongs, but Stagecraft was at the end of his tether and Environment Friend wore him down and got his nose in front. Then Stagecraft rallied again, but to no avail. Environment Friend won by a head.

Although he was not exactly the punters' choice, Environment Friend's victory was highly popular. Before the Derby, much had been made in the press of how the colt was George Duffield's best ever chance of winning the premier Classic, and the grey's dismal display was a bitter disappointment to his jockey. Here was handsome consolation, and a prize won through a brilliant riding performance. 'There's life in the old dog yet', observed Duffield in response to the crowd's appreciation of his effort.

Nor was it lost on many observers that this was a case of the pupil getting one over on the master, for winning trainer James Fanshawe was gaining his first Group One success in only his second season after a long period as assistant to Michael Stoute – trainer of Stagecraft. Fanshawe admitted that he had not expected his charge to get more than a place, and gave credit to owner Bill Gredley: 'It's thanks to Mr Gredley that we're here', he said in the unsaddling enclosure: 'He gave me a rollocking on Friday for not being positive enough.'

Of the beaten horses, Marju had suffered a recurrence of the problem which had blighted his performance in the Two Thousand Guineas, but the others had no specific excuses.

It was a classic Eclipse, a head-to-head clash of the generations on a sizzling summer's day, and a race which would long linger in the memory.

Coral–Eclipse Stakes (Group 1)

6 July 1991

1 mile 2 furlongs (going: good)

1st: £147,825; 2nd: £55,325; 3rd: £26,575; 4th: £11,575

1	ENVIRONMENT FRIEND	G. Duffield	28–1
2	STAGECRAFT	S. Cauthen	2–1 fav
3	SANGLAMORE	Pat Eddery	7–2
4	IN THE GROOVE	R. Cochrane	3–1
5	TERIMON	M. Roberts	14–1
6	MARJU	W. Carson	3–1
7	GREEN'S FERNELEY	W. R. Swinburn	500–1

7 ran

distances: head, 7 lengths
time: 2 mins 07.61 secs

Winner owned by W. J. Gredley, trained by J. R. Fanshawe (Newmarket, Suffolk), bred by Stetchworth Park Stud

Tote: win £28.70; places £4.20, £1.70; dual forecast £57.90

NEWMARKET JULY MEETING

Newmarket, 9–11 July 199

The Newmarket July Meeting has an atmosphere all of its own: sylvan surroundings, panama hats and summer dresses, sunshine more often than not, a track with that uphill grind of a finish which makes for so many exciting finishes, and above all three days of marvellous racing building up to the pinnacle of the July Cup on the final day.

The highlight of the opening day's programme was the Princess Of Wales's Stakes. Rock Hopper was having his fourth race in thirty-three days, having run second to Epervier Bleu in the Grand Prix de Saint-Cloud since his controversial win at Royal Ascot (page 101). His five rivals were Spritsail, the cause of much of his trouble in the Hardwicke Stakes, Nashwan's half-brother Mukddaam, who had notched up his first win of the season on the July course ten days earlier, Mountain Kingdom (beaten a neck by Rock Hopper in the Jockey Club Stakes on the other Newmarket course), the Vincent O'Brien-trained Splash Of Colour, and Sapience, who had won the Princess Of Wales's Stakes in 1990 but had run only twice (both unplaced) since.

The race was run at a very slow pace, but when the heat was turned on as the runners met the rising ground Mukddaam made rapid headway to take up the running. Rock Hopper could not immediately go with him, but as the post approached he started to claw back the deficit, and plugged on gamely as Mukddaam surged towards the line. For every stride bar the last it looked as if Mukddaam was sure to win, then Rock Hopper caught him at the last gasp and won by a head in a typical July Course finish.

The other Group race of the opening day was the Hillsdown Cherry Hinton Stakes for two-year-old fillies. This

Rock Hopper (Pat Eddery) just gets up to beat Mukddaam (Willie Carson, striped cap) in the Princess of Wales's Stakes.

The Cherry Hinton: Musicale (Steve Cauthen) beats Coffee Ice (Walter Swinburn, left) and Miss Bluebird (Michael Roberts, rails).

Savoyard (Walter Swinburn, rails) holds off Superoo (Nicky Adams) in the Bunbury Cup.

seemed a very open contest. Of the six runners only Miss Bluebird had not won, and she had been narrowly beaten by Marling in the National Stakes at Sandown on her only outing before Newmarket. Miss Bluebird was sent off the 3–1 favourite, with her main rivals Solar Star, Twafeaj and Musicale starting at 100–30, 4–1 and 9–2 respectively.

It was another desperately close finish, with Robert Sangster's Musicale showing great courage to hold off Coffee Ice – who had not had a clear run – by a head, with Miss Bluebird a close third.

Robert Sangster had already had a two-year-old winner by the time that his Musicale went to post. The Fairview Homes Chesterfield Stakes attracted a field of just three, but with betting of 11–8 Power Lake, 2–1 Bit-A-Magic and 9–4 Night Duty, this was likely to be a tight contest. Backers of the outsider of three collected after Night Duty had got up close home to beat Power Lake by a head.

And there was an even tighter climax to the opening day's big handicap, the Ladbroke Bunbury Cup, with Savoyard running on to beat Albert Finney's stongly fancied Superoo by a neck, with Gentle Hero a short head back in third and 33–1 shot Sharpalto finishing like a train to save his each-way backers in fourth.

Wednesday's feature was the Group Two Child Stakes over a mile for fillies. Only six runners, and this looked on paper a formality for Satin Flower, who had walloped a good field for the Jersey Stakes at Royal Ascot. On form she was a certainty, and was sent off the 9–4 on favourite. But form isn't everything, and when the crunch came up that hill she could find no extra under pressure. Only Yours, who had disappointed after running an excellent fifth in the One Thousand Guineas, took the lead at the two-furlong pole and kept on resolutely to beat Trojan Crown by one and a half lengths, with the favourite a deeply disappointing third.

From the right in the Child Stakes: Only Yours (Michael Roberts), Trojan Crown (Gary Carter), Satin Flower (Pat Eddery).

The Anglia Television July Stakes produced a field of only four, for a Group Three two-year-old race a poor turnout both numerically and in terms of quality. Showbrook, who had won well at Epsom on Derby Day and then run unaccountably badly when fifth to Dilum in the Coventry Stakes at Royal Ascot, was joint favourite with Made Of Gold, who had enjoyed a winning debut at Ripon in June. Computer Kid and Wilde Rufo had both been behind Showbrook in the Coventry.

Showbrook pulled for his head early on but settled down and proceeded to make all the running, staying on up the rising ground to beat Made Of Gold by three and a half lengths.

When he went out for his winning ride on Showbrook, jockey Bruce Raymond was still bristling from being on the receiving end of a controversial stewards' decision after the More O'Ferrall Stakes. His mount Nibbs Point moved off the rails with more than a furlong to go and brushed the 33–1 outsider Sobranie before taking the lead inside the final furlong and going on to win by half a length. Sobranie finished second. But the stewards decided – to general bewilderment – that the brush had affected the result. Nibbs Point was demoted, Sobranie got the race.

Some of the interest in the Carroll Foundation July Cup was removed with the news that Two Thousand Guineas winner Mystiko's blood was not right, and he would have to miss the race.

. . . racegoers who steamed in the sweltering heat . . . had a gripping race in prospect.

Showbrook powers home under Bruce Raymond in the July Stakes.

Princess Of Wales's Stakes (Group 2)

9 July 1991

1 mile 4 furlongs (going: good)

1st: £42,198; **2nd:** £15,713; **3rd:** £7,482; **4th:** £3,187

1	ROCK HOPPER	Pat Eddery	4–6 fav
2	MUKDDAAM	W. Carson	8–1
3	SPLASH OF COLOUR	L. Piggott	9–1
4	SPRITSAIL	S. Cauthen	11–2

6 ran

distances: head, 2½ lengths
time: 2 mins 33.47 secs

Winner owned by Maktoum Al Maktoum, trained by M.R. Stoute (Newmarket, Suffolk), bred by Gainsborough Stud Management Ltd

Tote: win £1.70; places £1.40, £2.50; dual forecast £3.70

None the less, racegoers who steamed in the sweltering heat on the Thursday had a gripping race in prospect. There was Elbio, fresh from his brilliant win in the King's Stand Stakes (page 99). There was Polish Patriot, who had just got up to land the other big sprint at Royal Ascot, the Cork and Orrery Stakes (page 97). Polar Falcon from France had beaten In The Groove in Newbury's Lockinge Stakes, and Lycius had run third when hot favourite in the Irish Two Thousand Guineas since going down by a head to Mystiko at Newmarket. There was also Chicarica, the filly with the huge white blaze on her face who had been caught in the last stride by Polish Patriot at Ascot. Even without Mystiko, this was a sprint to relish.

Polish Patriot was known to be an exceptionally volatile character, and he sported a net muzzle as Ray Cochrane nursed him through the pre-race parade and took him to the post ever so gently. Coming back there was no need for restraint, but Polish Patriot settled nicely in the early stages as Time Gentlemen set the pace. Elbio, who had been marginally preferred to Lycius in the betting and started favourite, found it more difficult to settle, and once the race began in earnest he could not muster the speed to get to the front. It was Polish Patriot who took affairs by the scruff of the neck and charged up the rising ground with only Lycius having any apparent chance of denying him, but such was the power of Polish Patriot's finish that Steve Cauthen soon accepted the inevitable. Nothing could match Polish Patriot's gallop, and he ran out an easy winner by two lengths from Lycius, with Elbio keeping on to claim third place. Polar Falcon was a never-dangerous fourth, and Chicarica a disappointing fifth.

After the race it was revealed that Polish Patriot had pulled a muscle in his back after winning at Ascot and had come right just in time for the July Cup. But the Newmarket showpiece itself had exacted a harsh price, for the

Hillsdown Cherry Hinton Stakes (Group 3)

9 July 1991

6 furlongs (going: good)

1st: £21,411; 2nd: £7,930; 3rd: £3,740; 4th: £1,554

1	MUSICALE	S. Cauthen	9–2
2	COFFEE ICE	W.R. Swinburn	8–1
3	MISS BLUEBIRD	M. Roberts	3–1 fav
4	TWAFEAJ	Pat Eddery	4–1

6 ran

distances: head, ¾ length

time: 1 min 12.62 secs

Winner owned by R.E. Sangster, trained by H. R. A. Cecil (Newmarket, Suffolk), bred by Swettenham Stud

Tote: win £5.70; places £2.30, £2.30; dual forecast £21.30

Anglia Television July Stakes (Group 3)

10 July 1991

6 furlongs (going: good)

1st: £20,979; 2nd: £7,764; 3rd: £3,657; 4th: £1,514

1	SHOWBROOK	B. Raymond	13–8 jt fav
2	MADE OF GOLD	A. S. Cruz	13–8 jt fav
3	WILDE RUFO	M. Roberts	14–1
4	COMPUTER KID	A. Munro	7–2

4 ran

distances: 3 ½ lengths, 2 ½ lengths

time: 1 min 14.16 secs

Winner owned by A. F. Budge (Equine) Ltd, trained by R. Hannon (East Everleigh, Wilts), bred by A. Watkins, Ireland

Tote: win £2.40; dual forecast £1.80

Child Stakes (Group 2)

10 July 1991

1 mile (going: good)

1st: £42,534; 2nd: £15,842; 3rd: £7,546; 4th: £3,218

1	ONLY YOURS	M. Roberts	10–1
2	TROJAN CROWN	G. Carter	10–1
3	SATIN FLOWER	Pat Eddery	4–9 fav
4	ZIGAURA	W. Carson	10–1

6 ran

distances: 1 ½ lengths, 1 ½ lengths

time: 1 min 40.43 secs

Winner owned by Mrs M. Butcher, trained by R. Hannon (East Everleigh, Wilts), bred by R.J. Gorringe

Tote: win £8.50; places £2.60, £2.70; dual forecast £45.90

Ray Cochrane and Polish Patriot at full stretch with the July Cup in the bag.

following day it was revealed that Polish Patriot had fractured his off-fore cannon bone during the race. He would not run again in 1991, and may have raced for the last time.

The July Cup apart, the final day had seen stirring stuff from Robert Sangster's Dr Devious in the Krug Superlative Stakes, a powerhouse performance from Jendali in the Bahrain Trophy, and a superbly gutsy effort from Richard Hannon's Rise Up Singing in the Qualitair Racing Welfare Handicap.

Rock Hopper, Musicale, Only Yours, and most of all Polish Patriot had made it a memorable July Meeting.

Carroll Foundation July Cup (Group 1)

11 July 1991

6 furlongs (going: good)

1st: £115,254; **2nd:** £42,693; **3rd:** £20,521; **4th:** £8,428; **5th:** £3,389; **6th:** £1,373

1	POLISH PATRIOT	R. Cochrane	6–1
2	LYCIUS	S. Cauthen	11–4
3	ELBIO	W. R. Swinburn	5–2 fav
4	POLAR FALCON	L. Piggott	12–1
5	CHICARICA	W. Carson	6–1
6	EXIT TO NOWHERE	F. Head	12–1
7	MAJLOOD	Pat Eddery	9–1
8	TIME GENTLEMEN	J. Reid	33–1

8 ran

distances: 2 lengths, ½ length

time: 1 min 12.98 secs

Winner owned by R. A. Kirstein, trained by G. Harwood (Pulborough, W Sussex), bred by Peters, Kaskel, Baker *et al*, USA

Tote: win £6.50; places £1.50, £1.50, £1.70; dual forecast £11.00

KILDANGAN STUD IRISH OAKS

The Curragh, 13 July 1991

The 50-1 victory of Jet Ski Lady in the Gold Seal Oaks (pages 84–7) had stunned many students of form, and her next appearance was eagerly awaited. Would that staggering ten-length Epsom demolition job prove a fluke, or the start of something big?

Jim Bolger's imposing filly faced nine opponents in the Irish Oaks. By far the most fancied was Third Watch, who had caused a bit of an upset herself when running away with the Ribblesdale Stakes at Royal Ascot (page 98). Possessive Dancer was unbeaten, but her best effort – winning the Italian Oaks – did not seem up to Jet Ski Lady's form. Polemic had run fifth to Caerlina in the Prix de Diane, Julie La Rousse second to Kooyonga in the Irish One Thousand, Jaffa Line fourth in the Oaks before flopping behind Third Watch at Ascot.

Jet Ski Lady's stablemate Trescalini did the donkey work for the first half of the race, then the Oaks winner took over and tried to make the best of her way home. But as the runners entered the straight Christy Roche on the favourite was already uneasy, taking a glance behind to see where the danger was coming from. They weren't exactly queueing up to attack, but Possessive Dancer had moved easily into third place and with a quarter of a mile to go came under pressure from Steve Cauthen to go on and catch the leader. This she did inside the final furlong, collaring Jet Ski Lady over a hundred yards out and running on to win by half a length. Eileen Jenny was three lengths further back in third.

It may have been disappointing to see the Oaks winner beaten, but she lost little caste in defeat on ground that was probably too lively for her. Her Epsom win had clearly been no fluke. As for the winner, Possessive Dancer was now unbeaten in five races. She brought trainer Alex Scott his biggest win and a particular sense of relief at a time when his horses had been widely affected by a virus. 'Possessive Dancer is an amazing filly', said the trainer: 'Her homework is dreadful – it's painful to watch. But she keeps doing it on the track.'

Possessive Dancer was bred by the jockey Walter Swinburn, and won her first two races in the colours of his mother before being sold to Sheikh Ahmed Al Maktoum.

Possessive Dancer (Steve Cauthen) gets the better of Jet Ski Lady (Christy Roche).

Kildangan Stud Irish Oaks (Group 1)

13 July 1991

1 mile 4 furlongs (going: good)

1st: IR£121,200; **2nd:** IR£39,400; **3rd:** IR£19,400; **4th:** IR£7,400

1	POSSESSIVE DANCER	S. Cauthen	8–1
2	JET SKI LADY	C. Roche	7–4 fav
3	EILEEN JENNY	J. P. Murtagh	12–1
4	OFTEN AHEAD	S. Craine	150–1
5	JULIE LA ROUSSE	L. Piggott	16–1
6	POLEMIC	Pat Eddery	11–2
7	JAFFA LINE	B. Raymond	20–1
8	BE A HONEY	M.J. Kinane	100–1
9	THIRD WATCH	J. Reid	2–1
10	TRESCALINI	W. J. Supple	100–1

10 ran

distances: ½ length, 3 lengths
time: 2 mins 31.1 secs

Winner owned by Sheikh Ahmed Al Maktoum, trained by A. A. Scott (Newmarket, Suffolk), bred by Walter Swinburn Ltd.

Tote: win IR£8.30; places IR£2.20, IR£1.30, IR£1.90; dual forecast IR£9.40

KING GEORGE VI AND QUEEN ELIZABETH DIAMOND STAKES

Ascot, 27 July 1991

Each racing season is characterised by moments, periods of (if we're lucky) a few seconds which will always come back into the mind as the events of that year are recalled and very occasionally will enter the pantheon of the sport's greatest memories.

For the 1989 Flat season, there was Nashwan going clear in the Derby. For the 1990 season, Salsabil leaving the Oaks field trailing in her wake or Dayjur thundering home at York.

In 1991 the first moment came shortly after the runners in the King George VI and Queen Elizabeth Diamond Stakes had straightened up for home. From a bunched field one shape emerged – a compact chestnut horse with flaxen mane and tail, on whose back crouched a diminutive figure in dark green so closely packed down into the withers that horse and jockey were as one creature. Generous and Alan Munro had dominated the season, but as they sprinted away from their rivals in the King George they wrote their part in the events of the 1991 Flat season in illuminated letters.

Generous beat eight rivals that brilliantly sunny Diamond Day, and started at 6–4 on so to do. Saddlers' Hall was second favourite at 6–1. But when the early books on the race had opened a fortnight earlier, it looked as if the opposition to the Derby winner would be a good deal stronger than turned out to be the case on the day.

Epervier Bleu, second to Saumarez in the 1990 Arc, was an intended runner

Generous (Alan Munro) leaves Sanglamore (Pat Eddery) behind . . .

and Stagecraft, In The Groove and two 1990 Classic winners, Quest For Fame and Snurge, were declared likely to take their chances. Then it was announced that Stagecraft would miss the race and go instead for the International at York, and that Sanglamore rather than Quest For Fame would represent Khalid Abdullah and Roger Charlton.

The weekend before Ascot came the news that Epervier Bleu would not run: trainer Elie Lellouche said that there was nothing wrong with the colt, 'we just believe the King George will be a very difficult race to win'. Daniel Wildenstein's colt would be aimed specifically at the Arc – but a few weeks later a setback caused his defection from that race as well. On the Monday before the King George, Snurge was removed from the reckoning: the expected fast ground would be against him, and he would not run. The following day In The Groove was announced a non-runner after her final piece of work had convinced David Elsworth that she was below par.

These defections removed a great deal of the edge from the race, and the absence of Epervier Bleu meant no overseas challenge for Britain's most prestigious all-aged middle-distance contest. None the less, Generous faced his stiffest opposition yet – Suave Dancer apart. Saddlers' Hall and Lester Piggott had streaked home in the King Edward VII Stakes at Royal Ascot (page 92). The 1990 Prix du Jockey-Club winner Sanglamore had run third in the Eclipse since taking the Prix d'Ispahan at Chantilly. Rock Hopper – ridden at Ascot by Bruce Raymond as Pat Eddery was claimed for Sanglamore – had proved himself a remarkably tough character by winning four of his six races in 1991, and was for the first time fitted with blinkers to assist his concentration. Then there was the ubiquitous Terimon and his stable-mates the Italian Derby winner

. . . and comes home alone.

Jockey Alan Munro, lad Robert Latham, and the object of their admiration.

Hailsham and Luchiroverte, who had landed the Churchill Stakes at Ascot on his last outing, and Jimmy Fitzgerald's good five-year-old Sapience. Tiger Flower, representing the Sheikh Mohammed–Henry Cecil combination whose Belmez and Old Vic had dominated the 1990 King George, had run just once in 1991, short-headed by Mukddaam at Newmarket.

If Generous could trample over the claims of that lot with the same authority that he had lorded it over his three-year-old contemporaries, we'd perhaps have to consider enlisting the overused word 'great'.

He did, and we did. With Hailsham setting a fierce opening pace, the field in the early stages was well strung out. Generous settled in fourth, then moved up as Lester Piggott took Saddlers' Hall into the lead half a mile out.

The bell that is rung as an Ascot field comes round the final turn heralded Generous's moment of greatness, for as Saddlers' Hall took the runners into the straight it was clear that the Derby winner could stamp his superiority on this race whenever he liked. His rivals may not have been the absolute cream of Europe's Thoroughbreds, but what he did to them in the next ten seconds placed him with the very best of post-war racehorses.

He simply left them for dead, powering clear in a few strides with a stunning burst of acceleration and hammering towards the post with the rest of the field strung out in his wake.

Her Majesty The Queen with Paul Cole and Alan Munro.

Sanglamore gave vain pursuit and Rock Hopper ran on stoutly to be third, but this King George was magnificent not as a race but as a scintillating individual performance. In a moment Generous had put lengths between himself and the others, and Alan Munro, having peered over his left shoulder for any hint of a challenge as he made for home, ducked his head and allowed himself the cheeky luxury of one last look back between his legs as the chestnut, seven lengths clear of Sanglamore, passed the post.

"He frightened the life out of me"

Great races come in all guises, and the huge Ascot crowd which witnessed Generous on Diamond Day knew they had seen one. The response as the Derby winner hammered up the Ascot straight was not like the frantic yelling home of Grundy and Bustino – it was the more controlled rapture which greets such a superlative individual performance. They knew they'd seen something very special, and after the gasp of astonishment as Generous went clear in the straight, what was required was an awed respect.

That respect was underpinned by the knowledge that Generous had joined an extremely elite group of horses who had won the Derby, the Irish Derby and the King George – Nijinsky, Grundy, The Minstrel, Troy and Shergar. Comparisons were not odious, they were required, and it was the placing of the feats of Generous within such exalted company which kept the Ascot bars buzzing that afternoon.

One thing which Generous's five predecessors had in common was that none of them raced as four-year-olds, and the excited talk of the greatness of Generous was tempered by the fear that he would be retired to stud at the end of the season.

Within the week those fears were realised, and all the specious claims that the horse 'had nothing left to prove' could not compensate for the disappointment felt when it was announced that Generous would be retired after running in the Arc. It was good, of course, that he would stand as a stallion in England at Newmarket's Banstead Manor Stud, where the syndication plans made public in August put him at a valuation a little short of £8 million. But after Ascot he would not be seen again in a race in England, and whatever the demands of commerce and whatever the records of recent Derby winners kept in training at four, that was a great shame.

Nothing left to prove? To have shown himself a great racehorse at four, as he had been at three, would have been something. To have exerted his crowd-pulling powers in 1992 as he saw off the aspirations of that year's Classic crop – that would have been something. To have been the first colt to have won the King George twice – now that *would* have been something.

But it was churlish to harp on what might have been, so we had to concentrate on what Generous was on his last competitive appearance on a British racecourse, and on King George day we could do no better than solicit the views of the jockeys who had ridden the first two home. Alan Munro: 'He frightened the life out of me, doing it with his ears pricked and in such style.' And Pat Eddery: 'Generous was fantastic.'

So he was. And whatever the arguments for and against his retirement at the end of the season, the way he pulled away from his rivals in the King George will live, for the 1991 Flat season in England, as The Moment.

King George VI and Queen Elizabeth Diamond Stakes (Group 1)

27 July 1991

1 mile 4 furlongs (going: good)

1st: £276,480; **2nd:** £103,024; **3rd:** £49,112; **4th:** £20,984

1	GENEROUS	A. Munro	4–6 fav
2	SANGLAMORE	Pat Eddery	7–1
3	ROCK HOPPER	B. Raymond	8–1
4	TERIMON	M. Roberts	18–1
5	SAPIENCE	W. Carson	40–1
6	SADDLERS' HALL	L. Piggott	6–1
7	LUCHIROVERTE	L. Dettori	66–1
8	TIGER FLOWER	S. Cauthen	25–1
9	HAILSHAM	R. Cochrane	100–1

9 ran

distances: 7 lengths, 1 length
time: 2 mins 28.99 secs

Winner owned by Fahd Salman, trained by P. F. I. Cole (Whatcombe, Oxon), bred by Barronstown Stud, Ireland

Tote: win £1.70; places £1.30, £1.70, £1.80; dual forecast £4.30

AMERICAN WAY IS ONLY A DREAM FOR US

Tony Stafford

Fewer European buyers made the journey to Lexington for last week's Keeneland summer yearling sales than in recent years. The Maktoums, contrary to some expectations, came to the domestic industry's rescue by contributing more than a third of the $73 million total at the two-day Select Sale, but American money was pretty scarce.

Thereby hangs an ironic tale. American racecourses have continued to increase prize money – funded by on-course pari-mutuel revenue built up from meetings which run for months.

So, the American yearling buyer does have at least a shot at retrieving his investment by way of prize money, yet still remains largely inactive.

The Maktoums, meanwhile, are content to bring most of their sales acquisitions and the bulk of their breeding programme to Britain, where prize money has actually declined, never mind taking account of inflation.

Appropriately, in a week when the top level of the market was being shored up to a degree, the Jockey Club managed to stave off a further drastic prize money cut proposed by the Levy Board.

Talking last week to top English trainers in Lexington – generally those with Maktoum family connections – it was hard to discern much optimism.

There has been criticism of the Dubai-based brothers' approach to British racing; that their policy has swamped the sport to an extent which gives smaller owners no chance. My contention is that the Maktoums themselves have the least chance of all

of making the seriously under-funded British racing pay.

They are, I am certain, in the sport for itself, for the excitement and for the love of the animals and the environment (Britain) in which they race.

If this seems romantic, naive nonsense, as evidence for the defence I recall a conversation I had eight or nine years ago with Sheikh Mohammed when he said: 'It does not take four years to put together a breeding programme, but forty years. We have the commitment to the sport to undertake that sort of programme.'

When asked 'why racing?' the Sheikh said, 'Why not? We could put our money into a building , but how long can you look at it and enjoy it. With a beautiful horse, you can look and admire him or her for a long time and never be tired of it.'

The bottom line for British racing is that the Maktoums provide an astonishing amount of employment for stable and stud staff and generate funding within all branches of the industry, without ever swamping it in terms of achievement.

How else could Jack Berry (who has no Maktoum horses) be well past 100 winners by mid-July? How else could Sheikh Mohammed still be without a colts' Classic winner in England, despite years of endeavour aided by the most talented trainers in the land?

Those trainers' views was that the autumn yearling sales in Britain and Ireland will much more accurately reflect the true doom and gloom situation of slump-stuck Britain.

Who in his right mind, they ask,

would pay £50,000 for a yearling and wait at least six months at £200 a week before getting it onto a racecourse, only to compete for a winner's prize of less than £2,000?

These dreaming optimists still exist, but not in sufficient numbers to prevent heavy casualties among the training ranks.

In the United States, the present figure of 45,000 foals a year reflects a decline roughly in line with the fall in stallion fees during the past seven or eight years. Those business people who saw bloodstock as a guaranteed investment have gone, leaving the true horse people at the forefront.

But there will still be more than 3,000 yearlings on offer at the September yearling sale at Keeneland. Even if the figures for that sale are down, too, Americans will still be secure in the knowledge that a $50,000 yearling could be running for a $15,000 winner's maiden purse in New York next spring.

Much of that is due to the fact that Americans can go to the track whenever they want. Almost all tracks there now have Sunday racing, matching availability to an identifiable demand.

This weekend, for example, Atlantic City racecourse staged a $500,000 race supported by Caesar's Palace, which has a casino at the New Jersey resort. Bob Levy, owner of the racecourse, is a shareholder in both the Fasig-Tipton sales company, which runs the Saratoga yearling sale in August, and also the Philadelphia Phillies baseball team.

His equine team includes such giants as Bet Twice and Housebuster, yet Levy, surely the type of American to look to British racing as an alternative target, merely has a half-share with Dick Duchossois, who runs Arlington racecourse, in a Luca Cumani two-year-old.

'It's ridiculous,' he says. 'Unless you have a champion in Britain, it's like haemorrhaging money. So we stay here and go for the purses.'

In Britain, people can only go racing when permitted to by the Government, who prefer to bow to the influence of the farcical lobbies than give the public its right to entertainment when it is free to attend.

A sample of what would happen if ludicrous objections to Sunday racing were overcome, was seen at Newmarket on Friday night when 12,000 people went along, despite a dull card, simply because it was a nice evening and Newmarket offered some post-racing entertainment.

Apparently, Chester did even better the previous week, with a crowd exceeding that of Chester Cup day, so big, people were even turned away.

Clearly, every racetrack could pull in a decent Sunday crowd, even if ten raced together.

Perhaps it's time for racing's tail to stop wagging the dog, because, make no mistake, soon there may only be a carcass of a dog to do any wagging.

The Daily Telegraph, 22 July 1991

BENTINCK SURE TO BE WATCHING OVER HIS BELOVED GOODWOOD

John Oaksey

If you happen to meet, or glimpse in the background of your TV screen, a tall, handsome, rather arrogant-looking ghost at Goodwood this week, don't bother asking his name.

It will almost certainly be Lord George Bentinck – and, if you are either a steward of the Jockey Club wanting a solution to racing's problems, or a losing punter in search of a winner, don't hesitate to ask the ghost's advice.

Because, between 1824, when Bentinck first visited his beloved Goodwood, and 1848, when he died of a heart attack, no single man did more for British racing – or for its most beautiful racecourse.

In the last ten of twenty dramatic, hyperactive years in racing, he not only became the sport's outstanding personality and administrator but also a highly successful owner-breeder and one of the most fearless gamblers in even that high-rolling era.

The Duke of Richmond created a racecourse near his home on the Sussex Downs in 1801, a year before Bentinck was born. The early Goodwood meetings, mostly 'Hunters' Plates' and matches, were informal entertainment for the Duke and his friends.

There was one (wooden) stand and the public was allowed to come. But at Goodwood, as at Newmarket and all other meetings in those days, the interests and requirements of the hoi polloi came a poor second to those of horsey nobs like the Duke and the group of rich men of whom the racing establishment then consisted. Lord George Bentinck seems to have been the first of them to recognise how much more fun it might be for all concerned if

a degree of organisation – and honesty – could be imposed.

I wonder what his ghost will make of it all this week. But however high those aristocratic eyebrows rise at some of the sights, much that we now take for granted will be familiar – and, for a lot of it, their owner can take a lion's share of credit.

It was Bentinck, for instance, who first insisted that races should start as near as possible on time. He fined clerks of courses ten shillings for every minute a race was late, invented the rule that each horse should have a number, had number boards erected and insisted that all runners should be saddled and mounted in the same area in front of the stands.

Weighing out and in was apt to be conducted so informally that early incarnations of John Francome could adjust their weight almost at will by judicious use of heel or toe. Bentinck soon altered that and, even more important, introduced his own revolutionary method of starting.

The old custom of simply shouting 'Go' led to disgraceful delays, multiple false starts and all sorts of crooked stratagems. Bentinck replaced it by equipping the starter (he often did the job himself) with a flag – and heavily fining any jockey who did not do his best to get away as soon as the flag was dropped.

It was a method which survived until the invention of the starting gate. In fact, this week's Goodwood Cup, run for the first time over two miles, will also be the first Cup started from stalls rather than à la Bentinck – by flag in front of the stands.

Although famous for the tireless and effective war he waged against the defaulters and crooks who then plagued riding, Bentinck was himself a massive and sometimes distinctly devious punter. He lost £26,000 (about £3.7m today) on the 1826 St Leger, and one of his greatest gambles, also on the final Classic, depended on the first known use in racing of a long-distance horsebox. Horses walked to the races in those pre-railway days and it invariably took at least a fortnight to walk from Goodwood (where the Bentinck horses were trained) to Doncaster.

So, by running his good colt Elis, first at Goodwood (twice in one day) and then at Lewes less than a fortnight before the St Leger, Bentinck was easily able to 'persuade' the bookies that Elis could not possibly run in the Classic.

But the horsebox had secretly been built and pulled by six-horse teams, it could cover eighty miles a day. So Elis got to Doncaster in plenty of time – and won the St Leger in style. The owner was on at 12–1.

By the time he amazed the racing world by selling his stable and studs so cheaply (including, as it turned out, the 1848 Derby winner Surplice), Bentinck had already done wonders to clean up the unsavoury image of nineteenth century racing. The best-known victory in his war on corruption was, of course, the exposure of Running Rein, the *four-year-old* who 'won' the Derby in 1844.

But great though his services in racing were, Lord George Bentinck was no plaster saint. If his ghost does cross your path this week, watch out.

'What a humbug it is,' his former friend Charles Greville wrote after the Running Rein affair. 'If everbody knew all that I know of his [Bentinck's] tricks and artifices, what a rogue he would be thought.'

Sadly, it seems that Greville was right. This brave, brilliant man, who twice narrowly escaped death in duels, did 'prescribe a different code of morals for himself than he did for others.'

I still rather wish he was here today – to take charge, perhaps, of the Jockey Club's negotiations with the bookmakers. With Bentinck in command, the big three might not know what hit them . . .

The Daily Telegraph, 30 July 1991

GOODWOOD JULY MEETING

Goodwood, 30 July–3 August 199

The racing world was still abuzz with the excitement of Generous's performance at Ascot when, three days after the King George, the caravan moved on to five days on the Sussex Downs.

But the wheels soon got stuck in the mud, for on the opening day Glorious Goodwood hardly lived up to its epithet. Rain lashed the racegoers, mocking the traditional notion of Goodwood as a garden party with racing tacked on, and such was the

Glorious Goodwood hardly lived up to its epithet.

ferocity of the downpour that after the second race the official going was changed from firm to good to firm.

The second race of the day was the Gordon Stakes, often an informative trial for the St Leger and won in recent memory by Commanche Run and Minster Son before Classic success at Doncaster. The 1991 field was dire by such standards – just three runners – of which only one appeared to have even remote St Leger pretensions. This was Le Corsaire, who had twice won well at

The Gordon Stakes: the blinkered Stylish Senor (George Duffield) beats Trebly (Michael Roberts, left) and Le Corsaire (Lanfranco Dettori).

Newmarket, and he was sent off the 5–2 on favourite. He looked certain to justify those odds three furlongs out when going past the outsider Trebly, but found nothing under pressure. Trebly came back at him and then Stylish Senor ran on to head Trebly by half a length, with the favourite finishing last. It transpired that Le Corsaire had coughed several times during the race, and trainer Luca Cumani's fears that the virus had tightened its stranglehold on his stable seemed confirmed.

The Stewards' Cup looked as impenetrable as ever, but produced an easy winner. Notley had been well fancied for the Royal Hunt Cup and ran well to finish fourth, then followed up with a narrow victory at Chepstow. At Goodwood he was steady in the market at 14–1 as money came in for the 1990 winner Knight Of Mercy (trained like Notley by Richard Hannon) and the Wokingham hero Amigo Menor, but once Notley had taken the lead he was never in danger. After sitting handy in the group on the far side of the track he took command with two furlongs to go and sailed home under five-pound claimer Richard Perham, who was riding his biggest winner.

Richard Hannon was the first trainer to land the Stewards' Cup in successive years with different horses since Fred Armstrong forty years ago, and he was quick to give credit to the vet John Walmsley, who had operated last year on Notley's knees, so badly injured that his trainer 'thought he was a shooting job'.

The other highlight of a dismal first day was the victory of Barry Hills' Himiko over the hot favourite Satin Flower in the Oak Tree Stakes.

On Wednesday the weather had improved, and the card featured the most glittering prize of the week, the Sussex Stakes. This looked a superb contest, with the Guineas winners in opposition plus the Derby third and a clutch of top–class mile specialists.

Neither Shadayid nor Mystiko had

Rain-soaked Notley and Richard Perham return after the Stewards' Cup.

won since Newmarket. The One Thousand winner had performed the more creditably – third in the Oaks and second in the Coronation Stakes – but Mystiko looked certain to benefit from the return to a mile after his uninspiring attempt at an extra half mile in the Derby.

Second Set had been beaten a head by Marju in the St James's Palace Stakes at Royal Ascot, only the third start of his life, and could be expected to improve. But the woeful performance of Le Corsaire in the Gordon Stakes had provided eloquent evidence of how the virus was affecting the Cumani stable, and in the betting ring confidence in Second Set evaporated almost visibly. He opened at 11-4 and drifted to as long as 6-1 before coming in to a starting price of 5–1 as Shadayid hardened to 5–2 favourite.

The top-class French miler Priolo was fresh from running a close second to Sanglamore in the Prix d'Ispahan, Star Of Gdansk had run second in the Irish Two Thousand Guineas and third in both the Derby and the Irish Derby. Sikeston had won the Queen Anne Stakes at Royal Ascot, Green Line Express had been second in the Sussex Stakes for the last two years and recently won well at Lingfield, and Radwell had beaten Sure Sharp at Newcastle.

Mystiko was keyed up in the paddock and during the parade, but Shadayid took the preliminaries well.

Green Line Express made the running for the first half of the race and was still in front as the field came sweeping down the straight, but it was soon obvious that Second Set was travelling like a winner, and with more

than quarter of a mile to go he quickened impressively and took the lead, with Shadayid on the stands side in grim pursuit. Willie Carson gave the One Thousand Guineas winner the full works, but Lanfranco Dettori always had something up his sleeve, and Second Set responded to hard riding by running on with great determination throughout the final hundred yards to score by one and a half lengths, with Priolo finishing fast to miss second place by a short head. Star Of Gdansk was a disappointing sixth, and Mystiko last.

For such an inexperienced horse, the performance which Second Set produced in one of Europe's top mile races was remarkable, and already there was talk of his consolidating his claim to be the best miler in Europe and then taking on the world in the

The Richmond Stakes: Dilum (Alan Munro) at his peak.

Breeders' Cup Mile. More immediately, the victory was a cause of special satisfaction and relief to Luca Cumani: one of his charges could still turn in a championship effort, no matter how sick some of the others were. 'He's got a great will to win', said Dettori in praise of his partner.

At this stage of the season the giant two-year-old Dilum hardly seemed to need a great will to win. He just switched his giant stride into overdrive and pulverised his opponents, and the contempt with which he had treated his rivals in the Coventry Stakes at Royal Ascot was repeated in the Scottish Equitable Richmond Stakes. He surged into the lead halfway through this six-furlong Group Two contest and found a turn of foot a furlong out to saunter home from Showbrook. He seemed invincible, and was best-priced 14–1 for the 1992 Two Thousand Guineas.

"He's got a great will to win."

The arguments persisted about whether the great staying races should be shortened, but ammunition for the reformers came in the turnout for the Dickins & Jones Goodwood Cup. Reduced in distance from two and a half miles to two, it attracted eleven runners – and had not seen a double-figure field for forty-five years.

They didn't exactly ooze class, but they did include some of the best stayers available. Great Marquess, winner of the Jockey Club Cup in 1990 and most recently an impressive scorer at York, was favourite, preferred to Shahi (undefeated in 1991 but having only his fourth race ever), Quest For Fame's full brother Silver Rainbow (narrowly beaten in the Queen's Vase) and Further Flight, winner of the 1990 Ebor and of two of his three races this

year: he was clearly a horse on the upgrade.

Further Flight was held towards the rear of the field as the pacemaker Play Games surrendered the lead to his stable companion Silver Rainbow half a mile out, then Shahi took it up, then Silver Rainbow had another crack, then Great Marquess – and then Michael Hills brought Further Flight through to put the issue beyond further doubt and give his father Barry his fourth Goodwood Cup.

Barry Hills' successor at Manton, Peter Chapple-Hyam, had his first

Group race winner when Robert Sangster's Dr Devious beat Made Of Gold in the Lanson Champagne Vintage Stakes. This race was also notable for a whopping bet – £22,000 to £20,000 (11–10) – about Thourios, who was backed from 11–8 to evens. He finished a distant fifth.

Robert Sangster netted another big prize on the Thursday when Title Roll, trained in County Tipperary by Tommy Stack, sped through a timely opening to land the Group Three King George Stakes from Food Of Love and Rivers Rhapsody.

Dr Devious (Willie Carson) battles past Made Of Gold in the Lanson Champagne Vintage Stakes.

The Schweppes Golden Mile, one of the big betting races of the meeting, proved a real argy-bargy, with Band On The Run the most notable victim. Trying to make his way through closely-packed rivals in the final furlong, Band On The Run suffered from the knock-on effect of eventual winner Sky Cloud veering across fifth-placed Superoo, and jockey of the moment Alan Munro took a crashing fall. Ironically, the winner Sky Cloud was ridden by Richard Quinn, replaced by Munro as jockey to Fahd Salman. One effect of the fall of Band On The Run was to hamper the hot favourite Desert Dirham, but the 2–1 chance had in any case all but left his chance behind in the stalls, rearing as the gates opened and in the process losing the sort of ground which simply could not be made up in such a competitive handicap.

The Schweppes Golden Mile: Alan Munro takes a tumble from Band On The Run, as Richard Quinn on Sky Cloud (light cap with dark star, centre) goes on to win.

The Schweppes Golden Mile proved a real argy-bargy

Alan Munro bounced back to land Friday's big race, the Leslie & Godwin Spitfire Handicap, on Lord Weinstock's Green Danube, who was having only the third race of her life. The only Group race of the meeting's fourth day, the Molecomb Stakes, went to another lightly raced filly, Sahara Star, who collared her market rival Another Episode inside the last furlong under strong handling from John Reid.

Dick Hern, who had been having a quiet time with runners from his new Kingwood stable in Lambourn in the early part of the season, confirmed his return to form by taking the first two races on Saturday – thus notching up six winners from the stable's last nine runners. None of the seven runners in the Vodapage Maiden Stakes had run before, which made the performance of Basma in beating Shaping Up by two and a half lengths difficult to assess, but this filly – bought for $375,000 as a yearling – looked highly promising to say the least.

Hern's double came with a much more exposed fellow. Ijtihaad had won a good handicap at Ascot only a week before, and now landed the Racal Chesterfeld Cup, taking the lead from Fire Top two furlongs out and responding to the drive of a Willie Carson finish to win by one and a half lengths from last year's winner Song Of Sixpence. Carson's double brought his total for the meeting to five, and

secured for him the Ritz Club Trophy for the most successful jockey at the meeting.

But there is no doubt that the most spectacular display of the final day – and for many the most eye-catching effort of the whole week – came from the fetching grey filly Ruby Tiger in the Vodafone Nassau Stakes. This ten furlong race for fillies and mares usually brings together a high-class collection

Gordon Stakes (Group 3)

30 July 1991

1 mile 4 furlongs (going: good to firm)
1st: £24,816; 2nd: £8,390; 3rd: £3,945

1	STYLISH SENOR	G. Duffield	11–4
2	TREBLY	M. Roberts	11–1
3	LE CORSAIRE	L. Dettori	2–5 fav

3 ran

distances: ½ length, 1½ lengths
time: 2 mins 41.62 secs

Winner owned by Dexa'tex (Decorations) Ltd, trained by J. R. Fanshawe (Newmarket, Suffolk), bred by Robert N. Clay and Michael J. Ryan, USA

Tote: win £3.90, dual forecast £5.00

Ijtihaad and Willie Carson (striped cap) land the Chesterfield Cup.

nd in 1991 the field included hamshir, second in the Oaks; Gussy Marlowe, winner of the Pretty Polly takes at Newmarket and the Musidora takes at York, and most recently third o Kooyonga in the Coronation Stakes; he good five-year-old Filia Ardross; and uby Tiger.

There had been some doubt about he participation of Ruby Tiger as she ad been suffering from a bruised foot, ut trainer Paul Cole was duly satisfied hat she was fit to take her chance, and er presence in the field added an iternational lustre. Now four, she had ot won in Britain since the age of two, ut had scored several notable uccesses abroad, in Italy, Canada, ermany and Ireland – where she had von the Group Two Pretty Polly Stakes t The Curragh.

Gussy Marlowe was favourite, but uby Tiger slaughtered her opponents, lisplaying a dazzling turn of foot to ome clean away in the final quarter aile and win by seven lengths from hamshir.

This victory took her earnings vorldwide beyond £400,000, and Paul ole announced an ambitious target of million pounds. But a week later it vas announced that she had suffered a racked bone in her knee when inning the Nassau and might never ace again.

It was a sad postscript to a oodwood meeting which had risen bove the gloom of that sodden first day o climax with Ruby Tiger providing one f the best individual performances of he season, and which along the way ad seen other memorable runs from econd Set and from Dilum.

It hadn't all been Glorious Goodwood y any means, but it had sure had its aoments.

Sussex Stakes (Group 1)

31 July 1991

1 mile (going: good)

1st: £108,580; **2nd:** £40,482; **3rd:** £19,316; **4th:** £8,273

1	SECOND SET	L. Dettori	5–1
2	SHADAYID	W. Carson	9–4 fav
3	PRIOLO	F. Head	6–1
4	SIKESTON	Pat Eddery	14–1
5	RADWELL	G. Duffield	25–1
6	STAR OF GDANSK	C. Roche	15–2
7	GREEN LINE EXPRESS	A. S. Cruz	12–1
8	MYSTIKO	M. Roberts	9–2

8 ran

distances: 1½ lengths, short head
time: 1 min 40.53 secs
Winner owned by Richard L. Duchossois, trained by L. M. Cumani (Newmarket, Suffolk), bred by J. P. and Miss M. Mangan, Ireland
Tote: win £8.00; places £2.60, £1.60, £1.30; dual forecast £7.60

Scottish Equitable Richmond Stakes (Group 2)

31 July 1991

6 furlongs (going: good)

1st: £51,710; **2nd:** £19, 391; **3rd:** £9,345; **4th:** £4,104

1	DILUM	A. Munro	2–7 fav
2	SHOWBROOK	B. Raymond	4–1
3	DIAMOND MINE	K. Darley	30–1
4	SILVIO ALFREDO	M. Roberts	20–1

4 ran

distances: 3½ lengths, 3½ lengths
time: 1 min 13.05 secs
Winner owned by Fahd Salman, trained by P. F. I. Cole (Whatcombe, Oxon), bred by Ron Con Ltd 1, USA
Tote: win £1.30; dual forecast £1.30

Dickins & Jones Goodwood Cup (Group 3)

1 August 1991

2 miles (going: good)

1st: £37,994; **2nd:** £14,133; **3rd:** £6,716; **4th:** £2,847

1	FURTHER FLIGHT	M. Hills	9–2
2	GREAT MARQUESS	Pat Eddery	3–1 fav
3	SHAMBO	M. Roberts	10–1
4	SILVER RAINBOW	W. Carson	9–2

10 ran

distances: 1 length, head
time: 3 mins 28.69 secs
Winner owned by S. Wingfield Digby, trained by B. W. Hills (Lambourn, Berks), bred by S. Wingfield Digby
Tote: win £5.10; places £1.80, £1.50, £2.50; dual forecast £6.20

Ruby Tiger (Richard Quinn) at full stretch in the Nassau Stakes.

Philip Cornes Molecomb Stakes (Group 3)

2 August 1991

5 furlongs (going: good)

1st: £21,330; **2nd:** £7,899; **3rd:** £3,725; **4th:** £1,547

1	SAHARA STAR	J. Reid	2–1 fav
2	ANOTHER EPISODE	Pat Eddery	5–2
3	REGAL CHIMES	A. Munro	33–1
4	REGAL SCINTILLA	S. Cauthen	10–1

7 ran

distances: 1½ lengths, head
time: 59.14 secs

Winner owned by T. E. Sellier, trained by M. R. Stoute (Newmarket, Suffolk), bred by T. E. Sellier

Tote: win £3.10; places £1.70; dual forecast £2.80

Vodafone Nassau Stakes (Group 2)

3 August 1991

1 mile 2 furlongs (going: good to firm)

1st: £50,335; **2nd:** £18,756; **3rd:** £8,940; **4th:** £3,819

1	RUBY TIGER	T. Quinn	11–4
2	SHAMSHIR	L. Dettori	7–2
3	NORTH WIND	W. Carson	16–1
4	GUSSY MARLOWE	R. Cochrane	9–4 fav

6 ran

distances: 7 lengths, 3½ lengths
time: 2 mins 08.71 secs

Winner owned by Mrs Philip Blacker, trained by P. F. I. Cole (Whatcombe, Oxon), bred by S. Stanhope and Sheikh M. Alamuddin

Tote: win £3.30; places £1.80, £2.20; dual forecast £5.70

YORK AUGUST MEETING

One figure dominated the York August Meeting in 1991. Not a jockey, trainer or owner – let alone a horse. The individual who stole the headlines in most reports of one of the Flat season's greatest weeks was the Clerk of the Course at York, John Smith.

In the opinion of several jockeys and trainers, his watering of the course in order to produce good going went too far, providing ground so uneven and false that the form book could be thrown out the window. After the shock defeat of the crack two–year–old Dilum in the Gimcrack Stakes on the second day, even the Jockey Club's senior handicapper Geoffrey Gibbs admitted that the ground was so patchy that he would be ignoring the form as far as his ratings were concerned.

As the meeting progressed, John Smith resolutely stuck to pronouncing the going officially good, though race after race returned a time significantly lower than standard. Whatever the rights or wrongs of the zeal with which Smith watered the track, the issue of the state of the going sadly overshadowed the many stirring performances which, as always, made York a landmark in the Flat season.

The main event on the Tuesday was the Juddmonte International Stakes, the race which began life in 1972 as the Benson and Hedges Gold Cup and since the earth–shaking defeat of Brigadier Gerard in the inaugural running has been famous for shock results.

The Derby winner Roberto won that 1972 race and Troy in 1979 followed in his hoofprints by adding the Benson and Hedges to Epsom glory as a three–year–old. But Quest For Fame in 1991 was attempting to become the first Derby winner to take the York race as a four–year–old. He had been re–routed to York – for the race sponsored by his owner Khalid Abdullah's Juddmonte Farms – from an alternative engagement in the Geoffrey Freer Stakes at Newbury the previous weekend, but two horses were preferred to him in the betting.

He might run into a place . . . but surely he couldn't win.

Stagecraft was all the rage in the market, and understandably so. After his brilliant victory in the Prince of Wales's Stakes at Royal Ascot (page 92) he had just gone under to Environment Friend in the Eclipse (pages 106–7) but it was widely felt that Sheikh Mohammed's four-year-old could overturn that form at York, and he started at 6–5 on favourite with his Sandown Park conqueror – who had not run since his memorable effort in the Eclipse – second best at 3–1. There were only four others in the field chasing a first prize of nearly £150,000.

Quest For Fame may have been a Derby winner, but the feeling that he was a moderate one had not been entirely dispersed by his encouraging run in the Coronation Cup. Topanoora had run second to Toulon at Maisons-Laffitte since his controversial disqualification in favour of Rock Hopper at Royal Ascot, and seemed better suited by a distance longer than the ten furlongs of the International. Mukaddamah had won well at The Curragh and was apparently returning to the form which for a short time had seen him favourite for the Two Thousand Guineas. But he seemed a little out of his own league against the likes of Stagecraft and Environment Friend, and at 16–1 he shared the outsider's role with Terimon.

In computer jargon, Terimon was the 'WYSIWYG' horse: what you see is what you get. Lady Beaverbrook's grey had been around for too long to hold any surprises up his sleeve, and that 500–1 second to Nashwan in the 1989 Derby by now seemed to be an appropriate prelude to the role he regularly filled – in the frame in the big races. Second behind In The Groove in the 1991 Coronation Cup, third behind Stagecraft at Royal Ascot, fourth behind Generous in the King George. He might run into a place at York, but surely he couldn't win.

He could, of course, and he did. The runners left the stalls as if setting out for a quiet Sunday morning hack, and with no one prepared to set a proper pace, Michael Roberts seized the initiative and stole the race. After a furlong he sent Terimon – not usually a front runner – up to take the lead, and proceeded to set what looked like a sensible gallop. Quest For Fame was in close attendance round the turn, but when the runners came into the straight the expected challenges from the more fancied horses simply failed to materialise.

With a furlong and a half to go Quest For Fame may just have appeared to be going better than the leader, but when roused to his final effort Terimon found a fresh turn of foot and shook off the Derby winner without undue difficulty, running on stoutly to the line, where he was two lengths clear of Quest For Fame. Stagecraft, who had come under pressure early in the straight, could never mount a serious challenge, and finished third, a head in front of Topanoora.

Roberts had ridden an inspired race to send Terimon into the lead after a

The International Stakes: Terimon (Michael Roberts) repels Quest For Fame (Pat Eddery) and gives his handlers something to celebrate.

furlong, and his enterprise was handsomely rewarded. Clive Brittain, for whose virus-hit stable this Group One success ended a thirty-seven-day period without a winner, was met with hearty if somewhat dumbfounded applause when he greeted his hero in the unsaddling enclosure. 'I knew it was going to be a tactical race so I left it to the tactician', he said in exultant tribute to his jockey, and although few students of the form book could have backed the winner, Terimon's success was highly popular. This was the five-year-old's first Group One win on his twenty-fourth start, and for a horse always campaigned at the highest level the moment of glory had not come before time.

Above all the International had been a jockey's race, and the day's other Pattern event, the Great Voltigeur Stakes, also saw riding expertise at its very best. For Pat Eddery, the York meeting marked the return from a six-day suspension, but his performances on Torrey Canyon in the Acomb Stakes and then on Corrupt in the Voltigeur showed that a short lay-off had not diluted his powers. Whether or not Eddery had learnt from observation of Michael Roberts earlier in the day, he employed similar tactics, sending Corrupt clear at the start and simply keeping going to deny his rivals any chance of getting to him. Saddlers' Hall, who looked so impressive in the King Edward VII Stakes at Ascot before keeping a respectful distance behind Generous in the King George, was six lengths back in second.

The winner had been joint favourite for the Derby when flopping comprehensively at Epsom, but now alternative Classic glory beckoned in the St Leger. Eddery announced that he would be happy to partner Corrupt at Doncaster if his retainer with Khalid Abdullah did not corner his services in the final Classic – and as things turned

Corrupt (Pat Eddery) out on his own in the Great Voltigeur.

ut, he would have no reason to regret that prior claim.

But on the first day of York, the prospect of Lester Piggott landing his thirtieth Classic in the Leger seemed at least conceivable after he had driven Micheletti to victory in the Melrose Handicap. Charles St George's colt was improving with every race, and Lester said that 'he could be a Leger horse'. Time would tell.

Highlight of the middle day of the meeting was the Aston Upthorpe Yorkshire Oaks, a re-match between Possessive Dancer and Jet Ski Lady, who had fought out the finish of the Irish Oaks in July. Possessive Dancer's surprisingly effective turn of foot at The

Curragh had preserved her unbeaten record, and she was slightly preferred in the betting to Jet Ski Lady – for whom the Oaks had, if nothing else, proved that her Epsom victory was certainly no fluke.

Five others took them on. Third Watch had won the Ribblesdale Stakes at Royal Ascot but flopped in the Irish Oaks, Shamshir had run limply behind Third Watch at Ascot and then been left flat-footed by Ruby Tiger in the Nassau Stakes at Goodwood, and Gussy Marlowe, winner of Musidora at York in the spring, had been fourth in the Nassau. Fife had been fifth in the Ribblesdale, and Magnificent Star had filled the same position behind Jet Ski

Lady at Epsom. Since then Magnificent Star had run Fly Away Soon to three quarters of a length in the Schroders Glorious Stakes at Goodwood, and was no forlorn hope in the Yorkshire Oaks – though she would have to improve to trouble Possessive Dancer or Jet Ski Lady.

It was a wonderful race. Fife led until Jet Ski Lady took over with about three furlongs to go, with several of her rivals looking likely to mount a challenge. But Possessive Dancer's effort soon fizzled out and it was left to Magnificent Star to launch the only serious threat to the Oaks winner. Never out of the first three, she made her bid a furlong and a half out, and although for a few seconds

Head to head: Magnificent Star (Tony Cruz, far side) gets to Jet Ski Lady (Pat Eddery) in the Yorkshire Oaks.

it seemed that the best she would get was an honourable second, eventually she wore down Jet Ski Lady after a sustained struggle throughout the final two hundred yards, and won by a short head. Shamshir was five lengths away third.

Winning trainer Mohammed Moubarak attributed his filly's two recent defeats to the courses at Epsom and Goodwood: 'All she wanted was a galloping track and some cut in the ground.'

But another trainer was deeply unhappy about that cut, and there began a murmuring of discontent which had reached a clamour by the end of the day. Alex Scott had assessed the effect of the going on the chance of the hitherto unbeaten Possessive Dancer, and was not best pleased. He said after the race: 'I walked the course at one o'clock and it was good to soft. I knew then that she had no chance.'

"I do think they have overwatered."

The race following the Yorkshire Oaks did nothing to dispel the notion that the going was becoming a problem. The Tote Ebor Handicap, the biggest betting race of the week, was almost literally turned into a procession once the young apprentice Francis Norton had let the visored Deposki take the lead around a mile and a half out. Nothing could get to him as he hogged the rail all the way up the straight to finish five lengths in front of Tidemark, who was subsequently deemed to have interfered with the third past the post, Roll A Dollar: their placings were reversed.

The 8–1 favourite Highflying finished

Francis Norton and Deposki land the Ebor.

a tailed-off last, and his trainer Alan Harrison criticised the state of the ground: 'I do think they have overwatered.'

What was becoming noticeable was that horses were finding it impossible to come off the pace to mount a late challenge. On the round course, most of the winners had made much or all of the running, or had been prominent throughout their races: horses trying to make a telling run late on were finding themselves held back in the sticky ground.

The Scottish Equitable Gimcrack Stakes provided perhaps the most unexpected outcome of the meeting – the complete eclipse of the much-vaunted two-year-old Dilum. Winner of the Coventry Stakes at Royal Ascot and the Richmond Stakes at Goodwood on his last two outings, Dilum was a heavily supported 7–4 on favourite for the Gimcrack, but was on edge in the paddock before the race and all at sea on the ground once the heat was turned up in the race. He made a vain attempt to get to the head of affairs two furlongs out but his effort soon evaporated, and River Falls, who had

Juddmonte International Stakes (Group I)

20 August 1991

I mile 2 furlongs 85 yards (going: good)

1st: £144,407; **2nd:** £52,913; **3rd:** £24,956; **4th:** £9,707; **5th:** £3,353; **6th:** £812

I	TERIMON	M. Roberts	16–1
2	QUEST FOR FAME	Pat Eddery	11–2
3	STAGECRAFT	S. Cauthen	5–6 fav
4	TOPANOORA	L. Piggott	14–1
5	ENVIRONMENT FRIEND	G. Duffield	3–1
6	MUKADDAMAH	W. Carson	16–1

6 ran

distances: 2 lengths, 3½ lengths
time: 2 mins 16.18 secs

Winner owned by The Dowager Lady Beaverbrook, trained by C. E. Brittain (Newmarket, Suffolk), bred by Hesmonds Stud Ltd

Tote: win £15.40; places £3.50, £2.40; dual forecast £21.70

Great Voltigeur Stakes (Group 2)

20 August 1991

I mile 3 furlongs 195 yards (going: good)

1st: £43,281; **2nd:** £16,036; **3rd:** £7,568; **4th:** £3,150

I	CORRUPT	Pat Eddery	5–1
2	SADDLERS' HALL	L. Piggott	11–8 fav
3	COLLINS AVENUE	M. Hills	18–1
4	RUNYON	W. Carson	9–2

7 ran

distances: 6 lengths, 2 lengths
time: 2 mins 34.16 secs

Winner owned by F. M. Kalla, trained by N. A. Callaghan (Newmarket, Suffolk), bred by Claremont Green, USA

Tote: win £4.70; places £2.20, £1.50; dual forecast £4.90

led from the start, ran on well to beat the 33–1 outsider Taylor Quigley by three and a half lengths, with Prince Ferdinand fourth and Dilum a desperately disappointing fourth of five.

Perhaps the going had found Dilum out, perhaps he had just had enough for the season. It was not until he turned in another below-par performance in the Mill Reef Stakes at Newbury in September that holders of ante-post vouchers on Paul Cole's colt for the 1992 Two Thousand Guineas would think of using them to light consoling mid-winter fires.

And another who found it difficult to quicken in the watered ground was the runner-up to Food Of Love in the Falmouth Handicap, Sarcita – of whom we would be hearing more.

By the end of the second day of the meeting complaints were rising to a crescendo. Paul Cole attributed the downfall of Dilum to the going. Luca Cumani described the ground as 'atrocious, a joke'. Bruce Raymond may have had little cause to grumble – he had won the Gimcrack on River Falls – but he stated that 'I have never known racing over two days when nothing has been able to make up ground from the back at all.'

On the Thursday the National Trainers' Federation announced that they had asked the Jockey Club to investigate the matter, and the day's results did little to improve John Smith's position. On going again officially returned as 'good', all seven races produced times slower than standard.

The most spectacular instance of a horse – and indeed a jockey – taking advantage of the conditions was the performance of Pontenuovo in the Bradford and Bingley Handicap. Drawn 1 on the inside of the round course for the one-mile trip, Pat Eddery shot the 1990 Royal Hunt Cup winner into the lead as soon as the stalls opened and simply stayed there. If horses found it difficult to challenge from off the pace at this meeting, it was almost impossible to peg back a resolute front-

Sheikh Albadou (Pat Eddery) at full stretch to beat Paris House (Darryll Holland) in the Nunthorpe.

runner like Pontenuovo, who kept on to win comfortably from Venus Observed.

After the race Pontenuovo gave connections a momentary scare when becoming somewhat shaky in the unsaddling enclosure through lack of oxygen, but he soon recovered.

The day's big race was the Keeneland Nunthorpe Stakes, the third Group One event of the meeting. Favourite was the French challenger Divine Danse, trained by Criquette Head. After a good two-year-old career (she was an unlucky third in the Cheveley Park Stakes), she had in 1991 run second in the Prix Imprudence and fourth in the French One Thousand Guineas before winning two good sprints, the Prix du Gros-Chene and the Prix de Ris-Orangis.

Her main rival in the betting was Elbio, having his first run since that slightly disappointing effort when his third in the July Cup had rather dented aspirations to being the season's top sprinter. Sheikh Albadou, a mightily impressive winner of a six-furlong handicap at York in June but only fourth in the Criterion Stakes at Newmarket when stepping up into pattern-race company, was quietly fancied, as was Jack Berry's speedy Paris House, bidding to become the first two-year-old to win the Nunthorpe since Ennis in 1956.

For all the form of such horses, perhaps the most interesting runner was Klassy Briefcase, trained in New Jersey by Phil Serpe and mounting an American bid in the Nunthorpe for the second successive year, following Mr Nickerson's fruitless pursuit of Dayjur in 1990. The winner of eighteen of her forty-one starts and holder of the American record for five furlongs on turf, Klassy Briefcase did not boast form which suggested that she could overcome her European rivals.

Title Roll, trained in Ireland by Tommy Stack and winner of the King George Stakes at Goodwood, completed the overseas challenge.

Klassy Briefcase left the stalls like a

Aston Upthorpe Yorkshire Oaks (Group 1)

21 August 1991

1 mile 3 furlongs 195 yards (going: good)

1st: £75,640; **2nd:** £27,760; **3rd:** £13,130; **4th:** £5,150; **5th:** £1,825; **6th:** £495

1	MAGNIFICENT STAR	A. S. Cruz	16–1
2	JET SKI LADY	Pat Eddery	7–4
3	SHAMSHIR	L. Dettori	9–1
4	THIRD WATCH	J. Reid	9–1
5	POSSESSIVE DANCER	S. Cauthen	13–8 fav
6	FIFE	W. R. Swinburn	50–1
7	GUSSY MARLOWE	M. Roberts	9–1

7 ran

distances: short head, 5 lengths
time: 2 mins 35.92 secs

Winner owned by Ecurie Fustok, trained by M. Moubarak (Newmarket, Suffolk), bred by Buckram Oak Farm, USA

Tote: win £25.60; places £5.30, £1.40; dual forecast £31.10

Scottish Equitable Gimcrack Stakes (Group 2)

21 August 1991

6 furlongs (going: good)

1st: £49,830; **2nd:** £18,593; **3rd:** £8,884; **4th:** £3,818

1	RIVER FALLS	B. Raymond	9–4
2	TAYLOR QUIGLEY	M. Roberts	33–1
3	PRINCE FERDINAND	J. Reid	20–1
4	DILUM	A. Munro	4–7 fav

5 ran

distances: 3½ lengths, 4 lengths
time: 1 min 13.72 secs

Winner owned by A. F. Budge (Equine) Ltd, trained by R. Hannon (East Everleigh, Wilts), bred by Mrs J. R. Hine and Miss J. Bunting

Tote: win £3.50; places £1.30, £3.00; dual forecast £22.00

Keeneland Nunthorpe Stakes (Group 1)

22 August 1991

5 furlongs (going: good)

1st: £89,262; **2nd:** £33,107; **3rd:** £15,654; **4th:** £6,547

1	SHEIKH ALBADOU	Pat Eddery	6–1
2	PARIS HOUSE	D. Holland	7–1
3	BLYTON LAD	S. Webster	40–1
4	DIVINE DANSE	F. Head	2–1 fav
5	ELBIO	S. Cauthen	11–4
6	DUPLICITY	J. Reid	100–1
7	POYLE GEORGE	L. Piggott	50–1
8	TITLE ROLL	W. Carson	9–1
9	KLASSY BRIEFCASE	J. Ferrer	9–1

9 ran

distances: 1½ lengths, neck
time: 58.21 secs

Winner owned by Hilal Salem, trained by A. A. Scott (Newmarket, Suffolk), bred by Highclere Stud Ltd

Tote: win £6.20; places £1.70, £1.40, £6.70; dual forecast £14.90

rocket and for one and a half furlongs had the legs off the rest, but when the race really started to heat up at halfway she was engulfed. Paris House took up the running and looked to be going like the winner until Sheikh Albadou, responding to a rousing ride from Pat Eddery, bore down on him inside the final furlong and ran on to score a gutsy win. Not bad for a horse who so recently was running in handicaps, and a great credit to trainer Alex Scott.

Hardly less credit attached to the runner-up, for Paris House had run superbly well for a two-year-old – even Pat Eddery acknowledged that Jack Berry's charge had run 'a hell of a race'.

The 40–1 outsider Blyton Lad was third, with Divine Danse plugging on to be fourth.

Klassy Briefcase was last, adding to the controversy about the ground. 'I have walked the course every day', said trainer Phil Serpe, 'and I don't understand how everything can be like cement around it and the course so wet.' In the midst of his disappointment and disenchantment, Serpe expressed a ready willingness to come back another year.

Despite a fine effort when second to Marling at Royal Ascot, Culture Vulture was not favourite for the Lowther Stakes, that privilege going to the unbeaten Sahara Star, winner of the Molecomb Stakes at Goodwood. But it was Culture Vulture who took up the running three furlongs out and ran on stoutly to win by four lengths from Poolesta and so set up her splendid autumn campaign.

She also completed a two-year-old double for Paul Cole, whose Great Palm overturned the hot favourite Wesaam in the Moorestyle Convivial Maiden Stakes.

Time would tell whether the York form was as dubious as some were claiming, though the trainers did not harbour any grudge against John Smith: the next fixture at the course was very well supported.

But the August meeting, the track's flagship event, was dominated by the furore over the watering, and certainly the form book made more curious reading after the meeting than before. Not that the backer of Terimon, Deposki, Pontenuovo and the rest of the winners who adapted so well to conditions were complaining.

Lowther Stakes (Group 2)

22 August 1991

6 furlongs (going: good)

1st: £38,439; **2nd:** £14,319; **3rd:** £6,822; **4th:** £2,910

1	CULTURE VULTURE	T. Quinn	85–40
2	POOLESTA	K. Darley	13–2
3	SAHARA STAR	Pat Eddery	11–8 fav
4	MISS BLUEBIRD	L. Piggott	4–1

4 ran

distances: 4 lengths, 1½ lengths
time: 1 min 12.44 secs

Winner owned by Christopher Wright, trained by P. F. I Cole (Whatcombe, Oxon), bred by Holtsinger Inc, USA

Tote: win £2.70; dual forecast £7.30

The Lowther Stakes: Culture Vulture (Richard Quinn) storms home.

LADBROKE SPRINT CUP

The sprinting scene had not quite been the same since the departure of Dayjur after his remarkable performance in the 1990 Breeders' Cup Sprint, and the big sprint races of 1991 were spent looking for a new star. By the time of the Ladbroke Sprint Cup, the third leg of the Group One sprints in Britain after the July Cup and the Nunthorpe Stakes, the picture was far from clear.

Polish Patriot had won the July Cup brilliantly but was now sidelined by injury. Sheikh Albadou had won the Nunthorpe over five furlongs, but the field he beat was, to be honest, substandard for that race, the ground had been questionable, and the horse himself had only recently graduated from handicaps.

Sheikh Albadou was one of six runners in the Ladbroke Sprint (reduced from seven upon the late defection of King's Stand Stakes winner Elbio), but the small field held the potential for an intriguing race. The Guineas winners Shadayid and Mystiko were in opposition for the second time since their Newmarket hours of glory – and neither had won a race since their respective Classics. Shadayid had done somewhat better than her male counterpart: she had run third in the Oaks, and second in both the Coronation Stakes and Sussex Stakes, in which race Mystiko had finished last. Mystiko, however, looked a real sprinter, and might just return to form over six furlongs.

Then there was Polar Falcon, who since beating In The Groove in Newbury's Lockinge Stakes had run fourth in the July Cup and fourth in the Prix Jacques le Marois at Deauville, beaten less than a length by the winner Hector Protector. Shalford looked out of his depth, as did the Wokingham Stakes winner Amigo Menor, winner most recently of a Group Three race at Leopardstown.

With hindsight Polar Falcon's starting price of 13–2 looked inordinately generous for a horse who had last time finished so close to Hector Protector, Lycius and Danseuse du Soir, but it was felt in some quarters that six furlongs was too short for him, and three of his rivals were preferred in the betting. Shadayid went off 13–8 favourite, with Sheikh Albadou at 9–4 and Mystiko uneasy in the market at 9–2.

Shalford led for the first half of the race, but weakened as Sheikh Albadou came with a powerful run with over two furlongs to go. Shadayid was running on, but a six-furlong sprint was too sharp for her and she could not accelerate as Cash Asmussen – who already ridden a winner earlier in the afternoon on his first ride in England since being injured in June – brought Polar Falcon through to take the lead. Asmussen switched the French-trained colt inside Sheikh Albadou with less than a furlong to go and Polar Falcon kept on impressively to win by one and a half lengths. Shadayid was well behind in third, and Mystiko a disappointing fourth.

Polar Falcon had lowered the course record for six furlongs and was clearly not inconvenienced by the distance, but immediate post-race plans signalled a return to a longer trip in the Breeders' Cup Mile. As far as Asmussen was concerned, distance was no object: 'From five furlongs to a mile he can find a furlong and a half of super speed.'

The three British Group One sprints had been won by three different horses, and the European sprinting crown was still there for the taking.

Ladbroke Sprint Cup (Group 1)

7 September 1991

6 furlongs (going: good to firm)

1st: £85,837; 2nd: £31,534; 3rd: £14,942; 4th: £5,892; 5th: £2,121; 6th: £612

1	POLAR FALCON	C. Asmussen	13–2
2	SHEIKH ALBADOU	B. Raymond	9–4
3	SHADAYID	W. Carson	13–8 fav
4	MYSTIKO	M. Roberts	9–2
5	SHALFORD	J. Reid	12–2
6	AMIGO MENOR	C. Rutter	20–1

6 ran

distances: 1½ lengths, 3½ lengths
time: 1 min 11.23 secs

Winner owned by David Thompson, trained by J. E. Hammond (France), bred by Edward A. Seltzer, USA

Tote: win £7.80; places £2.80, £1.70; dual forecast £8.00

DONCASTER SEPTEMBER MEETING

Doncaster, 11–14 September 1991

'Leger meeting's air of optimism', went the headline on the front page of the *Racing Post* on the opening day of Doncaster's biggest fixture of the year, and the course's new management team could certainly do with a dose of looking on the bright side after two years which had brought the meeting the very worst attention.

In 1989 holes in the track caused racing to be abandoned and the St Leger transferred to Ayr, while in 1990 came the horror of the doping of Bravefoot and Norwich.

But with the final Classic on the Saturday and the prospect of excellent sport leading up to it, there was plenty of ground for optimism.

That mood took a severe jolt as early as the third race on the opening day. Everything had started well enough. Sheikh Maktoum Al Maktoum's Ezzoud had won the graduation race by a short head from his brother Sheikh Mohammed's Lead the Dance, while Stewards' Cup winner Notley had stepped up into Listed company and landed the Doncaster Bloodstock Sales Scarborough Stakes from Northern Goddess and Blyton Lad in a finish of heads.

The third race was the Tote-Portland Handicap, one of the great sprints of the season but one which has had its fair share of controversy. There was the famous 1986 running with its two false starts and the Starter's anguished cry of 'Come back, you buggers!' More ominous was the 1989 race in which three horses fell, and in 1991 it was the memory of that day which came hurrying back after Farfelu had stumbled and crashed to the ground a quarter of a mile from the finish, giving jockey Simon Whitworth a heavy fall.

The race went to the 13–2 favourite Sarcita, ridden by Willie Carson, but Farfelu's fall had raised the spectre of

A nervous inspection of the course after the Portland Handicap.

1989, and a deputation of jockeys was dispatched to the scene of the incident to examine the ground before racing could continue. For several minutes Ray Cochrane, John Lowe, Nicky Carlisle, John Williams and Kevin Darley – accompanied by a pack of journalists – studied the area where Farfelu had fallen, and in particular a substantial hole into which television cameras had shown groundsman Terry Harrison submerging his arm.

But before the followers of the racing circus could start looking up the train times to Ayr – where the St Leger would again be run in the event of Doncaster being abandoned – the jockeys and stewards gave the ground the all-clear

The holes had been caused by – and were not the cause of – Farfelu's stumble, and Simon Whitworth told the stewards that his mount had struck into the heels of Plain Fact. So racing continued, but it had been a nasty moment, and trainer Liam Codd, whose Madraco had broken a leg in the 1989 Portland, withdrew his charge Sagaman from his intended race on the second day of the meeting.

Farfelu can hardly have been Simon Whitworth's favourite horse: the colt had crashed into the rails after finishing sixth in the Stewards' Cup, giving Whitworth another nasty fall. But both horse and jockey escaped injury in the Portland, and with a sigh of relief, racing went ahead.

Normal service resumed with the A.F. Budge Park Hill Stakes, which used to be known as the 'Fillies' St Leger' but in 1991 was opened up to fillies older than three and downgraded to Group Three from Group Two. Patricia, winner of her last three races, which included the Lancashire Oaks and the Prix de Pomone at Deauville, went off the 11–8 favourite and ran on strongly to account for Luca Cumani's improving Nibbs Point by a length and a half. Patricia had been bought by Sheikh Mohammed only the previous week from Charles St George.

The second day of the meeting belonged mainly to Lester Piggott, who did family connections a couple of good turns on Bog Trotter and Mudaffar. Bog Trotter, trained by Piggott's son-in-law William Haggas and winner of the Greenham Stakes (page 41) had not run since disappointing in the Two Thousand Guineas, but he surged back to form in the Kiveton Park Stakes by making much of the running and keeping on stoutly to beat Satin Flower and Only Yours.

Half an hour later it was Piggott's brother-in-law Robert Armstrong who was the successful trainer as the Long Fellow brought 16–1 chance Mudaffar through at the death to whip the People–Sporting Life Championship

Patricia (Steve Cauthen) dominates the Park Hill Stakes.

Handicap from under the nose of Pat Eddery and Troupe.

This was vintage Piggott, delivering his mount in the right place at the right moment to snatch a race which seconds before he seemed to have no chance of getting. The winning jockey had looked across at the doubtless startled Eddery as he sailed by, and later elaborated: 'I did not say anything, but as he had gone past me turning into the straight he looked at me and laughed!'

Laughter might have been one reaction to the prospect of the Champion Hurdler – even one as good as Morley Street – taking on specialist Flat stayers in a classy race like the Doncaster Cup. But Morley Street took his chance, starting at 33–1: the price was not really surprising, given that the opposition included the likes of Arzanni (winner of the Yorkshire Cup and narrowly beaten in the Ascot Gold Cup) and Great Marquess, second in the Goodwood Cup. Morley Street had

produced one of the craziest results of the 1990 Flat season when beating the 1989 St Leger winner Michelozzo at Goodwood, and in the Doncaster Cup he so nearly pulled off an even more remarkable feat.

Pat Eddery sent Great Marquess on three furlongs out and it seemed that none of his rivals had a chance of pegging him back – until John Williams galvanised Morley Street into action. Steaming up the stands side, the Champion Hurdler gained an extraordinary amount of ground in the final quarter of a mile and was catching Great Marquess relentlessly. But the post came just in time for the leader, and Morley Street was denied by a short head. He would certainly have won in another stride, and even in defeat his effort must go down as one of the most notable of the whole season.

The Laurent–Perrier Champagne Stakes is regularly one of the most significant two-year-old races of the year, and the field in 1991 was small but

quite select. Rodrigo De Triano (named after the look-out on the ship in which Columbus discovered the New World) was unbeaten in three races, in the second of which he had accounted for River Falls – who had subsequently gone on to land the Gimcrack Stakes at York (page 139). River Falls reopposed at Doncaster, but the weight of opinion was with Rodrigo De Triano.

Another colt unbeaten in three outings was White Blade, who had bolted with Pat Eddery on his debut at Sandown Park and subsequently withdrawn, but had since then struck up a good working relationship with Tony Clark, who had ridden the headstrong colt to all his victories. Artic Tracker was heralded as the best two-year-old of the season after easy wins at Newmarket and Newbury, but his reputation was tarnished after running third to Chicmond in the Solario Stakes at Sandown Park.

River Falls made the running until approaching the final furlong, where

Willie Carson brought Rodrigo De Triano through to win with such ease that owner Robert Sangster opined: 'I think I could have won on him.' Confident that Sangster would not be able to do the weight for the 1992 Two Thousand Guineas, the bookmakers installed Rodrigo De Triano the new favourite for the Classic.

Desert Sun had been hotly fancied for the 1991 Two Thousand Guineas in the dim distant months of the early spring, then had rather lost his way after finishing second to Marju in the Craven Stakes (pages 38–9). But he came good in the Sun Princess Graduation Stakes, showing an impressive turn of foot to sail home five lengths clear of Ristna. Within a few weeks that would look very good form.

The feature event on the Saturday was of course the Coalite St Leger (pages 146–8), but the supporting races provided some memorable moments.

Paris House was a well-backed odds-on favourite for the five-furlong Flying Childers Stakes on the strength of his magnificent second in the Nunthorpe Stakes at York. His only other defeat in seven outings had been by Magic Ring at Royal Ascot, and he was clearly a cut above his four rivals at Doncaster – though the Bill Watts-trained Colway Bold was unbeaten in his three races.

The result was never in doubt. Paris House made all the running and increased the pace at halfway to stride home two-and-a-half lengths clear of Power Lake and earn himself another crack at his elders in the Prix de l'Abbaye at Longchamp. Looking to the longer term, Paris House would clearly be a sprinter to be reckoned with in 1992.

The Coalite Handicap which followed the St Leger went to Sky Cloud, but the runner-up Mellottie ran on well enough inside the final furlong after encountering traffic problems to enhance his Cambridgeshire prospects: he had done his Newmarket chances no harm by missing picking up a penalty at Doncaster, and his odds for

the first leg of the Autumn Double contracted to a best-priced 14–1.

But even allowing for the feats of Toulon and Paris House, perhaps the most remarkable performance seen at Doncaster on the fourth day of the meeting came from the filly You Know The Rules in the Reference Point Sceptre Stakes – or rather came from her jockey Lester Piggott.

This was one of those Piggott rides which simply had to be seen to be believed. A 14–1 chance in a good field which included Hyabella, Susurration and Crystal Path, You Know The Rules

seemed to have little chance two furlongs out, labouring at the back as the leader Susurration was collared by Silver Braid. Inside the final furlong, You Know The Rules was running on but Silver Braid appeared to have the race sewn up until Piggott conjured the most extraordinary burst from his mount in the last few yards to put her nose in front a stride before the line and land the verdict by a short head.

This was the first time that Piggott had ridden for the filly's trainer, Mike Channon. After this effort he'd probably be asked again.

A.F. Budge Park Hill Stakes (Group 3)

11 September 1991

1 mile 6 furlongs 132 yards (going: good to firm)

1st: £22,734; 2nd: £8,437; 3rd: £3,994; 4th: £1,675

1	PATRICIA	S. Cauthen	11–8 fav
2	NIBBS POINT	L. Dettori	5–1
3	SESAME	W.R. Swinburn	14–1
4	ALWAYS FRIENDLY	C. Rutter	8–1

11 ran

distances: 1½ lengths, neck
time: 3 mins 05.37 secs
Winner owned by Sheikh Mohammed, trained by H.R.A. Cecil (Newmarket, Suffolk), bred by Maple Leaf Farm, USA
Tote: win £2.10; places £1.30, £1.80, £4.00; dual forecast £3.80

Laurent–Perrier Champagne Stakes (Group 2)

13 September 1991

7 furlongs (going: good to firm)

1st: £41,550; 2nd: £15,558; 3rd: £7,479; 4th: £3,264

1	RODRIGO DE TRIANO	W. Carson	11–8 fav
2	RIVER FALLS	B. Raymond	3–1
3	ARTIC TRACKER	J. Reid	5–2
4	CORALS DREAM	K. Fallon	50–1

5 ran

distances: 3½ lengths, 2½ lengths
time: 1 min 26.55 secs
Winner owned by R.E. Sangster, trained by P.W. Chapple–Hyam (Manton, Wilts), bred by Swettenham Stud
Tote: win £2.10; places £1.50, £1.30; dual forecast £2.90

COALITE
ST LEGER

Doncaster, 14 September 1991

There was, to be truthful, a rather second-division look to the ten-strong field for the St Leger, the first run under the sponsorship of Coalite.

None of the runners had won a Group One race, let alone another Classic, and several were untried at the highest level, their presence in the line-up justified by the hope that they might be improving.

At least there was little doubt about the ability of the favourite, Toulon. Trained in France by André Fabre, Khalid Abdullah's Top Ville colt had been practically unknown to British racing fans before his remarkable win in the Chester Vase (page 55), and then had lost a lot of friends when trailing in ninth when joint favourite for the Derby. Since Epsom he had redeemed himself with an easy victory over Topanoora and Our Account in the Prix Maurice de Neuil at Maisons-Laffitte, and with plenty of excuses available for his Derby flop, he seemed one of the few runners in the St Leger with genuine class.

Among his opponents at Doncaster was the horse with whom Toulon had shared the dubious privilege of Derby favouritism. Corrupt had fared little better at Epsom, finishing sixth behind Generous. He had then come a disappointing fifth behind Saddlers' Hall in the King Edward VII Stakes at Royal Ascot and second to Zoman in the Scottish Classic at Ayr. But he bounced back to his best with a vengeance with a six-length victory over Saddlers' Hall in the Great Voltigeur at York, and if on his top form would have a formidable chance.

Saddlers' Hall himself was also in the Leger field. After Royal Ascot he had finished a long way behind Generous in the King George and then seemed to confirm that his earlier promise had been a mirage with a disappointing run

Pat Eddery on Toulon looks around for dangers as John Reid and Saddlers' Hall plug on.

behind Corrupt in the Voltigeur. And it cannot have boosted the confidence of his supporters that his regular partner Lester Piggott had deserted him for Micheletti.

This was no great surprise, for Micheletti (a half brother to the 1989 winner Michelozzo) was owned by

Piggott's close friend Charles St George, and his victory in the Melrose Handicap at the York August Meeting had suggested that Piggott might find far worse partners for his bid for a ninth St Leger. This was the twenty-seventh year Lester Piggott had ridden in the race.

Of the others, Luchiroverte attracted

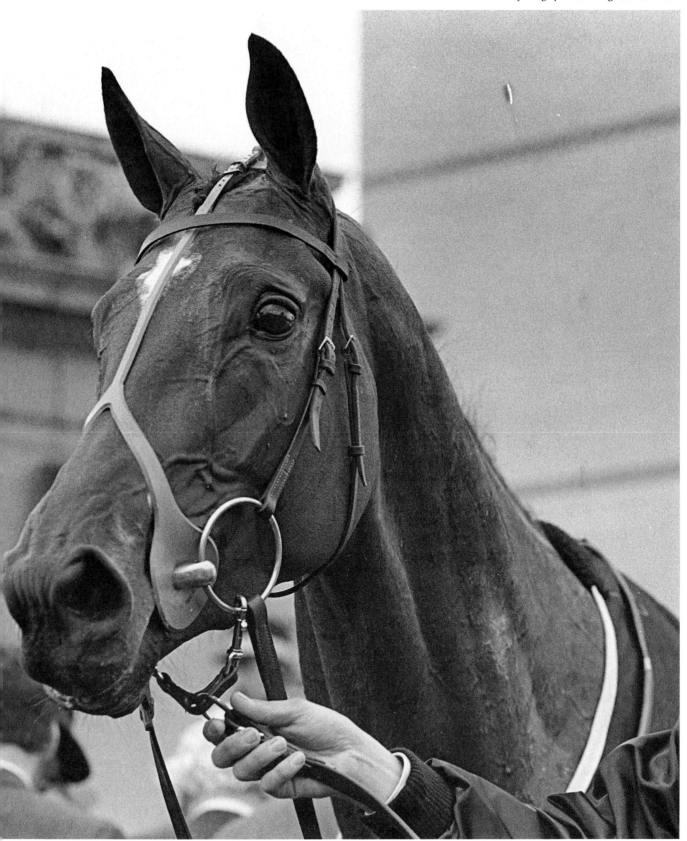

Toulon in the unsaddling enclosure.

some interest: he had won the Churchill Stakes at Ascot after running fourth behind Suave Dancer in the Prix du Jockey-Club and second to Toulon at Chester. Jahafil had won the March Stakes at Goodwood, Jendali the Queen's Vase at Royal Ascot and a Listed race at Newmarket's July Meeting. Arcadian Heights (winner of a Listed race at Chester and second to Jahafil at Goodwood) and Fly Away Soon (who had beaten Magnificent Star at Goodwood) were supplemented for the race on 3 September at a cost of £25,000 each, in itself some indication of the potential weakness of the field. Libk had been fourth of five behind Jahafil at Goodwood.

So it was by no means a great field, but a Classic is a Classic, and there was the usual sense of excitement as the runners set off – on a trip which after remeasuring of the course officially reverted to the traditional 1 mile 6 furlongs 132 yards.

After about two furlongs of that trip Jahafil had the lead and the rest were in fairly close proximity, when the runners were confronted by the sight of a man and a small boy sitting on the course, right in their path. Willie Carson on the leader took evasive action and steered round the pair, though some of the horses following had a less clear view of the obstruction and had to snatch up. (The man was subsequently arrested and charged with endangering the life of the boy.)

With that drama behind them, the St Leger field continued its way round towards the straight. Jahafil and Arcadian Heights were leading, then Jahafil faded and Arcadian Heights made the best of his way home until, three furlongs out, Saddlers' Hall took over.

For a few seconds it looked as if John Reid on Saddlers' Hall has stolen the St Leger. He went well clear of his rivals and was maintaining a tremendous gallop which seemed to be grinding all the others into defeat. Not quite all, though, for Pat Eddery had made

stealthy progress on Toulon up the straight and now, just inside the final furlong, collared the leader.

Saddlers' Hall had run a fine race but Toulon was simply too good, and after a brief struggle the issue was settled. Pat Eddery looked to his outside to check that nothing was coming late, to his inside to gauge how Saddlers' Hall was finishing, and let Toulon storm clear to victory by one and a half lengths. Micheletti was *fifteen* lengths back in third – some measure of the gulf between the two horses who made a race of the St Leger and the rest who just made up the numbers.

"It must have been a good race for us two to go clear of the others."

But Luchiroverte picked up £13,097 by finishing fourth, thus making Clive Brittain the third trainer in 1991 to exceed the million-pound mark in prize money. Corrupt finished sixth; jockey Lanfranco Dettori reported that he hated the firmish ground.

Because the final Classic had turned out to be, in effect, a two-horse race, it was difficult to know quite what to make of the form, but the consensus of opinion was that Toulon was a pretty good horse, and would be even better as a four-year-old. Meanwhile there was talk of a bid for the Prix de l'Arc de Triomphe.

Owner Khalid Abdullah and trainer André Fabre were unable to attend the St Leger, but Khalid Abdullah's racing manager Grant Pritchard-Gordon confirmed that Toulon would remain in training in 1992, adding, 'It has always been Prince Khalid's ambition to win this great race.'

And Pat Eddery should have the last word on the last Classic: 'It must have been a good race for us two to go clear of the others.'

Coalite St Leger Stakes (Group 1)

14 September 1991

1 mile 6 furlongs 132 yards (going: good to firm)

1st: £175,781; **2nd:** £65,297; **3rd:** £31,514; **4th:** £13,097; **5th:** £5,423; **6th:** £2,355

1	TOULON	Pat Eddery	5–2 fav
2	SADDLERS' HALL	J. Reid	13–2
3	MICHELETTI	L. Piggott	6–1
4	LUCHIROVERTE	M. Roberts	12–1
5	FLY AWAY SOON	T. Quinn	7–1
6	CORRUPT	L. Dettori	13–2
7	JENDALI	A. S. Cruz	15–1
8	ARCADIAN HEIGHTS	W. R. Swinburn	12–1
9	LIBK	R. Hills	25–1
10	JAHAFIL	W. Carson	11–1

10 ran

distances: 1½ lengths, 15 lengths
time: 3 mins 03.12 secs

Winner owned by K. Abdullah trained by A. Fabre (France), bred by Juddmonte Farms

Tote: win £4.00; places £1.60, £2.20, £1.80; dual forecast £16.80

TOULON bay colt, born 15 April 1988	Top Ville	High Top	Derring-Do
			Camenae
		Sega Ville	Charlottesville
			La Sega
	Green Rock	Mill Reef	Never Bend
			Milau Mill
		Infra Green	Laser Light
			Greenback

Pat Eddery in traditional headgear.

FINAL CLASSIC LIABLE TO DENT REPUTATIONS

Peter Scott

A framed cartoon, displayed in the smallest room of Dick Hern's house for twenty-five years, provides light-hearted warning that the St Leger result is by no means always a rubber-stamp of earlier form.

The cartoon depicts a man on crutches, with one arm in a sling and his free hand clutching a glass of beer. 'Odds-on Meadow Court beaten by ten lengths,' is the headline of a newspaper on the bar counter.

The man, discussing his injuries with a friend, explains: 'All I said to her was that after Provoke's St Leger win, your mother must have a good chance of being voted Miss World.'

Provoke, trained by Hern, and graduating from a handicap win, provided one of the St Leger's biggest post-war shocks.

He ploughed through the Doncaster mud to slam Meadow Court, who started at 11–4 on after his Irish Derby and King George VI and Queen Elizabeth Stakes wins had followed a Derby second to Sea Bird II.

The St Leger has been contested by eight more odds-on chances since Meadow Court's 1965 defeat, and only three have won.

Nijinsky completed his Triple Crown at Doncaster in 1970. Oh So Sharp and Reference Point also justified their short prices.

They, too, had previously won other Classics, but Shergar and Diminuendo have been Classic winners beaten at odds-on in the St Leger. Ile de Bourbon, Alleged and Connaught were other expensive failures.

The St Leger provides a stamina test severe by modern standards and is thus specially liable to dent reputations. Reference Point and Shergar have been the only Derby winners to tackle it since Nijinsky, but Doncaster's management is right not to tamper with tradition, because of a lean quality patch.

Both the Irish St Leger and France's counterpart, the Prix Royal-Oak, have lost rather than gained status by being opened to older horses. Shortening the St Leger distance would destroy its character.

Nashwan and Kahyasi, two of the last four Derby winners, both missed the St Leger in favour of Longchamp's Prix Niel. This mile-and-a-half trial for the Prix de l'Arc de Triomphe is run the day after the Doncaster Classic.

Nashwan and Kahyasi both carried seven-pound penalties in the Prix Niel, but it has now become a level-weights test and would no doubt have been favourably considered for Generous if an early September race was thought necessary before his Arc challenge.

Mill Reef, another Derby winner, did not run between his King George and Arc victories. Dancing Brave prepared for his 1986 Arc success by tackling a ten-furlong race at Goodwood on the eve of the St Leger.

Mr Louis Freedman, a staunch traditionalist, made no bones about aiming his Derby winner, Reference Point, at the St Leger. The Arc injury suffered by Reference Point cannot be blamed on his having run at Doncaster.

Nijinsky's Arc defeat was fuel for the St Leger critics. They chose to forget that Sassafras, who beat him so narrowly at Longchamp, had tackled the 15½-furlong Prix Royal-Oak three weeks earlier.

Several St Leger winners since Nijinsky's time have almost certainly shown improvement on their Doncaster form to be placed in the Arc.

Snurge, Sun Princess and Crow were cases in point. Alleged scored the first of his two Arc wins only three weeks after losing the St Leger to the Queen's Dunfermline.

For all its subsequent fame, the Doncaster Classic had obscure beginnings.

Most reference books give Allabaculia as the inaugural winner in 1776, but neither she nor the race was then named. There even remains some doubt as to the spelling of her subsequently-given name.

She ran as Lord Rockingham's brown filly, by Sampson, in an untitled 25 guineas sweepstake for three-year-olds instituted by Colonel Anthony St Leger. The race officially became the St Leger in 1778.

MEADOW MEATS
IRISH CHAMPION STAKES

Leopardstown, 14 September 1991

With the closure of Phoenix Park in 1990, Ireland's premier all-aged middle-distance race moved to a new home in 1991. Regrets about the demise of Phoenix Park may have hung in the air, but there can have been no complaints about the quality of the 1991 field.

While Generous had gone on from the Irish Derby to demolish his opponents in the King George VI and Queen Elizabeth Diamond Stakes (pages 114–8) and enter the discussions about who was the greatest horse of recent years, his principal victim at The Curragh did not reappear until the Irish Champion Stakes.

There was no doubt that Suave Dancer had been beaten on merit in the Irish Derby, but several factors were against him on that occasion and he was still a very live hope for the Prix de l'Arc de Triomphe – the race for which he had been primed all season. Generous's devastating display at Ascot had made him look a good thing for Longchamp in October, and it would need a top-notch display from Suave Dancer to keep alive hopes that he would be able to turn the tables on the English colt.

Of the six runners who opposed him, four had high-class form. Environment Friend and Stagecraft had fought out that memorable finish to the Coral-Eclipse Stakes (pages 106–7) but both had been beaten behind Terimon in the International Stakes at York. The Sandown Park winner Environment Friend had turned in one of his more lacklustre performances when fifth there; Stagecraft had run third when odds-on favourite, with Topanoora, the only serious hope of a home victory at Leopardstown, just behind in fourth. Zoman had won the Scottish Classic at Ayr since running second to Stagecraft at Royal Ascot.

Suave Dancer had not raced for eleven weeks, but he showed little sign of ring-rustiness as he slaughtered his opponents. Cash Asmussen – who had missed the ride at The Curragh through injury – kept the French horse in third place as Gogarty and Zoman made the running, then moved up into second at the home turn. A furlong out he sped past Zoman and went clear, and in an instant the race was over, with Asmussen easing his mount down in the final hundred yards. Environment Friend came very wide to take second place, but Suave Dancer was never in the remotest danger of defeat, and won by four lengths.

With just three weeks to go to the Arc, the Generous camp insisted that Suave Dancer's performance in Ireland gave them no cause for alarm; it was a very good effort, but no one expected anything less. With another two furlongs to race at Longchamp, and Generous making as much improvement as his rival since they met at The Curragh, why should Suave Dancer reverse the form?

And yet plenty of Suave Dancer's supporters for the Arc (for which his odds rapidly contracted from around 8–1 to 3–1) were hugely encouraged by his Leopardstown win. It proved the horse to be in good heart, it showed the great affinity which Cash Asmussen had with the colt, and most of all it clearly demonstrated that the electric burst of speed with which Suave Dancer had won the Prix du Jockey-Club was no flash in the pan.

Here was a horse with a phenomenal turn of foot, and he had used it to hammer other top-class ten-furlong specialists. If he could find it again in the Arc they'd all better watch out – Generous included!

Meadow Meats Irish Champion Stakes (Group 1)

14 September 1991

1 mile 2 furlongs (going: good to yielding)

1st: IR£92,300; 2nd: IR£28,800; 3rd: IR£13,800; 4th: IR£4,800; 5th: IR£3,300; 6th: IR£1,800

1	SUAVE DANCER	C. Asmussen	4–6 fav
2	ENVIRONMENT FRIEND	G. Duffield	8–1
3	STAGECRAFT	S. Cauthen	5–1
4	TOPANOORA	C. Roche	8–1

7 ran

distances: 4 lengths, 2 lengths
time: 2 mins 06.80 secs

Winner owned by Henri Chalhoub, trained by J. E. Hammond (France), bred by Lillie F. Webb, USA

Tote: win IR£1.40; places IR£1.30, IR£3.70; dual forecast IR£8.00

ASCOT
SEPTEMBER MEETING

Drum Taps (Lanfranco Dettori, white cap) holds off Rock Hopper (Pat Eddery, right) in the Cumberland Lodge.

For many devotees of Flat racing, the September Meeting at Ascot is one of the very best fixtures of the year. It features top-class racing for many different types of horse, and provides an attractive mixture of races: some are pinnacles in themselves, and some look forward to the big events later in the autumn.

In the second catergory comes the Hoover Cumberland Lodge Stakes on the opening day, which usually brings together at least a couple of horses being primed for the Prix de l'Arc de Triomphe in ten days' time, and progressive three-year-olds looking for a decent late-season prize.

In 1991 the only serious Arc contender in the line-up for the Cumberland Lodge was Rock Hopper. Michael Stoute's tough campaigner was having his eighth run of the season but had not been out since his good effort when third behind Generous in th King George VI and Queen Elizabet Diamond Stakes at Ascot two month earlier. Reunited with Pat Eddery, wh had partnered him to all his quartet victories in 1991, he faced fou opponents.

The one three-year-old in the fiel was Young Buster, who had lowere the colours of the 1990 Derby winne Quest For Fame in the Bonusprii September Stakes at Kempton Pai earlier in the month. Drum Taps had been an impressive winner of the Geoffrey Freer Stakes at Newbury, and the other two runners were both owned by Hamdan Al Maktoum: Azzaam (winner of the 1990 November Handicap) had won by ten lengths at Ayr on his last outing, and Hateel had come on a ton since being ridden by John Oaksey in a charity race at this Ascot meeting in 1989, most recently landing a Listed race at The Curragh.

Azzaam made most of the early running until Young Buster took over inside the final quarter of a mile, then Drum Taps and Lanfranco Dettori came storming through. But Pat Eddery was holding Rock Hopper for his famed last-gasp run and pulled out to challenge, only to find Drum Taps possessed of rather more tenacity than he had bargained for. Rock Hopper was hard ridden throughout the final furlong but could not quite get to the leader, and at the line Drum Taps had the verdict by a head.

The winner was not in the Arc (somewhat to the regret of his owner Lord Carnarvon), but despite this defeat Rock Hopper still looked a possible outsider for Paris. In the event he suffered a setback and missed the race.

The Blue Seal Stakes, which often pinpoints a potential Classic filly, went to Misterioso, who broke a sequence of five years of Luca Cumani-trained winners: Cumani's Petite Sirene was last.

Several Cesarewitch hopefuls used the Gordon Carter Handicap as their prep race, but the clues were not too obvious. Brandon Prince, 16–1 winner here, went on to run fifteenth at Newmarket, and one can only hope that the punter who struck a bet of £7,500 to £300 about the fourth horse in the Gordon Carter – Go South – remained loyal three weeks later.

The middle day of the meeting was Ascot's annual charity day, which nowadays traditionally opens with a race for veteran jockeys riding horses owned by the Maktoum brothers. The sextet of worthies who lined up for the ten-furlong Shadwell Estates Handicap were John Oaksey, Brough Scott, Bill Smith, Joe Mercer, Robin Gray and John Francome, and it was Gray on Magic Secret who looked for a moment to have stolen the race. Taking the lead six furlongs out and making the best of his way home, Magic Secret still held a distinct advantage early in the straight – but then John Francome and Shaleel came cruising up the outside.

Those who recall his win on Sea Pigeon in the 1981 Champion Hurdle know what a glorious sight Francome with a double handful was, but this time it was more a question of a single handful. As Shaleel swept past Magic Secret, Francome extended his right hand and goosed the startled Gray. (The Stewards decorously declined to enquire, and Ed Byrne mercifully does not have a photograph of this most unusual moment of the 1991 Flat season.)

When the serious business got under way, the day proved a bonanza for Newmarket trainer Mark Tompkins, who won three races with Virkon Venture, Gilt Throne (who beat Sarcita, carrying ten stone, by a neck), and Canny Chronicle. The Kensington Palace Stakes, won in 1990 by Shadayid, went to Robert Sangster's Red Slippers, who within days had been snapped up by Sheikh Mohammed and supplemented for the Prix Marcel Boussac on Arc day.

The final day of the meeting saw the Brent Walker Festival. That this was the richest day's racing run in Britain was in ironic counterpoint to the holding of the Annual General Meeting of the troubled Brent Walker company the day before. Nothing that transpired at that meeting directly affected the day's sport, but the climate did its best to spoil one of racing's top days, and one for which Ascot puts on plenty of side attractions. The star turn for the 1991 Festival was a demonstration by Monty Roberts of his extraordinary method of breaking – or in his own word 'starting' – horses, which held a large crowd enthralled despite the weather.

And what weather! The rain started early in the afternoon and became progressively heavier. By the time of the Queen Elizabeth II Stakes it was bucketing down, and resolutely refused to let up. But try as it might to ruin the day, the rain could not dilute the appeal of a glittering card – the only day's racing in Britain when two Group One races are run.

The first of these was the Queen Elizabeth II Stakes, now probably the top mile race in Europe. There was a truly international field, headed by the American-trained grey gelding Forty Niner Days. Although he was not in the very top bracket in the USA, his transatlantic challenge had attracted a great deal of attention – not least on account of the girth of his trainer Roger Stein. The twenty-seven stone Stein was in a different mould from most European trainers and was reportedly not in the habit of wearing a tie – which sent a frisson of excitement through those who anticipated a clash with the vigilant Ascot gatemen.

The clash on the racecourse was more interesting, and a real cracker of a race was in prospect from a field that oozed class. Favourite was Second Set, who had not been out since winning the Sussex Stakes in such brilliant style (page 129). Kooyonga had won at The Curragh since her wonderful victory in the Coronation Stakes (page 95), and her main rival at the Royal Meeting, Shadayid, reopposed here having in the meantime run second in the Sussex Stakes to Second Set and third in the Ladbroke Sprint Cup to Polar Falcon.

Hector Protector had been returned to a mile after failing to stay in the Derby and had narrowly landed the Prix Jacques le Marois at Deauville, one of Europe's top mile races. On that form he would go very close at Ascot, but had somewhat blotted his copybook with the worst run of his life when only eighth in the Prix du Moulin: it was suspected that he may have had enough racing for the time being.

Mukaddamah had at last begun to realise some of his potential in the Moulin, going down by only a short head to Priolo, with the Queen Anne Stakes winner Sikeston back in seventh. But with the going getting softer, the chances of Sikeston causing an upset at Ascot increased.

Then there was Selkirk. A horse of immense promise, he had been somewhat disappointing early in the season before springing back to form early in September when beating Susurration and Zonda at Kempton Park. It seemed that one of his testicles had not completely descended – making him a 'rig' – and when the offending gland was removed three weeks before the Kempton race, Selkirk suddenly found galloping a much less uncomfortable business.

It was a race to make the crowd forget the rain. Much as expected, Forty Niner Days made the early running, and was still in the front turning for home. Once in the straight, Willie Carson shot Shadayid into the lead and for a moment it looked as though we were to be treated to a re-run of that magnificent Coronation Stakes finish, for Kooyonga started to run on and get the better of the One Thousand Guineas winner.

Then from out of the scything rain came the white face and large sheepskin noseband of Selkirk, powering up the stands side to slam his way past the two fillies and, in the end, win fairly handily by one and a half lengths. Kooyonga was second, Shadayid a gallant third, and Second Set a never-dangerous fourth. The American raider Forty Niner Days finished a highly creditable fifth,

enough to have connections vowing to return.

Maybe the rain had so softened the ground as to deny the best horses the chance to give their true running, but Kooyonga and Shadayid produced almost a carbon copy of their earlier Ascot clash, and Selkirk had turned in a sterling performance in the conditions.

In the *Racing Post* on the Monday following the race, Tim Richards quoted how Kooyonga's trainer Michael Kauntze had reflected on Selkirk's performance: 'If I'd been running around all my life with an inflamed testicle and it was suddenly sorted out I'm sure I'd run faster.'

The other Group One race of the day was the Brent Walker Fillies' Mile, which was mainly remarkable for an extraordinary lapse by Pat Eddery.

The race had attracted a typical field of seven fillies with only nineteen

Selkirk (Ray Cochrane) lands the Queen Elizabeth II Stakes.

previous starts between them. Culture Vulture had won the Lowther Stakes at York but the consensus of opinion was that a better strand of form was to be found in the May Hill Stakes at Doncaster, where Midnight Air had beaten the subsequently disqualified Fern. Sheikh Mohammed's Mystery Play had run only once – beating Midnight Air at Newmarket in July – and could be anything.

The going was officially changed to soft from good to soft before this race, the fourth on the card – evidence enough of the battering rain.

Shortly after the turn into the straight Mystery Play was leading, with the others sorting themselves out to challenge her. Pat Eddery on Midnight Air was clearly going the best, but as he started to pull out to make his challenge Culture Vulture, who had been last into the straight, began to accelerate. The consequence was that

Midnight Air swerved right into Culture Vulture's path and gave her a hefty bump which nearly threw her jockey Richard Quinn out of the saddle and cannoned the filly into Baharlilys on her outside.

Once Quinn and Culture Vulture had righted themselves Midnight Air had gone clear, and though the victim of the scrimmage tried gamely to get back, at the post Midnight Air had the verdict by three quarters of a length.

No one expected her to keep the race, though – least of all Pat Eddery, who ruefully anticipated a suspension as he returned to the weighing room: 'I'm sure I'll get days.' He was right: an eight-day suspension for careless riding. Culture Vulture was awarded the race and Midnight Air placed last, which promoted Mystery Play to second and the 50–1 outsider Party Cited to third.

It had been an unsatisfactory ending to a Group One race, but few could

argue with the verdict – though it was widely felt that Midnight Air would have won had the race taken place along more placid lines.

The day's other big two-year-old race, the Royal Lodge William Hill Stakes, produced no such shenanigans, but its result did offer a hefty compliment to the top French two-year-old Arazi. Made Of Gold, who won the Royal Lodge after a splendid last-furlong battle with Mack The Knife and Twist And Turn, had been slammed five lengths by Arazi in the Prix de la Salamandre.

Made Of Gold's jockey Tony Cruz completed a double when Shalford ran away with the Diadem Stakes, coasting home three lengths clear of Montendre, with the hot favourite Bog Trotter out with the washing.

Though in those conditions, it was well past time to get the washing in.

The damage has been done as Midnight Air (Pat Eddery) holds off Culture Vulture (Richard Quinn) in the Fillies' Mile.

'I'm sure I'll get days': Pat Eddery after dismounting from Midnight Air following the Fillies' Mile.

The white face of Made Of Gold (Tony Cruz, second right) comes to the front rank in the Royal Lodge Stakes.

Queen Elizabeth II Stakes (Group 1)

28 September 1991

Old mile (going: good to soft)

1st: £228,135; **2nd:** £84,816; **3rd:** £40,270; **4th:** £17,029

1	SELKIRK	R. Cochrane	10–1
2	KOOYONGA	W. J. O'Connor	7–2
3	SHADAYID	Pat Eddery	9–1
4	SECOND SET	L. Dettori	3–1 fav
5	FORTY NINER DAYS	P. Valenzuela	20–1
6	HECTOR PROTECTOR	F. Head	11–2
7	SIKESTON	M. Roberts	15–2
8	LA GRANGE MUSIC	W. R. Swinburn	50–1
9	MUKADDAMAH	W. Carson	15–2

9 ran

distances: 1½ lengths, neck
time: 1 min 44,34 secs

Winner owned by George Strawbridge, trained by I. A. Balding (Kingsclere, Hants), bred by George Strawbridge jr, USA

Tote: win £13.80; places £3.00, £1.60, £1.90; dual forecast £23.00

Brent Walker Fillies' Mile (Group 1)

28 September 1991

Old mile (going: soft)

1st: £91,125; **2nd**: £34,006; **3rd**: £16,253; **4th**: £6,991

1	CULTURE VULTURE	T. Quinn	5–2 fav
2	MYSTERY PLAY	S. Cauthen	4–1
3	PARTY CITED	D. Holland	50–1
4	FERN	L. Dettori	3–1
5	SUPER SARENA	W. Carson	12–1
6	BAHARLILYS	M. Roberts	100–1
1d	MIDNIGHT AIR	Pat Eddery	11–4

7 ran

Following a stewards' enquiry and an objection by the runner-up to the winner, Midnight Air, the race was awarded to Culture Vulture and Midnight Air disqualified and placed last; the remaining horses were all promoted a place.

distances: ¾ length, 2 lengths

time: 1 min 46.11 secs

Winner owned by Christopher Wright, trained by P. F. I. Cole (Whatcombe, Oxon), bred by Holtsinger Inc, USA

Tote: win £2.80; places £1.80, £2.10; dual forecast £5.60

Royal Lodge William Hill Stakes (Group 2)

28 September 1991

Old mile (going: good to soft)

1st: £86,328; **2nd**: £32,352; **3rd**: £15,576; **4th**: £6,823

1	MADE OF GOLD	A. S. Cruz	4–1
2	MACK THE KNIFE	W. Carson	6–1
3	TWIST AND TURN	S. Cauthen	7–4 fav
4	TORREY CANYON	Pat Eddery	4–1

8 ran

distances: ¾ length, 1 length

time: 1 min 46.66 secs

Winner owned by Ecurie Fustok, trained by M. Moubarak (Newmarket, Suffolk), bred by Buckram Oak Farm, USA

Tote: win £5.60; places £1.60, £1.50, £1.40; dual forecast £15.50

RANDOM REFLECTIONS
OF A RACEGOER

SEAN MAGEE *considers what 1991 meant*
for those who go racing simply for the fun.

In 1991 the needs of 'the ordinary racegoer' fought their way to within at least shouting distance of the top of the sport's agenda of pressing concerns.

It was about time, too, as in the opinion of many observers, racecourses had sold part of their souls to the corporate hospitality clients during the Eighties, with the regular racegoer left – sometimes all too literally – out in the cold.

But corporate hospitality would always be subject to the whims of the economy, and reports that business had nosedived in 1991 were graphically illustrated. The boxes in the Epsom grandstand were refurbished in time for Derby Day, but windswept racegoers on the ground gazing covetously up at the champagne swiggers had few targets for their envy: scarcely half the boxes were occupied. The row of hospitality tents adjoining the Horse Racing Abroad pavilion at Longchamp on Arc day shrank in length from over one hundred yards in 1990 to scarcely twenty in 1991.

Times were hard.

They had long been thus for the ordinary racegoer, and now came the turn to have his or her opinions sought. At the Sandown Park conference on the racing industry in April 1990, Ian Pithers, Director of Publicity at the Racecourse Association, had stressed the need for proper market research into racing: what do existing customers think of the product, and why do people who don't go racing manage to resist its allure?

In early July 1991 the RCA published the results of an extensive market research effort carried out on its behalf by National Opinion Polls, who interviewed over 20,000 people, in their homes and on the racecourse. In the latter case, racegoers were invited to fill out the questionnaire and place it in a box on the course – which doubtless accounts for one of the survey's more curious findings: 79 per cent of on-course respondents expressed satisfaction with the ease of parking at racetracks. But they were being asked after they'd got *in:* they'd yet to experience trying to get *out*, and a supplementary survey of motorised racegoers attempting to leave Sandown Park after the Whitbread or Eclipse might have seen a significant swing.

The major findings of the survey gave the racing industry plenty of food for thought. Women formed a larger proportion of attenders and potential attenders than for other sports, but young people were disproportionately uninterested in racing. Three out of five racegoers considered they had overall value for money, and the same proportion had something to eat on the course – though scarcely more than a third were satisfied with the quality and range of food on offer – and fewer than two in five were impressed by the helpfulness of the catering staff. Betting was indulged in by 95 per cent of racegoers, with 67 percent using the Tote, 61 per cent bookmakers, and 12 per cent the on-course betting shop. And 55 per cent expressed themselves satisfied with the cleanliness of the toilets.

Standing room only at the Chester May Meeting.

On the wider issues examined, there was a perception that the highest social grades are disproportionately represented in the average race crowd – in other words, racing was still viewed by many as a sport mainly for toffs. Sunday racing would be welcomed by 85 per cent of respondents, and 78 per cent of on-course respondents attended evening meetings. But only 25 per cent of the age group 15–34 had ever gone racing, and an alarming 50 per cent of all those interviewed complained that lack of information about forthcoming fixtures severely reduced the chances of their going.

This was all very interesting, but scarcely had the survey been published than the sceptics had their say. John Oaksey in *The Daily Telegraph* wrote: 'Sixty per cent of British racegoers feel they get good value for money – as a non-paying Press-pass hack I find that almost as hard to believe as I do that the Racecourse Association got real value for the £40,000 they spent on opinion polls.' He went on to speculate whether the survey asked the right questions: 'We are, after all, in the entertainment business and the product we have to sell is the spectacle and gambling medium of horse racing. The RCA ought to be every bit as keen to find out what *kind* of racing their customers prefer as cinema owners are to discover which films most people will pay to watch.'

Within days the *Racing Post* had taken the initiative and launched its own survey of its readers, putting to them such questions about the actual product they were consuming as:

'When do you normally make the decision to go to a race meeting?'

'Assuming it stayed light until 9 p.m., what would be your ideal time for the first afternoon race?'

'How long would you ideally like the gap to be between races?'

Nearly nine hundred readers replied. Gratifyingly, it was the prospect of seeing famous horses in action which came out as the best reason for going racing, with witnessing a major race just getting the verdict over betting for the minor placings in that category. Racegoers – or at least those who read the *Post* – were happy with half an hour between races, were scornful of the potential effect of free parking or free racecards, and thought pensioners should be allowed free entry to racecourses, but not the unemployed.

Three respondents found racecourse entrance charges 'much too low'. Presumably a routine dope test was ordered.

Back on the racecourse, Ascot gatemen at the Royal fixture hit the pages of *The People* in a story exposing how the custodians had taken backhanders from certain undesirables to get them into the course. 'Ascot Nabs Bowler Hat Fiddlers', rang out the headline, and sackings and disciplinary action followed.

The People quoted an unnamed 'course official' who took it upon himself to pronounce that 'the Queen will be horrified'. Not half as horrified, though, as she must have been if reports were true that her mother had momentarily had her way barred by a scrupulous bowler-hatted vigilante who had not recognised her.

Remember, this was the year when the opinion poll revealed that more people recognised Desert Orchid than the Chancellor of the Exchequer, but recognition was not the issue, nor fame the answer, when the England footballer Paul Gascoigne accompanied the connections of a Susan Piggott runner at Doncaster in July. Gazza or no Gazza, no tie meant no admittance to Members, but a friend (so it was reported) bought him the neckwear Doncaster keeps against just such oversights, and he was let in. He can't have thought much of Donny's dress sense, though, for he was seen to take it off every time he left the Members' Enclosure.

Less publicised but much more sombre in its implications was an incident in a Goodwood car park on the Thursday evening of the July Meeting, when a fight involving golf clubs led to two racegoers undergoing hospital treatment for facial injuries and landed three in court charged with assault and public order offences.

Mercifully such incidents are few and far between on British racecourses, and as this book is about the year on the Flat we have no need to concern ourselves with the behaviour of the snooker player Alex 'Hurricane' Higgins at a Uttoxeter eveing meeting in August: he was arrested and released on police bail following a ruckus with a security guard.

There was plenty to be optimistic about on behalf of racegoers in 1991. At most of the big meetings, crowd numbers held up reasonably well in the light of the economic climate. At the major meetings at Chester, Goodwood and York attendances were slightly higher than in 1990. The Doncaster September Meeting increased its crowd by 11 per cent, and Eclipse day at Sandown was up 10 per cent. The most spectacular drop was recorded at Epsom on Derby Day, where the attendance plummeted by over 25 per cent. The Festival of British Racing at Ascot in September saw a substantial downturn compared with the same day in 1990, but in 1991 the weather was appalling – certainly the worst conditions on any of the big race days of the Flat season.

There were also grounds for optimism in the initiative which some courses took to attract the crowds, and to show appreciation of their loyal following.

On the Friday of the October fixture, its last Flat meeting of the year, Ascot gave a presentation to its Annual

Umbrellas and open-topped buses at Epsom on Derby Day.

Members. The event was heavily oversubscribed, and the lucky several hundred Members who sent their acceptances in sharply and so gained a place were treated to a slick and well-staged performance. Colonel Sir Piers Bengough, Her Majesty's Representative at Ascot, started the proceedings with a few facts and figures about Ascot. The statistic that it takes half a million gallons to water the course by an inch, and one and a half million gallons to flush the loos throughout Royal Ascot, was greeted by the audience with particular appreciation. This was just as well, for matters lavatorial loomed large for the rest of the presentation – even accompanied at one point on the screen behind the speaker by the famous saucy picture of three bare-bottomed young ladies in *al fresco* squatting position at the 1894 Royal Meeting.

'Talk and Listen', read a more solemn message on the screen, and that was exactly what the presentation was about. After Sir Piers came Clerk of the Course Nicholas Beaumont, Ascot Trustee Lord Hartington (who fielded questions about general Turf matters, including Sunday racing), and George Lehrian, chief executive of the caterers Ring & Brymer, who handle the Ascot Members' Enclosure.

Inter alia, Sir Piers explained the Ascot Authority's insistence that the Gold Cup should remain at two and a half miles, and asked for a show of hands from anyone in the audience who took the opposite view. *Nem Con.*

This was an excellent initiative by Ascot, giving its Members up-to-date information about facilities and plans, and allowing them to put questions – some sent in advance and some from the floor – on a variety of topics, large and small.

Longchamp on Arc day.

Could the course be used to stage simulcasting of big races overseas? Why is there never a policeman after racing at one of the exits from Number 1 Car Park? Why can there not be an electronic number board? Why, said a gentleman from the audience, could the Iron Stand (erstwhile refuge of divorcés and like reprobates) not be renamed to become something 'more elegant', such as the Britannia Stand? Why could smoking not be banned in sections of the Members' Stand? Then came the really burning issue. 'I am at a loss when it comes to the toilets', began one question, and off we went again.

Following the presentation the Members were treated to champagne and canapés, and wandered away for their afternoon's racing feeling that the course was genuinely glad of their support.

Ascot attracts a great deal of adverse comment over its supposed attitude to its racegoers – the ludicrous ban on jeans in Tattersalls being only one example – but the presentation to its Annual Members was a substantial step in the right direction.

There is a waiting list for Ascot membership (not surprising: the food at the presentation was pretty good), but other courses have been deploying all sorts of initiatives to market themselves and increase public awareness of the joys of racing.

Charlie Murless is marketing manager of International Racing Management, who are responsible for promoting the St Leger meeting at Doncaster. As part of his drive to raise local consciousness, he offered free life membership to the first Doncaster baby born on the opening day of the Leger meeting. First out of the stalls (as it were) were the twins born to Gillian Beazley, and both had membership at Donny to look forward to.

In an effort to reassure first-time racegoers that a day at the races need not be a baffling maze, Haydock Park's evening meeting on 16 August featured demonstrations by a bookmaker and a

Tote representative on how to make a bet, and talks by others professionally involved in the sport – including an explanation of training by Jack Berry.

The Newmarket July Course put on a series of free post-race entertainments after its midsummer evening meetings, which proved highly popular: on 19 July some 12,000 people basked in a glorious evening, tolerated some very ordinary racing and stayed on for an open-air concert from Alan Price.

A week earlier at Chester the gates to Tattersalls had to be closed before the Saturday afternoon meeting when the safety limit was reached, and a crowd of nearly 17,000 packed the Roodee the previous evening, despite there being only thirty-seven runners.

Under the right conditions people love to go racing, and there were signs enough in 1991 that the sport was at last coming to realise the importance of marketing. But the *Racing Post* survey showed that there is nothing like big races and great horses to set the turnstiles clicking, and main events of the year provided the usual patchwork of racegoing memories.

Derby Day mocked its traditional position as popular celebration, London's unofficial public holiday, etc., with weather almost as dismal as in 1990, a liberal covering of builders' dust caused by the construction of the new Members' Stand, and a curious lack of atmosphere. This first manifested itself on The Road to Epsom, that emblem of the British class system so beloved of Victorian illustrators. In 1991 the road was so extraordinarily free of hold-ups, even quite late into the morning, that you yearned for a decent traffic jam on the approach to the course so that you could convince youself that it was a special occasion.

The explanation for the absence of severe snarl-ups came the following day: the paying crowd was a little over 26,000, and the sparsely populated Downs in the middle of the course couldn't have multiplied that number by very much. Even Generous's

memorable performance couldn't get the crowd going, and he returned to unsaddle to a polite rather than rapturous reception.

By the time of the King George at Ascot racegoers knew how good Generous was, but were still taken aback by the surge of power with which he came away from his field. The whoops of excitement came at that moment, and decorum reigned again by the time the colt reached the unsaddling enclosure.

In an odd way, the September

... there is nothing like big races and great horses to set the turnstiles clicking ...

Saturday at Ascot was more memorable as a racegoing experience. This was the Brent Walker Festival, when the weather played a cruel trick on one of the season's showpieces. Doom-laden early morning forecasts proved all too correct as the rain lashed down, forcing soaked racegoers to pack into the bars, where many stayed for the afternoon.

Less sheltered from the storm was John McCririck, 'master of ceremonies' in the Silver Ring. Despite the lashing rain forcing most of his potential audience to keep well away from the podium from which he conducted the day's business, he ploughed ahead, dispensing a mixture of information, encouragement and bonhomie to the sodden groundlings. As the Stewards' Enquiry into the Midnight Air–Culture Vulture incident dragged on, McCririck could be heard yelling: 'Why haven't the

stewards made their decision yet? Have they had too much port for lunch?' What a trouper!

Eight days later came the British racegoer's annual excursion to Paris for the Arc. Some ten thousand fans, about a third of the crowd, make the pilgrimage. They represent a fair cross-section of the racegoing public, and get to the Bois de Boulogne by various means.

Arriving at Gatwick for the day trip with Horse Racing Abroad, you could easily tell which check-in queue to join: the Paris-bound punters were much the best turned-out bunch in the terminal. The captain greeted the trippers with a genial 'Good morning, sports fans!' and if behaviour on the return trip that evening was a little more ragged – an element at the back of the plane made a feeble attempt at 'Here we go, here we go, here we go' before falling asleep – the hours between the two flights presented the usual Arc day kaleidescope of sights and sensations.

There was the customary elegance of the Parisian racegoers, the wonderfully sylvan Longchamp parade ring, the band consisting of Welsh Guards, Scots Guards, and 17th/21st and 16th/5th Queen's Royal Lancers.('They English, then?', asked Essex Woman as the band struck up), the never-ending queues at the betting windows, and – again – there was McCririck. Fully a hundred yards from the hospitality tent where he was performing, you could hear the harangue as he gave his masterclass in tic-tac: 'Right arm! *Right* arm, you halfwit!'

Small knots of British racegoers found a suitable position and simply stayed there (apart from forays to try and place a bet), staking out their territory with crisp packets and lager cans. This operation transformed the lower reaches of the grandstand into a makeshift picnic area, into which other racegoers hoping to find a place from which to watch a race ventured at their peril. An element in the crowd –

apparently part of the British contingent – took it upon themselves to boo Alan Munro and Generous when the pair came back past the stands after their desperately disappointing run in the Arc. *L'enfer, c'est les autres.*

As always, some of the brightest chips in the mosaic of the racegoing year were snatches of conversation overhead in the crowd, and as always these illustrated the class divide which remains at the heart of British racing. The man caught greeting Steve Cauthen heroics at Newmarket in the autumn with 'lovely jubbly!' cannot have gone racing often with the woman who proclaimed to her friend, as they were watching the runners for the Greenham Stakes at Newbury walk round the paddock: 'I find these horses breathtaking in their beauty.' Her friend countered with: 'They are *sae* beautiful'. At which the first lady rounded off the exchange with: 'They give me *such* pleasure.'

This is on the same level as Nigel Molesworth's classmate Fotherington-Thomas at the races: 'Hurrah hurrah how good it is to be alive and the horse is the frend of man!'

Or to put it another way, 'Lovely jubbly!'

Finally, a word of appreciation to the executive at Newmarket for latching on to the notion that public address announcements warning racegoers that 'pickpockets are in operation in all enclosures' tend to play into the hands of the light-fingered brigade: the potential victims respond to such announcements by feeling that part of their clothing which harbours their valuables, thus showing the malefactor where to aim.

On Two Thousand Guineas day at the Rowley Mile came the brief public announcement which proves that courses really are thinking about the welfare of their racegoers: 'Please take care of your valuables and *don't* pat your pockets.'

Generous

NEWMARKET OCTOBER MEETING

Newmarket, 2–5 October 1991

On Wednesday 2 October began the most hectic five days in the European racing calendar: four days of top racing at Newmarket, overlapping on the Saturday with the first day of the Ciga Weekend at Longchamp which culminated in the Prix de l'Arc de Triomphe on the Sunday. Throughout the week the build-up to the Arc was cranked up cog by cog, and the sport at Newmarket took place against a backdrop of trainers' intentions and travel arrangements.

Billed as the richest two-year-old race in the world, the Tattersalls Tiffany Highflyer Stakes was the second running of a race under whose controversial terms huge bonuses were awarded to runners who had been purchased at the Tattersalls Highflyer Sales in 1990. The owner of the first Highflyer-sold runner to finish in the race would get £500,000 in addition to the prize money – plus an extra £100,000 if that runner were a filly – and the prizes went well down the field: even the tenth-qualified runner earned £10,000 (twice that if a filly).

The scheme had raised objections after the 1990 running, mainly because of the distorted values it involved, and the 1991 race was to be the last such event in Britain for the time being.

Unsurprisingly, in view of the gargantuan amount of money on offer, the race attracted the maximum of thirty runners, and they included some pretty good performers, notably Robert Sangster's Dr Devious, who started 5–2 favourite after attracting heavy support in the ring.

But it was Young Senor, beaten by Dr Devious at the July Meeting, who scooped the £30,218 winner's prize money – plus that half-million-pound bonus – by making rapid headway in the last quarter-mile and running on boldly up the hill to catch the favourite close home, with Alnasr Alwasheek just a neck away in third.

Robert Sangster cannot have been too downhearted by the defeat of his colt, as he picked up £200,000 for Dr Devious being the second Highflyer yearling home, and another £100,000 with his filly Soiree, sixth in the race but the first filly.

Young Senor's trainer Geoff Wragg was back in the winner's enclosure thirty-five minutes later after an even more prestigious victory in the Tattersalls Cheveley Park Stakes, the top race of the season for two-year-old fillies.

Wragg's Marling deservedly started favourite after an unblemished trio of races which had brought victories at Newmarket, Sandown Park and Royal Ascot (the Queen Mary), but she faced apparently stiff oposition in the form of the French raider Absurde, herself unbeaten in two races. Basma and

Twafeaj also had good form, but it looked a two-horse race on paper.

In reality it was more like a one-horse race. Basma set a useful pace but had no answer when Marling made her effort going down into the Dip, and once the Wragg filly hit the front it was all over. She ran on to record a one-and-a-half-length verdict over Absurde, who stayed on well without ever threatening the winner.

Since the War eight winners of the Cheveley Park had gone on to land the One Thousand Guineas the following spring, but the bookmakers' reaction to the 1991 running as a Classic trial was decidedly mixed. Corals made Marling

12–1 favourite for the Guineas, William Hill 14–1, Victor Chandler 16–1 – and Ladbrokes took the view that she would not truly stay a mile, offering the daughter of Marwell (fourth in the 1981 One Thousand and subsequently a brilliant sprinter) at 25–1.

Walter Swinburn had ridden Marwell to win the Cheveley Park in 1980, and said of her offspring: 'Marling is the spitting image of her mum.' How her exploits as a three-year-old would compare with Marwell's was just one of the intriguing prospects for 1992.

The juvenile colts had their day on the Thursday with the Newgate Stud Middle Park Stakes. Traditionally one of

the most important two-year-old races of the season, the quality of runners in the Middle Park had sunk in recent years, and there were even calls for its demotion from Group One. But the 1990 winner Lycius had run well (without quite winning) in many big races in 1991, and the latest renewal attracted the horse widely held to be the best two-year-old in Britain.

This was Rodrigo De Triano, unbeaten in four races and fresh from winning the Laurent-Perrier Champagne Stakes at Doncaster. In that race he beat the Gimcrack winner River Falls, who reopposed here. Sheikh Mohammed's Lion Cavern, third to Arazi in the Prix Morny at Deauville, was supplemented for the Middle Park and would provide a valuable link between the top British and French form – though it was not anticipated that he would trouble Rodrigo De Triano too much, and he started fourth favourite in a field of six.

Willie Carson had the mount on Rodrigo De Triano for Robert Sangster and Peter Chapple-Hyam, and the colt turned in a brilliant display, taking up the running over a furlong out and responding to Carson's inimitable pump-action finish to power up the hill. Behind him Lion Cavern had anything but a clear run, but once Steve Cauthen had found daylight and got his mount balanced, the French raider tore up the rising ground in pursuit of the favourite – who was not hard ridden to get home by a length.

Strict interpretation of the form suggested that Arazi was a superior horse to Rodrigo De Triano, though strict interpretation can mask other possibilities. 'Arazi would beat us at six furlongs,' said Chapple-Hyam, whose first Group One victory this was: 'At seven furlongs I don't know, but at a

Rodrigo De Triano (Willie Carson) strides home from Lion Cavern (Steve Cauthen) in the Middle Park Stakes.

mile Rodrigo might be the better horse.'

And Willie Carson drew an illuminating comparison between the Middle Park winner and Dr Devious, beaten in the Highflyer race but who a fortnight later would land Newmarket's other great two-year-old event, the Dewhurst Stakes: 'Rodrigo De Triano has class and speed while Dr Devious is more of slogger.'

The main interest on the Friday centred around the Main Reef Stakes and the long-awaited course reappearance of Cruachan, who had won the Glasgow Stakes at the York May Meeting in such devastating style (beating Saddlers' Hall by six lengths) but had then suffered an injury just before the Derby.

Weak in the market – he drifted from even money to 2–1 starting price – and unlikely to be fully wound up after such a long lay-off, Cruachan was not pressed by Ray Cochrane once it was clear that Pat Eddery on Lord Howard de Walden's Rudimentary had got the race sewn up. But it was none the less a highly promising outing, and boded well for Cruchan's next race, the Champion Stakes.

Saturday had triple peaks. Top of the bill in terms of class was the Cheveley Park Sun Chariot Stakes, which so often went to a top-notch filly or mare. The 1991 field was slightly below par, although the five runners included the Ribblesdale winner Third Watch, Filia Ardross (who on her last outing had beaten Gai Bulga and In The Groove at Goodwood), and Dartrey, sixth in the Oaks. Ristna was having only the fourth race of her life, after winning her Newbury maiden, then running fourth in the Musidora Stakes and a well-beaten second to Desert Sun at Doncaster.

Of the quintet, just Sipsi Fach started at odds longer than 9–2, but once Ristna found her stride a furlong out there could only be one result. She stormed on under Willie Carson to win in a highly impressive manner by four lengths from Dartrey and Third Watch.

Tattersalls Cheveley Park Stakes (Group 1)

2 October 1991

6 furlongs (going: good to firm)

1st: £91,651; **2nd:** £34,112; **3rd:** £16,531; **4th:** £6,941; **5th:** £2,945; **6th:** £1,347

1	MARLING	W. R. Swinburn	15–8 fav
2	ABSURDE	F. Head	5–2
3	BASMA	W. Carson	5–1
4	TWAFEAJ	Pat Eddery	5–1
5	STORM RING	L. Dettori	20–1
6	NIMBLE DEER	D. Holland	100–1
7	SWELLEGANT	M. Hills	20–1
7dht	SARATOGA STAR	M. Roberts	50–1
9	AFFAIR OF STATE	T. Quinn	12–1

9 ran

distances: 1½ lengths, head
time: 1 min 11.17 secs
Winner owned by E. J. Loder, trained by G. Wragg (Newmarket, Suffolk), bred by E. J. Loder
Tote: win £2.10; places £1.50, £1.30, £1.50; dual forecast £2.40

Newgate Stud Middle Park Stakes (Group 1)

3 October 1991

6 furlongs (going: good to firm)

1st: £77,644; **2nd:** £28,799; **3rd:** £13,875; **4th:** £5,734; **5th:** £2,342; **6th:** £985

1	RODRIGO DE TRIANO	W. Carson	Evens fav
2	LION CAVERN	S. Cauthen	7–1
3	RIVER FALLS	B. Raymond	9–2
4	POWER LAKE	J. Reid	25–1
5	BALLA JIDAAL	Pat Eddery	4–1
6	EDEN'S CLOSE	R. Hills	66–1

6 ran

distances: 1 length, 2 lengths
time: 1 min 11.11 secs
Winner owned by R. E. Sangster, trained by P. W. Chapple-Hyam (Manton, Wilts), bred by Swettenham Stud
Tote: win £1.70; places £1.30, £2.30; dual forecast £3.80

Cheveley Park Sun Chariot Stakes (Group 2)

5 October 1991

1 mile 2 furlongs (going: good to firm)

1st: £40,182; **2nd:** £14,941; **3rd:** £7,095; **4th:** £3,002

1	RISTNA	W. Carson	4–1
2	DARTREY	W. R. Swinburn	5–2
3	THIRD WATCH	J. Reid	9–2
4	FILIA ARDROSS	M. Roberts	9–4 fav

5 ran

distances: 4 lengths, short head
time: 2 min 03.47 secs
Winner owned by George Strawbridge, trained by J. H. M. Gosden (Newmarket, Suffolk), bred by George Strawbridge
Tote: win £3.80; places £1.50, £1.60; dual forecast £4.50

For such an inexperienced horse this was a cracking performance, and the daughter of Roussalka looked sure to go on to greater things. The result was especially significant for the filly's owner George Strawbridge, who had won big races on three consecutive Saturdays – with Turgeon in the Irish St Leger, Selkirk in the Queen Elizabeth II Stakes, and now Ristna in the Sun Chariot.

Barry Hills's good stayers Further Flight and Supreme Choice fought out the finish of the Jockey Club Cup, with the Goodwood Cup winner Further Flight eventually getting the better of a good tussle by one and a half lengths.

Then it was time for the William Hill Cambridgeshire, one of the big betting races of the season. As usual there were almost as many opinions as runners, but the manner in which Peter Easterby's Palatial Style had won his last three races – most recently slaughtering a good field of handicappers at Newbury by seven lengths – made him seem something of a good thing, even in such an ultra-competitive race. He opened the betting at 6–1 and momentarily touched 7–1 before a flood of money brought his price down to 9–2.

The bookmakers went 10–1 bar one, and among the 10–1 shots was the 1990 runner-up Mellottie. Those who quietly fancied Mellottie's chances of going one better and managed to resist the rush to get on Palatial Style had the last laugh. John Lowe brought Mellottie through in the final furlong and engaged in a rousing battle with Darryll Holland on High Premium before getting the verdict by a head. Vague Dancer was third, and as the runners returned to unsaddle, the smell of burnt fingers hung above Newmarket Heath, for Palatial Style was never really in the hunt and finished eighth.

One curious aspect of the Cambridgeshire result was that the first three home were all trained by women: the winner by Mary Reveley and the second and third by Lynda Ramsden.

Mrs Reveley had herself driven the horsebox down to Newmarket from Saltburn, and professed herself amazed that Mellottie could succeed where last year he had failed behind Risen Moon. The winner's dam Lottie Lehmann had been the trainer's first horse, winning eight races before being sent to the stallion Meldrum, who stood at a fee of £250. Mellottie was the outcome.

Many racegoers left Newmarket early that afternoon. They had planes to catch for Paris.

... as the runners returned to unsaddle, the smell of burnt fingers hung above Newmarket Heath ...

William Hill Cambridgeshire Handicap

5 October 1991

1 mile 1 furlong (going: good to firm)

1st: £59,885; **2nd:** £18,080; **3rd:** £8,790; **4th:** £4,145

1	MELLOTTIE	J. Lowe	10–1
2	HIGH PREMIUM	D. Holland	14–1
3	VAGUE DANCER	J. K. Fanning (3)	40–1
4	AGE OF MIRACLES	K. Fallon	100–1

29 ran   (Palatial Style 9–2 fav)

distances: head, 1½ lengths
time: 1 min 49.24 secs

Winner owned by Mrs J. G. Fulton, trained by Mrs G. R. Reveley (Lingdale, Cleveland), bred by Mrs G. R. Reveley and partners

Tote: win £13.70; places £3.60, £4.00, £6.90, £13.50; dual forecast £164.50; trio £4,955.60

CIGA WEEKEND

Longchamp, 5–6 October 1991

A feast of high-class racing is crammed into the Longchamp programme for the first weekend of October, with the hotel group Ciga sponsoring both days and giving its name to the whole event. Two Group One races on the Saturday and three, including, of course, the Prix de l'Arc de Triomphe (pages 175–82), on the Sunday make this weekend the climax of the European season.

Although the six-length victory of Victoire Bleue in the Group One Prix du Cadran on the Saturday was a superb performance, the abiding memory of the first day was of France's top two-year-old Arazi, trained by Francois Boutin and ridden by Gerald Mosse, slaughtering a good field in the Ciga Grand Criterium. This was Arazi's seventh race, and he had been beaten only on his debut outing, with the Prix du Bois, Prix Robert Papin, Prix Morny and Prix de la Salamandre among his victories.

Defeat for Arazi in the Grand Criterium was not seriously entertained – his returned odds were 5–1 on – but it was none the less impossible not to be impressed by the way in which he won, going to the front three furlongs out and quickening very well to finish three lengths ahead of Rainbow Corner. Just a short head further back in third came David Elsworth's Seattle Rhyme, who had come a long way since winning a maiden race at Ascot on King George day as a 12–1 outsider. The British raider had tried to get on terms with the winner a furlong out but was always fighting a losing battle – though he was to get handsome consolation and pay a huge compliment to Arazi in the Racing Post Trophy later in the month.

Arazi's owner Allen Paulson had had good horses before – including Estrapade and Theatrical – so his post-race comment when asked whether this colt was the best he had ever owned was significant: 'No. He's the best horse anyone has ever owned.'

Sheikh Mohammed, who knows a thing or two about owning good horses, obviously took such remarks in, for within a couple of weeks he had bought a half share in Arazi. The plan was to run the colt (in Paulson's colours) in the Breeders' Cup Juvenile and then to

The Bois de Boulogne provides the backdrop for the start of the Abbaye.

contemplate an adventurous three-year-old programme which could take in the Kentucky Derby. Running in the Two Thousand Guineas in the Sheikh's colours was another possibility – Sheikh Mohammed had never won an English Classic with a colt – and Ladbrokes' immediate reaction was to make Arazi 4–1 with a run for the Newmarket race. That price did not last long.

Cash Asmussen had a busy start to

the Sunday. He won the opener on Polista, and on Goofalik was beaten a nose in the second, the Prix Rond-Point, by Bistro Garden.

The third race was the Prix Marcel Boussac, which in previous years had become something of a benefit for British runners, and specifically for John Dunlop, Hamdan Al Maktoum and Willie Carson, who had won it with Ashayer (1987), Salsabil (1989) and Shadayid (1990), the latter two of whom

had gone on to take the One Thousand Guineas the following year.

This combination was not represented in 1991, though there was a strong English challenge none the less. Paul Cole's Culture Vulture had won the Lowther Stakes at York, and had been awarded the Brent Walker Fillies' Mile on the disqualification of Midnight Air only the previous weekend. Perfect Circle, trained by Michael Stoute, had won well at Kempton, as had Luca Cumani's Red Slippers at Ascot – since when the filly had been bought by Sheikh Mohammed and supplemented for the Marcel Boussac at a fee of £8,000. The best of the French appeared to be Verveine, unbeaten in two races, including the Prix du Calvados, Kenbu (second to Arazi in the Prix Morny) and Hatoof, just beaten by Guislaine (an outsider here) in the Prix d'Aumale.

Culture Vulture took the lead a furlong out and held on grimly to win by a short head from Hatoof, who finished like a train and was undoubtedly unlucky not to get up: she had been badly hampered in scrimmaging on the run towards the home straight, during which Lady Normandy broke a hind leg.

It would be churlish to temper admiration of Culture Vulture's remarkable feat of winning two Group One races within the space of nine days by making too much of the luck – if such it was – which attended both. She had proved herself a wonderfully tough and courageous filly, and a credit to Paul Cole and to her jockey Richard Quinn. 'She may be small, but she's got a big heart,' said Quinn, and there had been abundant evidence of that in the Prix Marcel Boussac. Nor was she necessarily finished with yet, for Churchill Downs and the Breeders' Cup Juvenile Fillies beckoned.

Churchill Downs was also on the itinerary for Keen Hunter after the Ciga Prix de l'Abbaye. The sprinting scene was still looking for a new star after the retirement of Dayjur, and an impressive

victory in the Abbaye fostered hopes that John Gosden's colt might just be it. The four-year-old had run only once before in 1991, winning at Newbury, and had then succumbed to the virus.

But he came back with a vengeance at Longchamp, taking up the running a furlong and a half out after the two-year-olds Paris House and Bradawn Breever had blazed the early trail, and running on well to beat Sheikh Albadou by a length, with another two-year-old Magic Ring (who started favourite) just a head away in third. Keen Hunter was Sheikh Mohammed's first Group One winner in England or France in 1991.

Fire The Groom, winner of the Beverly D Stakes at Arlington Park in Chicago, was on a $500,000 bonus if she could win the Ciga Prix de l'Opera. But the Bill Shoemaker-trained filly (who used to be with Luca Cumani at Newmarket) could finish only fourth behind the 66–1 German-trained three-year-old Martessa, who got home from Colour Chart and Polemic in a tight finish.

But by the time of the Prix de l'Opera, the sixth race of the afternoon, Longchamp was all abuzz after a sensational Arc . . .

Culture Vulture unwinds after the Prix Marcel Boussac.

CIGA PRIX DE L'ARC DE TRIOMPHE

Longchamp, 6 October 1991

'The cat-bird seat' was a new phrase to enter racing terminology in 1991, though it did not require much definition. Cash Asmussen had told us that he looked forward to being in the cat-bird seat on Suave Dancer in the Prix de l'Arc de Triomphe, and his ride in Europe's richest race provided the perfect illustration – the cat waiting to pounce on the bird.

The Arc always promises to provide a culmination to the European racing season, but in 1991 there was additional spice. Since the day Generous had won the King George at Ascot and set in motion the debates about just how good he was and how he could be rated against the great horses of the past, the

It takes three men to keep Suave Dancer calm in the Arc parade.

Arc had been the target, the conclusive test of his ability. Never mind the scorn heaped on the notion that as a four-year-old he would have nothing left to prove: he still had something to prove at three, and the Arc demanded that proof.

If he could win it, he was a great horse. If he joined those other much vaunted recent English challengers in defeat – narrow or comprehensive – the sceptics would again come muttering out of the shadows.

No horse had ever won the Derby, Irish Derby, King George and Arc. Nijinsky had won the first three and been beaten at Longchamp. So had Troy. Shergar had never even got to Paris. The last Derby winner to land the Arc was Mill Reef in 1971. In recent years, Nashwan had fallen by the wayside, and Kahyasi, Reference Point and Shahrastani had been well beaten. The omens were not good.

And yet how could Generous not fare better than those predecessors? He had proved invincible in the summer, and what's more, he had comprehensively beaten the one horse who might provide a real danger, Suave Dancer.

This was another fascinating facet of the 1991 Arc. Generous and Suave Dancer had met at The Curragh for the Irish Derby as two Derby winners, giants who towered above the three-year-old generations of their respective countries. Defeat for either seemed a little difficult to swallow, yet Generous had seen his opponent off without too much ado, and if he was fit and willing, why should he not do so again?

The Suave Dancer camp could think of a couple of reasons. Their colt had been specifically aimed at the Arc all season, and would be much stronger on the first Sunday in October than he had been at The Curragh on the last Sunday in June. With a bigger field than in Ireland, the race was more likely to be run to suit him, and – without any disrespect to Walter Swinburn – having his regular pilot Cash Asmussen on his back would be an additional advantage.

Swinging towards home in the Arc, Alan Munro has Generous in the right position.

Suave Dancer had shown by his brilliant win in the Irish Champion Stakes at Leopardstown (page 150) that he was in top form, but that race had been over ten furlongs, and he had weakened when the heat had been turned on by Generous in the twelve-furlong trip at The Curragh. True, he had won over a mile and a half at Chantilly, but did he really stay? Might he not again be found out by the relentless gallop of the Derby winner?

Such questions exerted a magnetic fascination in the days leading up to the Arc. Rarely in recent years has a race generated such an intense build-up of excitement, and come the day of the race the wonder was that the key battle – Generous versus Suave Dancer – was still intact.

That was not all there was to the Arc, by any means, for the twelve other runners included the cream of Europe's middle-distance horses.

Generous apart, four of the runners had won English Classics. There was Quest For Fame, Derby hero of 1990 but without a victory in three outings in 1991 and most recently a disappointing second to Young Buster at Kempton. The 1990 St Leger winner Snurge had won all three of his races this season – at Newbury, San Siro and Deauville – and was quietly fancied: he had, after all, run a wonderful race to be third in the 1990 Arc behind Saumarez. And there were the 1991 Oaks winner (Jet Ski Lady) and St Leger winner (Toulon).

El Senor had been sent over from the USA. He had won his last three races, and had a link with European form through his third behind In The Wings in the 1990 Breeders' Cup Turf at Belmont Park, but was not expected to figure prominently in the Arc.

Then there was In The Groove, winner of the Coronation Cup earlier in the year but a trifle disappointing since. The word was, though, that she was coming back to her best, and her old friend Steve Cauthen had the ride. Pistolet Bleu had been hailed as a top-class three-year-old earlier in the season before injury had kept him out of the Prix du Jockey-Club: his second to Subotica in the Prix Niel in September was his first run since May, and he could be expected to improve on that. Magic Night (whose dam had cost just 2500 francs and who had been unwanted at birth) had won the Prix Vermeille, so often a significant Arc pointer.

Of the fourteen runners, seven were trained in France, five in England, one in Ireland and one in the USA: truly an international field.

Generous was drawn on the outside of the field, and much of the pre-race speculation hinged around whether he would be able to keep a decent position in the early stages. Despite his not having raced since the King George, there seemed little doubt that he was fit enough: a post-racing gallop at Newbury a couple of weeks before the Arc had shown him to be in great shape, and he certainly looked like a horse on the brink of greatness as he was led into the parade ring.

But so did Suave Dancer, much more the bundle of pent-up energy than Generous and like his rival a wonderful sight to behold.

In a *Daily Telegraph* interview with J. A. McGrath earlier in the year, trainer John Hammond had said of Suave Dancer: 'He's a horse who likes to be left alone. He's just a professional racehorse. You feed him, go through the motions with him, let him do his own thing. He is not a pet in any way, nor is he an affectionate horse.'

Suave Dancer had his supporters, but the confidence behind Generous was immense. His lad Robert Latham put the significance of the Arc in perspective when talking to Marcus Armytage for the *Racing Post:* 'Horses like this only come in ones, for trainers and for us lads alike. I want him to do it so badly because it would make him one of the greatest horses of all time.'

Most of the British contingent at Longchamp had no doubt that Generous would deliver, and backed him down to odds-on favourite. To the chagrin of ante-post punters who had fallen over themselves to take 7–2 about Suave Dancer after his Leopardstown win, John Hammond's colt started at 37–10.

But the odds play only the most peripheral part in the story of the 1991 Arc, for this race was about a great individual performance.

"... it would make him one of the greatest horses of all time."

Art Bleu, pacemaker for Pistolet Bleu, led the field from the start, with Generous keeping his position on the outside then easily moving in to keep in the front rank. Apart from El Senor, who was outpaced in the early stages, the field was well bunched as they climbed the hill past the Petit Bois and started the descent towards the straight, and each time the course commentator called the name of Generous an expectant cheer rang out from the British racegoers.

As Art Bleu pulled wide turning for home to let Pistolet Bleu up the rails, with Quest For Fame going well and Suave Dancer still tucked in at the back, Generous looked ready to go on and make his run, but suddenly Alan Munro was having to push the horse along, and the wonted surge of acceleration never materialised. With two furlongs to go Generous had nothing left, and there was Cash Asmussen, poised to unleash his winning effort.

Here was the cat-bird seat in all its inevitability, and as soon as Asmussen asked his mount to quicken the Arc was over. With a furlong to go Suave Dancer produced a breathtaking burst to go clear of his rivals in a few strides, and although once in front he veered towards the inside rail (as he had done at Chantilly), he had only to be pushed out to win the race.

Behind him Magic Night plugged on gamely to take second place ahead of Pistolet Bleu, with Toulon running on to get fourth. Pigeon Voyageur, who had been hampered early in the straight was fifth, and In The Groove a highly creditable sixth. Then came Quest For Fame.

Generous was eighth, and his running had clearly been too bad to be true. Had he run third or fourth, had he succumbed to Suave Dancer after producing his own powerhouse finish, it would have been accepted that he was not quite the horse that we had thought. But his lifeless performance in Paris left the task of relating his ability to that of Suave Dancer somewhat problematic.

Of much more immediate importance was the legacy of the race itself. If Generous's surge away from his rivals in the King George had seemed at the time The Moment of the season, the explosion of speed which brought Suave Dancer the Arc provided at the very least a few seconds to dispute that claim. Arguments could rage later about which colt was the better, about whether Generous's flop could be excused when rating the respective merits of the two horses, but there was no denying that Suave Dancer had beaten a much stronger field than Generous had faced at Ascot and had slammed it no less comprehensively.

But the showdown between the big two had not taken place, and although there was consolation enough in the sheer brilliance of the acceleration which brought Suave Dancer the Arc, the disappointment over Generous ran deep. What had happened? For Alan Munro, 'He suddenly ran out of gas.' But why? Some thought that the colt was disadvantaged by not having had a race between the King George and the Arc: he was ring-rusty. For others, he had been on the go for too long, having started his season in the Two Thousand Guineas on 4 May. Those who wheeled out this excuse ignored the fact that Suave Dancer had been on the go a month longer – his first race in 1991 had been on 7 April, the day after Seagram

had won the Grand National. Suave Dancer had run six times in 1991 before the Arc, Generous four.

Fahd Salman, owner of Generous, simply said, 'You cannot win them all', and he was right. It subsequently transpired that Generous had registered an abnormal blood count, but he recovered and plans were laid to

give him one more run, in the Champion Stakes, to rehabilitate his reputation. Then a less than glittering gallop in the week before the Newmarket race ruled that out, and he was retired to stud.

But Longchamp on Arc day belonged to Suave Dancer, to Cash Asmussen ('This is the best horse that I have

Suave Dancer and Cash Asmussen at their moment of triumph.

ridden'), to owner Henri Chalhoub and to trainer John Hammond. It had been announced earlier in the season that the colt would stay in training in 1992, and the Arc victory added immeasurably to the excitement of that prospect. (There was even talk of another race in 1991. 'We'll discuss the Breeders' Cup after we've got over our hangovers', said John Hammond, but no one was surprised when it was later decided that Suave Dancer had done enough for the year.)

After the race the presentations were made on an elaborate dais wheeled into position on the racecourse itself in front of the President's box, and following the ceremonies – complete with speeches from winning jockey and trainer – Asmussen and Hammond, besieged by photographers, walked back down the track towards the entrance to the parade ring. The jockey was due to ride in the next race, and after posing for several shots detached himself from the crush and made for the weighing room.

At this moment the huge screen on the far side of the course was showing yet another re-run of Suave Dancer's victory. For a few seconds John Hammond just stood and watched enraptured, sharing the awe of all who witnessed Suave Dancer's Arc, before turning away to sprint back towards the paddock.

'I did it my way.' Having vacated the cat-bird seat, Cash Asmussen takes the plaudits.

Ciga Grand Criterium (Group 1)

5 October 1991

1 mile (going: good to soft)

1st: £122,200; **2nd:** £48,880; **3rd:** £24,440; **4th:** £12,220

1	ARAZI	G. Mosse	1–5 fav
2	RAINBOW CORNER	Pat Eddery	48–10
3	SEATTLE RHYME	C. Asmussen	58–10
4	ST JOVITE	C. Roche	12–1

6 ran

distances: 3 lengths, short head
time: 1 min 41.4 secs

Winner owned by A.E. Paulson, trained by F. Boutin, bred by Ralph Wilson jr, USA

Pari-mutuel: win FF1.20; places FF1.10, FF1.10; straight forecast FF2.60

Prix Marcel Boussac (Group 1)

6 October 1991

1 mile (going: good to soft)

1st: £81,466; **2nd:** £32,587; **3rd:** £16,293; **4th:** £8,147

1	CULTURE VULTURE	T. Quinn	4–1
2	HATOOF	Pat Eddery	74–10
3	VERVEINE	D. Boeuf	36–10 jt fav
4	GUISLAINE	E. Legrix	26–1

14 ran   (Red Slippers 36–10 jt fav)

distances: short head, 1 length
time: 1 min 40.6 secs

Winner owned by Christopher Wright, trained by P.F.I. Cole (Whatcombe, Oxon), bred by Holtsinger Inc, USA

Pari-mutuel: win FF5.00; places FF2.20, FF2.30, FF1.80; dual forecast FF31.60

Ciga Prix de l'Abbaye de Longchamp (Group 1)

6 October 1991

5 furlongs (going: good to soft)

1st: £71,283; **2nd:** £28,514; **3rd:** £14,257; **4th:** £7,129

1	KEEN HUNTER	S. Cauthen	115–10
2	SHEIKH ALBADOU	B. Raymond	3–1
3	MAGIC RING	A. Munro	21–10 fav
4	ARCHWAY	W.R. Swinburn	43–1

14 ran

distances: 1 length, head
time: 59.4 secs

Winner owned by Sheikh Mohammed, trained by J.H.M. Gosden (Newmarket, Suffolk), bred by Indian Creek, R. Beasley et al, USA

Pari-mutuel: win: FF12.50 (coupled with Katies First); places FF4.50, FF1.80, FF2.30; dual forecast FF32.00

Ciga Prix de l'Arc de Triomphe (Group 1)

6 October 1991

1 mile 4 furlongs (going: good to soft)

1st: £509,165; **2nd:** £203,666; **3rd:** £101,833; **4th:** £50,916

1	SUAVE DANCER	C. Asmussen	37–10
2	MAGIC NIGHT	A. Badel	102–10
3	PISTOLET BLEU	D. Boeuf	68–10
4	TOULON	Pat Eddery	95–10
5	PIGEON VOYAGEUR	T. Jarnet	26–1
6	IN THE GROOVE	S. Cauthen	32–1
7	QUEST FOR FAME	W.R. Swinburn	95–10
8	GENEROUS	A. Munro	9–10 fav
9	EL SENOR	M.J. Kinane	48–1
10	SHAMSHIR	L. Dettori	91–1
11	MISS ALLEGED	E. Legrix	43–1
12	ART BLEU	C. Aubert	62–1
13	JET SKI LADY	C. Roche	40–1
14	SNURGE	T. Quinn	8–1

14 ran

distances: 2 lengths, 1 length

time: 2 mins 31.4 secs

Winner owned by H. Chalhoub, trained by J.E. Hammond, bred by Lillie F. Webb, USA

Pari-mutuel: win FF4.70; places FF1.80, FF2.40, FF2.20; dual forecast FF27.70

SUAVE DANCER (USA) Bay colt, born 7 February 1988	Green Dancer	Nijinsky	Northern Dancer
			Flaming Page
		Green Valley	Val de Loir
			Sly Pola
	Suavite	Alleged	Hoist The Flag
			Princess Pout
		Guinevere's Folly	Round Table
			Lodge

NEWMARKET HOUGHTON MEETING

Newmarket, 17–19 October 1991

The first day of the Newmarket Houghton Meeting, the second leg of the course's great autumn programme, saw a very welcome return to form by Mystiko. The grey had not won in three outings (the Derby, the Sussex Stakes and the Ladbroke Sprint Cup) since beating Lycius in the Two Thousand Guineas at the beginning of May, but a return to Newmarket and a new distance of seven furlongs for the Challenge Stakes obviously suited Clive Brittain's charge.

The late withdrawal of the Queen Elizabeth II Stakes winner Selkirk due to a joint problem left Mystiko favourite to beat six opponents, including Bog Trotter, who had taken the Greenham Stakes and Kiveton Park Stakes, Only Yours, winner of the Child Stakes and Hungerford Stakes, and Volksraad, unbeaten in two races but untested in such company.

Mystiko shot out of the stalls and

The rehabilitation of Mystiko (Michael Roberts) in the Challenge Stakes.

made every inch of the running, Michael Roberts simply needing to push him out to beat Only Yours by two lengths, with Volksraad third. It was wonderful to see Mystiko's raking stride eating up the Rowley Mile again, and it came as no surprise (taking into account the strong tail wind) that the time for the race was a course record. There was an added bonus in Clive Brittain's announcement that Mystiko would remain in training in 1992. (If that plan is adhered to, Mystiko would be the first Two Thousand Guineas winner to race as a four-year-old since Known Fact in 1981.)

Friday's feature was the Three Chimneys Dewhurst Stakes, still the top two-year-old race of the season and with its reputation as a Classic-producer high after the exploits of Generous, 50–1 winner of the race in 1990.

The nine runners did not include the acknowledged best of England (Rodrigo De Triano) or France (Arazi), but they none the less formed a good field. Young Senor and Dr Devious, separated by a head when first and second in the Tattersalls Tiffany Highflyer Stakes over course and distance sixteen days earlier, were in the line-up, and Dr Devious – sold by Robert Sangster since the Highflyer to Luciano Gaucci – was confidently expected to turn the tables. He went off 3–1 favourite, with Young Senor twice those odds.

Fahd Salman and Paul Cole, owner and trainer of Generous, were

Willie Carson and Dr Devious dominate the Dewhurst.

this time represented by the grey Great Palm, who had won his only start at York. Another colt unbeaten in one outing was Zaahi, a seven-length winner at Sandown Park. Thourios had been beaten by Dr Devious at Goodwood after winning on his debut at Salisbury, and Henry Cecil's Pursuit Of Love, whose victory in a Newmarket maiden had impressed many experts, attracted some significant each-way money.

Thourios took up the running after a quarter of a mile and still led approaching the final furlong, but he was unable to quicken the pace when attacked by Dr Devious, who showed great resolution under strong driving to stay on well up the hill as Great Palm tried to mount a challenge. But Paul Cole's leggy and inexperienced colt never looked at ease in the closing stages and at the line Dr Devious had two and a half lengths to spare. Thourios stayed on to be third.

Those who had been snooty about the Dewhurst form in 1990, and had been proved so wrong, knew better than to quibble about the 1991 result, but few felt that Dr Devious was the best two-year-old of the year. Trainer Peter Chapple-Hyam, who had enjoyed a tremendous season with his juveniles, felt that the colt could well turn into a Derby horse, though he might go for the Two Thousand Guineas if forward enough in the spring. Bookmakers made him a best-priced 25–1 for the Epsom Classic, secure in the knowledge that candidates as yet unknown would be staking their claims over the next seven months.

Asked to compare Dr Devious with his other good two-year-old Rodrigo De Triano, Peter Chapple-Hyam said: 'Rodrigo is the sharper colt and the Doctor will get the trip.'

But it was not even certain that Dr Devious would turn out best of the Dewhurst runners: many pundits felt that Great Palm, who had run very green, had the rosier long-term prospects.

Though beaten on Great Palm, Alan Munro had a memorable afternoon, Petite-d-Argent giving him his one hundredth winner of the season – his maiden century.

Other highlights of the middle day were Susurrations's first victory in Listed company in the Baring International Darley Stakes, and Musicale's brilliant effort under Pat Eddery in the Rockfel Stakes, beating Mystery Play and Snow Forest in a manner which set owner Robert Sangster thinking about the 1992 Classics. With Musicale and Rodrigo De Triano (each unbeaten in five starts) to go into battle with, Sangster could afford not to worry too much about having let Dr Devious go.

The result of the opener on Saturday threatened to take up more column inches on some racing pages than the Champion Stakes and Cesarewitch combined. Pelorus, winner of the Severals Apprentice Handicap, numbered among his owners the racing journalists Geoff Lester, George Ennor, Rodney Masters, David Mort – and 'Hotspur' himself, J.A. McGrath, who was providing racecourse commentary that afternoon and called his horse home without any audible hint of partiality.

The Dubai Champion Stakes lacked Generous but offered a field well up to scratch for the last great middle-distance race of the season in Europe.

In The Groove's encouraging run when sixth in the Arc – she was the best-placed British-trained horse – engendered high hopes that she could repeat her Champion Stakes victory of 1990, and with Cash Asmussen on board she started the 4–1 favourite for what appeared to be an open race.

'Merci!' Thierry Jarnet shows his appreciation to Tel Quel after the Champion Stakes.

Marju, second in the Derby but without a run since finishing lame in the Eclipse Stakes, was well fancied, as was the Sun Chariot Stakes winner Ristna. But the filly became very stirred up on leaving the paddock and Lester Piggott elected to skip the parade: the stewards adopted a sympathetic view and took no action.

Others among those who did have to endure the parade on a bitterly cold afternoon were Cruachan, thought to be back to his highly promising best after running second in his warm-up race at the last Newmarket meeting; Stagecraft, third at Longchamp in the Prix Dollar and before that beaten when odds on for the International Stakes; Young Buster, third in the Cumberland Lodge since beating Quest For Fame at Kempton; Terimon, who had not been out since springing a shock in the International; Dolpour, favourite for the Champion Stakes in 1989 but now a 100–1 chance; and the Eclipse winner Environment Friend, second to Suave Dancer at Leopardstown.

Star Of Gdansk, third in the Derby and the Irish Derby but a flop in the Prix Rond-Point on Arc day, formed the Irish challenge, and there were two French-trained runners – Glity, who did not look up to this class, and Tel Quel.

Trained by André Fabre and giving jockey Thierry Jarnet his first ride in England, Sheikh Mohammed's Tel Quel was almost unknown to British racing fans. He had won his last two races, at Evry (beating the Rond-Point winner Bistro Garden) and at Maisons-Laffitte, but did not look a Group One performer and was easy to back at 16–1.

Terimon set the early pace, but never looked like being able to repeat his York victory, and three furlongs out Ray Cochrane pushed Cruachan into the lead and set sail for home. Coming into the Dip it looked as if Cruachan would hold on, but then out of the pack came Thierry Jarnet and Tel Quel, who was flying as the leaders hit the rising ground and grabbed the lead close home to beat Cruachan by half a length.

The blinkered Go South (Nicky Carlisle) surges to a Cesarewitch upset.

In The Groove had been held up in the early stages and then met with interference when Cash Asmussen brought her out to make her run, but once clear she ran on with tremendous gusto, failing by only half a length to peg back the second. Running her best race since the Coronation Cup, In The Groove booked herself a trip to Churchill Downs for the Breeders' Cup. She was widely regarded as unlucky in the Champion Stakes, not a race that Cash Asmussen will remember with too much affection. The cat-bird seat does have its drawbacks.

If a 16–1 winner of the Champion Stakes left punters licking their wounds, worse was to follow in the Cesarewitch, one of the big betting races of the season.

With Lester Piggott booked to ride, Martin Pipe's Tamarpour was all the rage here, a solid 5–1 favourite preferred in the market to Hieroglyphic, from the in-form stable of John Gosden, and the Chester Cup winner Star Player. But in the closing stages of the daftest contest of the Flat year – over half the race is effectively invisible from the stands – it was Nicky Carlisle and the 33–1 outsider Go South who came to the front inside the final furlong to score an easy win from Bardolph and Farsi.

This was Nicky Carlisle's biggest winner, but some indication of the perceived chance of Go South is supplied by the fact that trainer John Jenkins was not at Newmarket, preferring to saddle a runner at the Kempton Park jumping meeting. It was left to Jenkins's father to give the post-Cesarewitch quotes about Go South: 'It just depends what sort of mood he's in. He runs his own races.'

The Houghton Stakes attracted only five runners, but may have thrown up a future champion in the winner Shuailaan, trained for Sheikh Ahmed Al Maktoum by Alec Stewart. He ran on well to beat the Sadler's Wells colt Masad by a length and a half, and shaped with a great deal of promise.

Ears pricked, Shuailaan (Michael Roberts) lands the Houghton Stakes.

Challenge Stakes (Group 2)

17 October 1991

7 furlongs (going: good to firm)

1st: £42,192; **2nd:** £15,711; **3rd:** £7,481; **4th:** £3,186

1	MYSTIKO	M. Roberts	9–4 fav
2	ONLY YOURS	W. Carson	7–1
3	VOLKSRAAD	Pat Eddery	7–2
4	HIMIKO	M. Hills	16–1

7 ran

distances: 2 lengths, 1½ lengths
time: 1 min 22.77 secs

Winner owned by The Dowager Lady Beaverbrook, trained by C. E. Brittain (Newmarket, Suffolk), bred by Kingston Park Stud Inc, USA

Tote: win £2.90; places £1.60, £2.20; dual forecast £9.20

Three Chimneys Dewhurst Stakes (Group 1)

18 October 1991

7 furlongs (going: good to firm)

1st: £130,195; **2nd:** £48,732; **3rd:** £23,841; **4th:** £10,264; **5th:** £4,607; **6th:** £2,344

1	DR DEVIOUS	W. Carson	3–1 fav
2	GREAT PALM	A. Munro	7–2
3	THOURIOS	R. Cochrane	8–1
4	PURSUIT OF LOVE	Pat Eddery	13–2
5	ZAAHI	R. Hills	4–1
6	FREE FLYER	A. S. Cruz	20–1
7	YOUNG SENOR	J. Reid	6–1
8	STRONG SUIT	B. Raymond	33–1
9	TONY SAN	M. Roberts	100–1

9 ran

distances: 2½ lengths, short head

time: 1 min 23.45 secs

Winner owned by Luciano Gaucci, trained by P. W. Chapple-Hyam (Manton, Wilts), bred by Lyonstown Stud, Ireland

Tote: win £3.60; places £1.30, £1.80, £3.00; dual forecast £3.90

Dubai Champion Stakes (Group 1)

19 October 1991

1 mile 2 furlongs (going: good to firm)

1st: £262,350; **2nd:** £97,650; **3rd:** £47,325; **4th:** £19,875; **5th:** £8,437; **6th:** £3,862

1	TEL QUEL	T. Jarnet	16–1
2	CRUACHAN	R. Cochrane	8–1
3	IN THE GROOVE	C. Asmussen	4–1 fav
4	RISTNA	L. Piggott	11–2
5	STAR OF GDANSK	C. Roche	33–1
6	YOUNG BUSTER	J. Reid	15–2
7	STAGECRAFT	S. Cauthen	12–1
8	DOLPOUR	L. Dettori	100–1
9	TERIMON	M. Roberts	10–1
10	ENVIRONMENT FRIEND	G. Duffield	8–1
11	GLITY	A. Lequeux	50–1
12	MARJU	W. Carson	11–2

12 ran

distances: ½ length, ½ length

time: 2 mins 01.93 secs

Winner owned by Sheikh Mohammed, trained by A. Fabre (France), bred by Marystead Farm Ltd, France

Tote: win £22.60; places £4.30, £2.60, £1.90; dual forecast £146.80

Tote Cesarewitch (Handicap)

19 October 1991

2 miles 2 furlongs (going: good to firm)

1st: £48,965; **2nd:** £14,720; **3rd:** £7,110; **4th:** £3,305

1	GO SOUTH	N. Carlisle	33–1
2	BARDOLPH	F. Norton (5)	33–1
3	FARSI	J. Quinn	12–1
4	HIEROGLYPHIC	W. Carson	6–1

22 ran   (Tamarpour 5–1 fav)

distances: 2½ lengths, ¾ length

time: 3 mins 52.76 secs

Winner owned by Rex Joachim, trained by J. R. Jenkins (Royston, Herts), bred by M. E. Wates

Tote: win £41.00; places £7.10, £7.30, £2.30, £2.30; dual forecast £296.00; trio £2,542.80

RACING POST TROPHY

Doncaster, 26 October 1991

In the three decades of its existence only one horse has won what is now the Racing Post Trophy and gone on to land the Derby the following year – Reference Point in 1986/87. That peak in the race's fortunes was followed by a distinct trough: the 1987 winner Emmson failed to live up to his promise, Al Hareb (1988) and Be My Chief (1989) each finished last in one race as a three-year-old before being retired, and the 1990 winner Peter Davies was a sore disappointment in 1991.

But hope springs eternal, and after the latest running of the Racing Post Trophy the winner Seattle Rhyme was installed as favourite for the 1992 Derby at odds as low as 16–1. Despite the historical record being loaded against the horse, this was a perfectly reasonable reaction to a fine performance in Britain's last Group One race of the season.

There were eight runners. Seattle Rhyme was favourite on the strength of a campaign which had shown distinct improvement through the season: winner of his maiden at Ascot, second to Chicmond in the Solario Stakes, winner of the Stardom Stakes at Goodwood, then a very good third to Arazi in the Grand Criterium at Longchamp. To have been beaten just over three lengths by the best two-year-old in France was form a cut above that of any of his rivals, and this tough son of Seattle Dancer (who at $13.1 million was the most expensive yearling ever sold) looked a good thing.

The rest of the field included Mack The Knife, second to Made Of Gold in the Royal Lodge Stakes, Thourios, third in the Dewhurst after leading for much of the trip, and Ninja Dancer, who had beaten the highly regarded King's Loch (another taking his chance here) at Ascot eight days earlier. Peter Walwyn's

Anchorite had won well at Haydock, and Assessor had taken a graduation race at the Ascot September Meeting. The only runner without a win to his name was the rank outsider Beldi.

Ninja Dancer and Mack The Knife made the early running, and were joined by Thourios at the entrance to the straight. Just as in the Dewhurst, however, Thourios could not maintain the pace, and as he weakened before the two-furlong marker Mack The Knife started to make a forward move. But it was now all too clear that only one horse would be winning the Racing Post Trophy – Seattle Rhyme, on whom Cash Asmussen was simply exuding confidence. With a furlong to go David Elsworth's colt hit the front, and any worries that he had suffered too hard a race in the Grand Criterium were soon dispelled: running on with great gusto, he sailed home by three and a half lengths from Mack The Knife, who had been in vain pursuit for the final two hundred yards, and Assessor, who had never been close enough to threaten but kept on dourly for third place.

This is the time of year when big events come thick and fast. A week

earlier David Elsworth had been reacting to In The Groove's luckless run in the Champion Stakes, a week later he would be with the same filly at the Breeders' Cup. In between he could celebrate a fine performance by Seattle Rhyme (Elsworth's first Group One winner with a colt), and speculate about the future.

'He's obviously very exciting – he could be anything', was the trainer's immediate post-race comment. Further reflection revealed that Seattle Rhyme would be trained for the Derby but might well take in the Two Thousand Guineas if he was forward enough come the spring.

But the Guineas might also be a target for Arazi, whose stock had been given a huge boost by the result of the Racing Post Trophy: if he could beat this winner by more than three lengths, he must be some horse!

There was no doubt that Seattle Rhyme was an exciting prospect, and it was only the memory of similarly hopeful speculation about the potential of Al Hareb and Be My Chief and Peter Davies which kept some punters sitting on their hands if ante-post vouchers were near.

Racing Post Trophy (Group 1)

26 October 1991

1 mile (going: good)

1st: £135,994; **2nd:** £50,746; **3rd:** £24,698; **4th:** £10,490; **5th:** £4,570; **6th:** £2,202

1	SEATTLE RHYME	C. Asmussen	2–1 fav
2	MACK THE KNIFE	W. Carson	5–1
3	ASSESSOR	J. Reid	14–1
4	ANCHORITE	M. Birch	9–1
5	NINJA DANCER	B. Raymond	11–2
6	KING'S LOCH	W. Ryan	7–1
7	THOURIOS	R. Cochrane	4–1
8	BELDI	G. Duffield	66–1

8 ran

distances: 3½ lengths, 1½ lengths
time: 1 min 39.58 secs

Winner owned by H. J. Senn, trained by D. R. C. Elsworth (Whitsbury, Hants), bred by Meadow Grove Farm

Tote: win £2.80; places £1.30, £1.40, £2.40; dual forecast £5.30

Second Set (Lanfranco Dettori) goes clear in the Sussex Stakes at Goodwood.

More glories of Goodwood. *Above:* **The grey Further Flight (Michael Hills) gets the better of the favourite Great Marquess (Pat Eddery, black colours with white cap) in the closing stages of the Dickins & Jones Goodwood Cup.**

Below: **Title Roll (Willie Carson) on the far side comes to tackle Food Of Love (Richard Quinn) in the King George Stakes, with the fourth horse Be Fresh (Lanfranco Dettori) trying to get on terms on the right.**

Arazi (Gerald Mosse) goes down for the Prix Morny Agence Francaise at Deauville ... and comes back!

Former champion jockeys shine at the Doncaster September Meeting. *Above:* **Lester Piggott drives Bog Trotter clear of Satin Flower (Steve Cauthen) in the Kiveton Park Stakes.**

Below: **Willie Carson and Rodrigo De Triano are well in command at the end of the Laurent–Perrier Champagne Stakes.**

The Coalite St Leger. Pat Eddery on Toulon glances sympathetically across at John Reid on Saddlers' Hall.

A delay before the start of the Mallard Handicap at Doncaster affords Lester Piggott and Native Magic *(above)* **and Pat Eddery and Naswara** *(opposite page)* **a respite. But once in the stalls** *(overleaf)* **Naswara gets stirred up.**

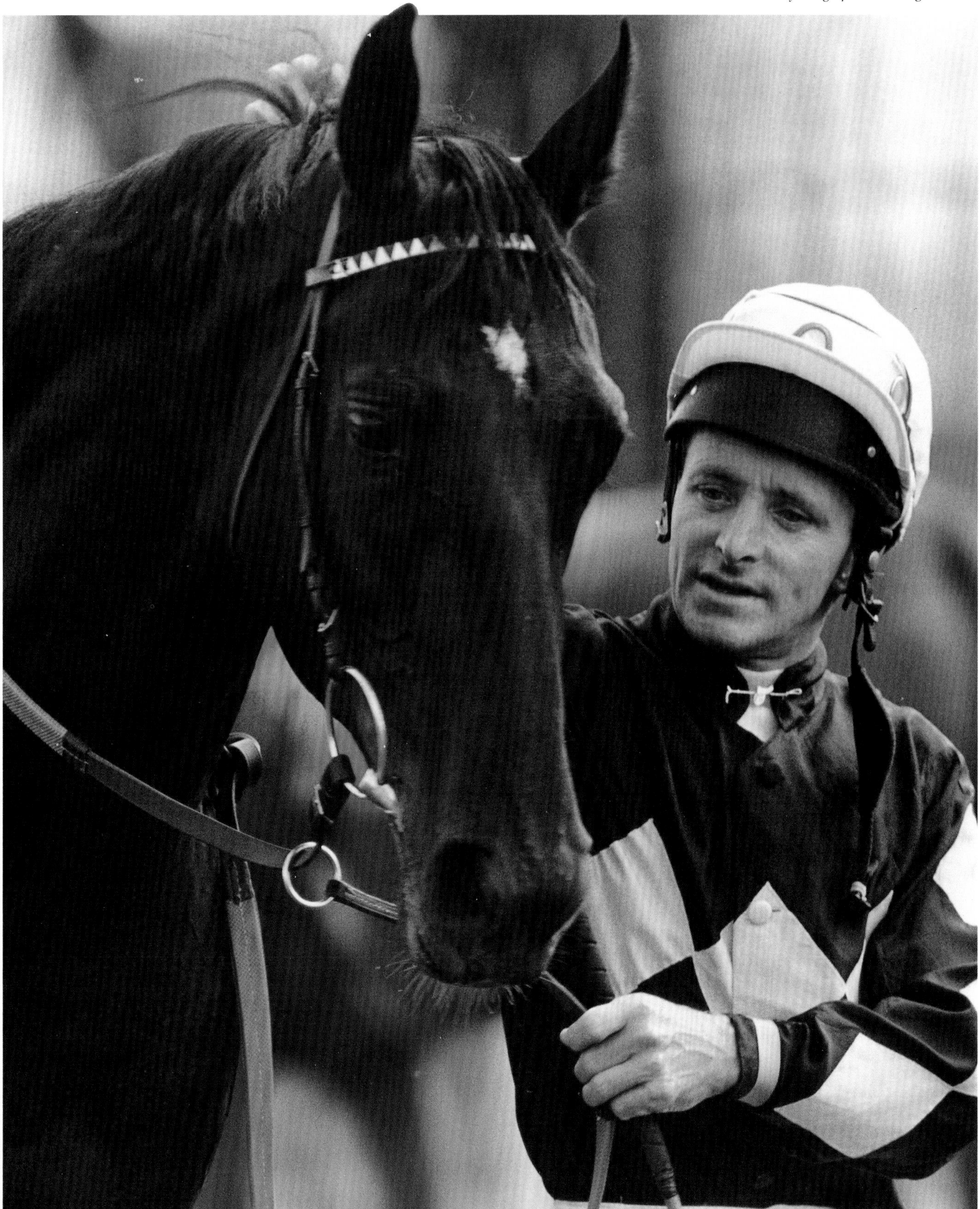

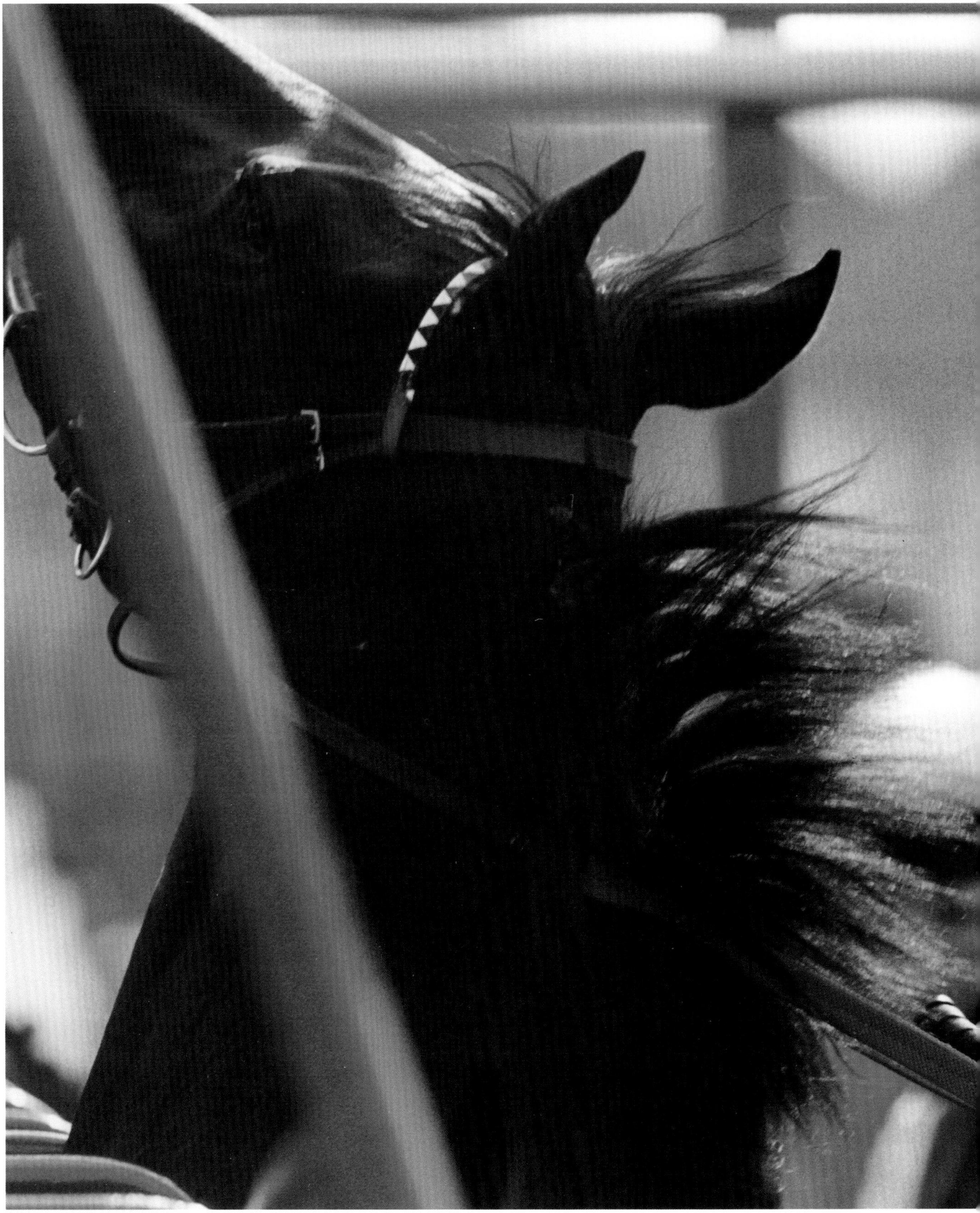

A big–race double for trainer Geoffrey Wragg and jockey Walter Swinburn on the opening day of the Newmarket October Meeting. Above: Young Senor comes between Dr Devious (Willie Carson, far side) and Alnasr Alwasheek (Steve Cauthen, yellow colours) to win the Tattersalls Tiffany Highflyer Stakes. The blinkered Ruhr (Lanfranco Dettori) is fourth.

Below: Marling strides away from Absurde (Freddie Head, black cap) and Basma (Willie Carson) to take the Tattersalls Cheveley Park Stakes.

Two English victories on Arc day at Longchamp. *Above:* **Richard Quinn and Culture Vulture just hold off Pat Eddery and Hatoof in the Prix Marcel Boussac, with Verveine (Dominique Boeuf) third.**

Below: **Keen Hunter (Steve Cauthen, white sleeves) beats Sheikh Albadou (Bruce Raymond, rails) and Magic Ring (Alan Munro, green colours) in the Ciga Prix de l'Abbaye.**

The contrasting sights and moods of Arc day.

The Ciga Prix de l'Arc de Triomphe field heads for the straight. The blinkered Art Bleu (Christo Aubert) leads from Quest For Fame (Walter Swinburn, pink cap), with Generous (Alan Munro, green colours) apparently poised. Suave Dancer and Cash Asmussen (blue and white hooped cap) are in no hurry at the rear of the field.

After the Arc: the heroes return.

SOUTH AFRICAN TRACKS PUT US ALL TO SHAME

John Oaksey

When did you last take your wife or girlfriend racing, have a losing bet apiece – and take home change from a tenner? With five rands to the pound, you can do it easily at any one of Johannesburg's four flourishing racecourses.

At Gosforth Park on Saturday, and Turffontein this week, admission to the Silver Ring costs 50 cents (10p). The Tote's minimum – for a whole variety of attractive high-dividend pool bets on a nine-race programme – is one rand (20p) and at Turffontein, where the drink is slightly cheaper than off-course, 15 rands (£3) will buy as much curry as anyone can eat.

In Britain of course, 'Silver Ring' conjures up horrid memories of noise on a good day, loneliness on a bad one and comparative squalor on either. At Gosforth on Saturday, it meant a good view from a seat on the first floor of a sunlit grandstand less than 100 yards short of the finish – with bars, fast food and Tote windows at your elbow.

The next-best enclosure cost only three rands (60p) and in the Members – admission seven rand (£1.40) – 35 rands (£7 a head) could buy a three-course lunch at a table looking out across the course. Each table is equipped with its own television screen and an internal telephone for bets with the 28 bookies who pay to stand on course.

In South Africa, already hit by sanctions, the recession is biting hard, Yet, amazingly, the bargain basement racegoing I have described is not being subsidised by unwilling and complaining owners.

If they complain at all, I have not heard it – and no wonder. The average basic cost of training a horse is 12,000 rands a year; and for winning one of the least-important maiden races on Saturday's card, the first of five prizes was 14,375 rands.

'After all deductions, and counting all training extras, we reckon to structure our prize-money so that one win pays at least threequarters of an owner's annual bill,' said Colin Dunn, Turffontein's chairman.

He is understandably proud of the operation he controls – and has no doubt at all what makes it possible.

'Betting is our life blood,' he said, 'and, most of all, we depend on the TAB or Tote.'

The track takes 7½ per cent of on-course Tote turnover, so every conceivable step is taken to attract the biggest possible crowd, make them comfortable and encourage them to bet. Average attendances at Gosforth and Turffontein are 14,000 and , with closed-circuit television relaying the action to other courses, it is possible for a nimble-witted punter to have an interest in 27 races on one day.

If you think that sounds excessive, do not forget that horse racing is *the* only legal medium for gambling in South Africa. No football pools, no lottery, no bingo and no casinos. So the TAB are catering for some fairly hungry and deprived enthusiasts.

Another crucial difference is that South African racing and betting are controlled and taxed, not centrally from Pretoria but locally by the provincial government of the area. Racing, in fact, is the Transvaal's second highest source of revenue industry. That makes for a very different, much closer, relationship than the Jockey Club or Levy Board has ever established in Britain with the Home Office. What is more, quite apart from percentages racing clubs are allowed to take from their own betting, the province put 2½ per cent of their betting tax receipts into a central Development Fund.

This must not be confused with our own Levy Board. The Transvaal already let racing deduct its own 'levy'. The Development Fund is an extra contribution made out of betting tax – precisely the all important re-investment in racing which successive British governments have always stubbornly refused to acknowledge.

All these factors – a friendly local government, imaginative Tote operation and control of bookmakers – plus energetic marketing of superlative yet cheap racecourse facilities, combined with a heavenly climate, make it impossible for an Englishman to go racing in South Africa without turning green with envy.

As for South Africa's eternal and still, sadly, unsolved problems, there was no trace of them at Gosforth Park. Racing was the first sport to become completely non-racial in 1976 and has been doing its best ever since to set an example. On Saturday, the cheapest, 50 cent, enclosure was almost entirely black and the three-rand 'Gold Ring' largely so. And in the seven-rand 'Members', the mixture looked a perfectly-contented 50–50.

RETURN OF THE LONG FELLOW IS COMPLETE

J.A. McGrath

Where were you when J. F. Kennedy was assassinated? What were you doing when man first set foot on the Moon? Silly, unimportant questions, I know, but it is amazing how many of us remember the mundane matters to which we were attending when an event of monumental significance has occurred in our lifetime.

For some curious reason, of which I have only the faintest suspicion, until a year ago the sporting paralled to J. F. K. and the Moonmen was always the Muhammed Ali–Joe Frazier 'Thriller in Manila' fight, which kept me and a few friends glued to a television set in a dingy Wanchai bar in Hong Kong as we watched two great fighers trade punches beyond what seemed the limits of human endurance.

But now my cluttered collection of sporting memories is dominated by one event – a year ago today – which came as the most pleasant surprise to racing people and added a colourful dimension hitherto regarded as lost for ever. That event was the Lester Piggott comeback.

After more than four and a half years in retirement, Piggott, at the age of fifty-four, decided to attempt the impossible, a return to race riding. The news that he had been licensed to ride again by the Jockey Club came in a short press release from Portman Square late one autumn afternoon, just after I had finished watching horses plough through heavy ground, almost up to their ears, at Haydock Park. Funny how you remember the mundane.

Pat Eddery, who was ahead of schedule to become the first jockey in thirty-eight years to ride two hundred winners in a season, gave that cheeky, mischievous, disbelieving laugh when told of Lester's comeback plan. 'He must be mad – good old Lester!' Eddery chirped. At the end of a day which had been cold, wet and miserably wintry, such a reaction was not hard to understand. Why should a silver-haired grandfather want to return to all this? But return he has, in typically dramatic style.

Lester Piggott has just completed the first year in the most remarkable comeback seen in sport in this country and tomorrow, he celebrates the occasion by attempting to win his 'own' race, the Lester Piggott All-Aged Stakes, over six furlongs, at Chepstow on Shafouri, a three-year-old trained by his wife, Susan.

Last year it was merely the Biddlestone All-Aged Stakes, but the race took on special significance – and a new name – after racing's legendary Long Fellow came home victorious on a tough sprinter called Nicholas, registering his first win on a British racecourse in nearly five years.

Quite simply, Piggott has achieved the impossible, going straight back into competition at the highest level; not merely holding his own, but proving the same, dominant player he was in the Fifties, Sixties and Seventies. The fact that his career spans six decades – he rode his first winner in 1948 – is, in itself, remarkable.

Some will argue that Piggott today is not the same as Piggott of yesteryear, but those critics were obviously unable to attend last year's incredible Breeders' Cup Day at Belmont Park, New York, and were probably out of town when the Doncaster St Leger meeting took place last month.

Just ask Pat Eddery, or any of Lester's other weighing room rivals, whether the Long Fellow has 'gone' (racing parlance for over-the-hill). He certainly did not look a spent force on Royal Academy in America, or You Know The Rules and Mudaffar when riding up north.

The Long Fellow in action, winning the King Edward VII Stakes at Royal Ascot on Saddlers' Hall . . .

It is totally unnecessary to ask Piggott how he feels about the comeback. The grin, seen in the past more often than legend would have you believe, is even more forthcoming these days. The boyish, athletic gait when he strides into the paddock has a certain spring to it. This racing legend is a happy man.

'I have enjoyed this past year a lot,' says Lester. 'And I would have to say that it has worked out much better than I could have hoped. I really never thought I would have had so many rides.'

No matter how confident the genius is in himself, often the hard part is convincing others the talent is still there. Lester returned with the good wishes of the great majority in racing but without a firm contract or retainer with a leading owner or trainer. Getting rides was a matter of popularity in the marketplace. Suddenly, the desire to be sought after became important again.

Domestically, Piggott has ridden 49 winners from 322 rides since he returned, but wins in Ireland, America and on the Continent swell the total beyond the century mark.

Piggott nominates his first win back on Nicholas at Chepstow, the glorious triumph of Royal Academy in the Breeders' Cup in New York and the victory of Saddlers' Hall at Royal Ascot this year, as his major milestones in the past twelve months. 'They have all meant something to me, but the Breeders' Cup was the best,' he says without hesitation.

Lester always was a good judge, and nobody would argue with his choice of Royal Academy as the win he treasures most this time round. The fact that the colt was trained by Vincent O'Brien, with whom he had combined during the glory days of Sir Ivor, Nijinsky, Roberto and The Minstrel, added a special element of satisfaction, as the Wizard of Ballydoyle gave Lester both encouragement and rides – and if he didn't need too much of the former, mounts such as Royal Academy certainly came in handy.

. . . and in conversation with John Oaksey at Longchamp on Arc day.

Coming from near last on the inside rail in the first furlong to storm home up the centre of the course, Royal Academy snatched a memorable win, which, if probably going over the heads of hard-bitten New Yorkers, had virtually reduced those from the other side of the pond to tears.

The Americans had to make a meal of the fact that Lester had 'done time' for tax offences in Britain, and if it had escaped the tabloids at the time, it certainly wasn't missed by the on-track television form experts, one of whom slated Piggott beforehand.

After Piggott had triumphed, one of the experts asked his fellow critic: 'Well Bill, what have you got to say now about a fifty-four-year-old ex-con riding again?' Bill was suddenly struck dumb.

Piggott was inwardly delighted at the reception he received from the public on his return to race riding. Prior to the full professional comeback, he had ridden in two veterans' invitation races at Tipperary and The Curragh – plus a couple of earlier mounts in Peru – and still, the warmest welcome he has received has been in Ireland. 'I think it has given the elderly people some interest,' says Piggott, who completed a double for Vincent O'Brien at The Currragh on Saturday and landed a big prize on the British-trained Colway Bold there yesterday, as well as another win for O'Brien.

But when the starting gates fly back and the race is on, there are no welcoming committees among his riding companions – it is every man for himself and his horse, and Piggott has been able to give the new breed a display of the old magic. 'Basically, riding in races is much the same as it always has been, although these days they go a bit quicker,' he observes. 'But the world has changed a lot.'

But there is one thing that hasn't changed in nearly forty years in Britain. It is a ritual that takes place every summer in early June, guaranteeing lots of guesswork and a certain amount of intrigue. This year – as they no doubt will for a few more to come – a new generation asked: 'What does Lester ride in the Derby?'

BREEDERS' CUP

Churchill Downs, 2 November 1991

For its eighth running the Breeders' Cup returned to Churchill Downs, home of the Kentucky Derby, for the second time in four years. The last running at the Louisville track, immortalised in Turf terms by the exploits of Personal Ensign, Miesque and Alysheba, is famous locally for the appalling weather – temperatures near freezing and relentless rain and gloom.

So it was with one eye on the barometer and the other on the form books of two continents that Louisville prepared for its second hosting of what is now widely accepted as the world championship of racing, seven races with a total prize money of $10 million, the fulfilment of the dream of breeder John Gaines to establish a racing event to match the SuperBowl or the World Series.

The attention of the racing world was on Louisville, and she knew it. On the main approach roads to the city, huge billboards clocked the countdown: '4 Days to the Breeders' Cup . . . 3 Days to the Breeders' Cup . . .'. Banners waved in the streets to announce the staging of racing's greatest day in the state where over forty thousand thoroughbreds are foaled each year. On the Wednesday before the races was held the Breeders' Cup Bash, a $20-a-head public party to whip up more local enthusiasm. Not that it needed much encouraging: the Louisville economy stood to reap the Breeders' Cup benefit to the tune of many millions of dollars.

The Bash took place indoors, of course. By the end of October the Kentucky weather could and would do anything, and the day before the Breeders' Cup teased with a compendium of conditions: driving rain, piercing wind, then sunshine and a little warmth. The forecast for Saturday was cold but clear, so it proved.

A crowd of 66,204 poured into Churchill Downs on the Saturday morning, with one preliminary race to keep them amused before the Breeders' Cup itself got under way with the Sprint at 12.16, the early post time being an attempt to end the tradition of running the final Breeders' Cup event – the Classic – in light ranging from dusk to darkness.

Tradition has a strong pull at Churchill Downs, where before each racing day the crowd stands to attention for the singing of the national anthem, but so does the need to meet the requirements of the modern racegoer: a room in the rear of the Clubhouse is labelled: 'Diaper Changing Facility – for our young guest.'

If our young guest were still in diapers he or she was probably one of the fortunate few immune to Pick Seven fever. The Pick Seven was a new pool bet in which punters throughout the nation could go for a huge payout by predicting the winners of all seven Breeders' Cup races, and with a predicted jackpot of at least $10 million, the newspapers in the days leading up to the races were full of advice on selections and staking plans. Syndicates were formed in order to boost the betting power and cover more possible outcomes than any sane individual would hazard for: it was estimated that to cover all the possibilities would involve an outlay of over $60 million.

On Breeders' Cup eve a panel of experts from the *Racing Times*, the new American Turf daily, held a 'seminar' in the Clubhouse to enlighten prospective Pick Seven punters, and from this it was obvious – as it had been from all the newspapers and lounge bar chat – that the European challenge was being taken very seriously.

Well it might, for in 1991 the European raid on the Breeders' Cup was the strongest numerically it had ever been. Twenty-one horses made the trip across the Atlantic. From England came Sheikh Albadou, Culture Vulture, Showbrook, Second Set, Shadayid, In The Groove, Quest For Fame and Saddlers' Hall. From France, Arazi, Ken de Saron, Polar Falcon, Priolo, Danseuse du Soir, Pistolet Bleu, Pigeon Voyageur, Dear Doctor, Miss Alleged, Saganeca

The splendour of Churchill Downs.

and Cudas. From Ireland, Kooyonga and Star Of Gdansk.

The form experts – 'handicappers', in local parlance – acknowledged that the Europeans had a major chance of lifting the Mile and the Turf, but the controversial horse was Arazi in the Juvenile. Clearly the best two-year-old in Europe, he had the outside draw for a race which involved negotiating two 180-degree bends, and had never worked on dirt before. According to one of the top American pundits at the *Racing Times* seminar, 'Arazi is one of the worst bets on the card' at his projected morning line odds of 3–1.

In common with many of his fellow raiders from Europe, Arazi would be racing for the first time with the aid of drugs – in his case the pain-reducer Bute. The use of Bute and the anti-coagulant Lasix is sanctioned in Kentucky (though not in New York, host state of the 1990 Breeders' Cup at Belmont Park), and brought back into the limelight a controversial issue central to the growing internationalisation of racing. But 'when in Rome' was good enough for plenty of the European trainers.

What seemed to be solidly uncontroversial was that the great American sprinter Housebuster was a certainty for the first Breeders' Cup race, the Sprint. Practically every on-track horse player would be looking to set himself up for the other six races by plunging on this four-year-old, and the vast majority of Pick Seven punters around the nation would have made only one choice for the Sprint, and that choice was Housebuster.

There had been a vague rumour before the race that Housebuster was not right, but he none the less went off the 5–2 on favourite in what would be his last race before retirement. None of his opponents seemed to have form remotely as good as his, and the relative merit of his sole European-trained rival Sheikh Albadou was impossible to assess. Alex Scott's colt had run a fine second to Keen Hunter in the Prix de

l'Abbaye, but he was clearly not in the same league as Dayjur – so freakishly unlucky in the Sprint in 1990 – and most of the on-track punters, including many in a hefty British contingent, felt it was safe to ignore him.

They were wrong, for Pat Eddery and Sheikh Albadou dominated the race from early in the straight, storming up the outside to win very easily by three lengths from Pleasant Tap.

Housebuster had made his move at the beginning of the straight but his effort was short-lived, and it transpired that he had torn a ligament in his left foreleg.

Before the race, an American photographer was overheard talking to his assistant. 'If there's a Go For Wand situation', he had instructed her, referring to the appalling death of that great filly in front of the Belmont Park stands at the climax of the 1990 Distaff, 'get straight out onto the track.' The injury to Housebuster was mercifully the nearest that the 1991 Breeders' Cup would come to a Go For Wand situation. As he returned towards the stands after finishing ninth, jockey Craig Perret pulled up near the winning post and dismounted. The horse ambulance – eerily reminiscent of the one which had carried Go For Wand away a year before – was drawn up, and sympathetic applause rippled through the stands as Housebuster was loaded in. It was subsequently confirmed that the injury was not as bad as had originally been feared, and Housebuster would be able to pursue his stud career.

The injury to Housebuster rather overshadowed the momentous achievement of Sheikh Albadou. He was only the second British-trained horse ever to win a Breeders' Cup race on the flat, after Pebbles in the Turf in 1985 (also ridden by Pat Eddery). And he was

Sheikh Albadou (Pat Eddery) storms clear in the Sprint . . .

. . . and his historic achievement is duly recognised by trainer Alex Scott (left) and Joe Mercer (right), racing manager to owner Hilal Salem.

the first European-trained horse to win a Breeders' Cup race on dirt – though he would be joined by another before very long.

Alex Scott revealed after the race that when owner Hilal Salem had suggested an attempt at the Breeders' Cup after Sheikh Albadou's second to Polar Falcon in the Ladbroke Sprint Cup, the trainer had assumed he meant the Mile. The Sprint provided an altogether more difficult proposition against the top American speed horses, but Sheikh Albadou's glorious victory vindicated the decision to take the bold course. Not bad for a horse who in April had opened his 1991 account with victory in the Levy Board Maiden Stakes at Pontefract, worth £3,028 to the winner!

British visitors to Churchill Downs hoping to play up Sheikh Albadou winnings on Culture Vulture in the Juvenile Fillies' did not get much of a run for their money. Paul Cole's tough filly, looking to add to a remarkable Group One sequence of the Brent Walker Fillies' Mile and the Prix Marcel Boussac, was slowly away for the 1 mile 110 yards trip and never looked completely at ease on the dirt. From a position in the rear during the early stages she fought her way towards the leaders at the entrance to the straight, but faded to finish ninth behind Pleasant Stage.

Trained by English-born Old Etonian Chris Speckert and ridden by Eddie Delahoussaye (trainer and jockey of the Sprint runner-up Pleasant Tap), Pleasant Stage just got up in the very last stride of a rousing finish to deny La Spia by a head.

There was no European runner in the Distaff, but the race did not stay in the USA. The Canadian-trained three-year-old filly Dance Smartly had won her last seven starts, including the Triple Crown in Canada, and was sent off the 2–1 on favourite. Always holding a handy position, she made up ground towards the end of the back stretch, continued to improve coming up the straight and hit the front with about a furlong to go, keeping going well to hold off Versailles Treaty without undue fuss.

'We think we have something magic', said owner Ernie Samuel, and no one who saw her win would disagree, while trainer Jim Day voiced the possibility of her challenging for a big race in Europe in 1992.

Meanwhile Dance Smartly had reached two milestones – the first Canadian-bred horse to win a Breeders' Cup race, and the richest filly or mare in racing history. The $3,083,456 to which her Distaff victory brought her career earnings passed the total accrued by 1986 Distaff heroine Lady's Secret.

Then came the Mile, which on paper looked a strong race – 'They don't get any better than this', a racegoer was

Pat Day and Dance Smartly capture the Distaff.

heard enthusing – and probably rich pickings for the European challenge. But a spanner was thrown into the works at the post-position draw on the Wednesday before the race with the declaration for this event of In Excess.

Trained as a two-year-old in England by Bill O'Gorman and some way below the top class, In Excess had developed under American trainer Bruce Jackson into arguably the best horse in the USA. In his last four starts he had become only the second horse ever to win the Metropolitan Handicap, the Suburban Handicap, Whitney Handicap and the Woodward in the same season: the first was the immortal Kelso. Entered for the Sprint and the Classic on dirt as well as the Mile on turf, In Excess was clearly a horse of great versatility, but it had been generally assumed that he would run in the Classic (worth three times more

than the Mile), and it came as a major surprise when he was announced as a starter for the Mile.

Of the home team, Tight Spot, narrow winner of the Arlington Million in September, seemed the strongest rival. But what a European bid for the Mile! Shadayid, Danseuse du Soir, Kooyonga, Second Set, Polar Falcon – their earlier exploits in 1991 have been described in these pages. They were joined by Priolo, winner of the 1991 Prix du Moulin and a close third to Royal Academy in the 1990 Breeders' Cup Mile at Belmont Park, who had been specifically trained by Francois Boutin for this race.

There was also Opening Verse, well remembered by British racing fans as the 200–1 pacemaker for Indian Skimmer in the 1989 Eclipse Stakes who had caused a minor sensation at Sandown by staying on to run a five-

length second to Nashwan, beating Indian Skimmer herself by a short head.

Now owned by Allen Paulson and trained in the USA by Dick Lundy, Opening Verse started an outsider at nearly 27–1, but ran on under pressure in the straight to beat Val des Bois and Star Of Cozzene. The French One Thousand Guineas winner Danseuse du Soir ran best of the Europeans to come fourth, just ahead of Priolo. Shadayid, who met severe interference close home, was seventh, with Polar Falcon, Second Set and Kooyonga all deeply disappointing.

In the race in which they were most expected to show their colours, the Europeans had been thrashed.

Would the same fate await Arazi in the Juvenile? The instant after the starting gate in front of the stands had

Opening Verse (Pat Valenzuela) powers up the stretch to win the Mile.

The Juvenile. Still in Allen Paulson's colours, Valenzuela guides Arazi out of the gate . . .

crashed open, the bell clanging the runners on their way, it seemed as if the pessimists would be proved right. Arazi did not exactly miss the break, but he did not explode from the stalls with the force which would ensure the required handy position at the first turn, and going into the Clubhouse turn he was second last of the fourteen runners.

What happened over the next minute and a half put the 1991 Breeders' Cup Juvenile into that select group of one of the universally acknowledged greatest racing moments of all. For the spectators at Churchill Downs it was one of those 'I can only thank God I was there' races. For the press, it was a rare occasion on which the superlatives never quite seem to match what the writers had seen. For anyone who saw it, the performance of Arazi was all but unbelievable.

In front of Arazi as he hammered into that first bend were the cream of America's two-year-old colts (plus Richard Hannon's Showbrook, well beaten by Arazi in the Prix Robert Papin and now, sporting a pair of equine goggles to protect his eyes from the dirt, providing Lester Piggott with his only 1991 Breeders' Cup ride). There was no way of relating the form which had made him the undisputed juvenile king of Europe with the form of his rivals, but Bertrando, who vied with Arazi for favouritism, was clearly a hot property – unbeaten in three races and the best two-year-old on the continent.

The questions of how Arazi had coped with the travel from France, of how he would cope with his outside draw, of whether he would race as well on dirt as he did on turf – these became completely irrelevant as jockey Pat Valenzuela headed the colt towards the inner going into that first bend and then, having looked distinctly in trouble early in the back stretch, started to collar the horses in front of him.

A third of the way down the back stretch Arazi was still second last. Then he started to slalom in and out of his rivals, moving to the outer to pick off a

few, then briefly back inside to pass a couple more, then between horses to come to the top of the home turn with only Bertrando, going hell for leather on the inside, still to pass.

Coming wide into the home straight, Valenzuela seemed to be taking a pull, but Arazi was by now in full flight and scorched past the leader, making the best American two-year-old look as if he were one of the outriders' ponies inadvertently drawn into the race.

Once clear of his market rival, Arazi barrelled up the straight and moved towards the inside rail, going further and further clear of his field without apparent effort. Valenzuela eased him down approaching the wire, but the official winning margin of five lengths still seemed to err strongly on the conservative side.

It had been a stupendous performance, and it raised the twin-spired roof of Churchill Downs. The crowd was aghast at what it had witnessed, and instant comparisons with Secretariat – the last colt to be named Horse of the Year as a two-year-old – did not in any way appear fanciful. Arazi was simply breathtaking.

In the aftermath of this overpowering performance, thoughts inevitably focused on a return visit to the track on the first Saturday of May 1992 for the Kentucky Derby, and even a unique bid for the Derbies at Churchill Downs and Epsom. The half share sold to Sheikh Mohammed by owner Allen Paulson – after Opening Verse in the Mile, the first owner to have back-to-back Breeders' Cup winners – made such a future at least something to dream about.

But for the moment all that mattered was Arazi in the Juvenile.

Pat Valenzuela said: 'He has the greatest turn of foot I have ever experienced.'

. . . off into the Clubhouse turn and round and back again . . .

Bruce Headley, trainer of Bertrando, said: 'He blew by us. What a monster. I saw Swaps and Secretariat run like that, but never from that far back. That was amazing.'

Top American trainer Shug McGaughey said: 'That was the greatest performance I've ever seen.'

Jockey Club handicapper Geoffrey Gibbs said: 'It's the best performance I've ever seen from a two-year-old, and one of the most amazing performances I've seen in twenty-eight years as a handicapper.'

No one who saw Arazi at Churchill Downs could disagree with any of them.

The Juvenile had set Breeders' Cup Day 1991 alight, but the two richest races were still to come.

The $2 million Turf had been at the centre of a row earlier in the week after the owners of Cameroon announced that they would be taking legal action over their horse's being excluded from the race under the rules of entry. (Cameroon ran at Churchill Downs on the day after the Breeders' Cup and was well beaten.)

Those who did run formed a truly international field, featuring the first time an Epsom Derby winner had competed in a Breeders' Cup race. Quest For Fame, not the most lauded hero of the Blue Riband, ran a marvellous race despite starting at the insulting odds of 58–1, and for an instant in the straight looked like winning. But he had no answer to the late surge of the French-trained Miss Alleged (running on Bute and Lasix 'the Kentucky Cocktail'), who to almost universal surprise proved the best of eight European raiders when responding to a strong ride from Eric Legrix to beat Itsallgreektome (second to Royal Academy in the 1990 Mile) by half a length. Quest For Fame came a gallant third, the Canadian Sky Classic

. . . to an unforgettable victory.

fourth, and Arc third Pistolet Bleu fifth. In The Groove, ridden by Kentucky-born Steve Cauthen, was a never-dangerous seventh, and Saddlers' Hall was tenth.

The Breeders' Cup ended with the Classic, with prize money of $3 million the richest horse race in the world. This attracted two European runners, the Derby and Irish Derby third Star Of Gdansk and Francois Boutin's Cudas, who had beaten Suave Dancer in the Prix Lupin in May. But they were unconsidered outsiders against the likes of Unbridled, winner of the Kentucky Derby and the Classic in 1990, the 1991 Kentucky Derby winner Strike The Gold, the 1990 Preakness winner Summer Squall, the 1991 Jockey Club Gold Cup winner Festin, and the five-year-old grey Black Tie Affair, winner of his last five races.

Run over the Kentucky Derby distance of one and a quarter miles, with the runners starting at the entrance to the home stretch and coming past the stands before making a complete circuit of the track, the Classic raised the Churchill Downs spectators to increasing paroxysms of ecstasy as Black Tie Affair led from the start. Coming back into the straight he still held the lead, though he looked a sitting duck to the challenge of Twilight Agenda. But Black Tie Affair found a fresh turn of foot once straightened up for home and kept on gamely to win by one and a quarter lengths, with Unbridled making a late run from a seemingly impossible position early in the race to claim third. After running prominently for much of the race, Star of Gdansk beat Cudas for last place.

And that was the 1991 Breeders' Cup. With long-priced winners in Sheikh Albadou, Opening Verse and Miss Alleged, it was not a day that many horse players would remember through their pockets with relish. To no one's surprise, the Pick Seven was not won, though several bettors picked up a hefty consolation for choosing six of the seven winners. The total pool nationally for the Pick Seven was disappointing – just over $8.5 million.

Of the seven Breeders' Cup winners, three – Pleasant Stage, Opening Verse and Black Tie Affair – had been trained in the USA. Three – Sheikh Albadou, Arazi and Miss Alleged – in Europe. And the other – Dance Smartly – in Canada. The event's claim to be the world championship of racing had been vindicated.

Yet the abiding memory of the 1991 Breeders' Cup at Churchill Downs was not so much those races which saw international competition at its height. Rather it was the sight of one superlative, staggering, overwhelming performance by Arazi.

Like one of those daft races in a Marx Brothers or even a George Formby film when the plot demands that one horse overcomes all sorts of trouble in running and still comes through to win and achieve the happy ending, the Juvenile provided all the circumstances of defeat for the best horse and yet saw him gloriously triumphant in the end.

Whatever his future might hold, no one who saw Arazi win the Breeders' Cup Juvenile at Churchill Downs will ever forget it.

Eric Legrix is understandably pleased with himself after the Turf.

Breeders' Cup Sprint (Grade I)

2 November 1991

6 furlongs – Dirt (going: fast)

1st: £269,430; **2nd:** £103,627; **3rd:** £62,176; **4th:** £29,016

1	SHEIKH ALBADOU	Pat Eddery	263–10
2	PLEASANT TAP	E. Delahoussaye	88–10
3	ROBYN DANCER	L. Pincay jr	22–1
4	SENOR SPEEDY	J. F. Chavez	19–1

11 ran (Housebuster 2–5 fav)

distances: 3 lengths, ½ length
time: 1 min 09.2 secs

Winner owned by Hilal Salem, trained by A. A. Scott (Newmarket, Suffolk), bred by Highclere Stud Ltd

Pari–Mutuel (including $2 stake): win $54.60; places (1-2) $21.60, $8.20; show (1-2-3) $15.20, $6.60, $10.00; exacta (SF) $546.40

Breeders' Cup Juvenile Fillies (Grade I)

2 November 1991

1 mile 110 yards – Dirt (going: fast)

1st: £269,430; **2nd:** £103,627; **3rd:** £62,176; **4th:** £29,016

1	PLEASANT STAGE	E. Delahoussaye	58–10
2	LA SPIA	A. Solis	29–1
3	CADILLAC WOMEN	P. Compton	28–1
4	SPEED DIALER	P. Day	38–10

14 ran (Preach 24–10 fav)

distances: head, 2½ lengths
time: 1 min 46.4 secs

Winner owned by Buckland Farm, trained by C. Speckert, bred by Mrs Thomas Mellon Evans

Pari–Mutuel (including $2 stake): win $13.60; places (1-2) $7.40, $29.60; show (1-2-3) $5.60, $15.40, $10.40; exacta (SF) $386.20

Black Tie Affair (Jerry Bailey) holds off Twilight Agenda (Chris McCarron) in the Classic.

Breeders' Cup Distaff (Grade 1)

2 November 1991

1 mile 1 furlong – Dirt (going: fast)

1st: £269,430; **2nd:** £103,627; **3rd:** £62,176; **4th:** £29,016

1	DANCE SMARTLY	P. Day	1–2 fav
2	VERSAILLES TREATY	A. Cordero jr	48–10
3	BROUGHT TO MIND	P. Valenzuela	48–1
4	FIT FOR A QUEEN	R. D. Lopez	20–1

13 ran

distances: 1½ lengths, 2½ lengths
time: 1 min 50.8 secs

Winner owned by Sam-Son Farm, trained by J. Day (Canada), bred by Sam-Son Farm, Canada

Pari–Mutuel (including $2 stake): win $3.00; places (1-2) $2.40, $3.20; show (1-2-3) $2.40, $3.20, $8.40; exacta (SF) $9.60

Breeders' Cup Mile (Grade 1)

2 November 1991

1 mile – Turf (going: firm)

1st: £269,430; **2nd:** £103,627; **3rd:** £62,176; **4th:** £29,016

1	OPENING VERSE	P. Valenzuela	267–10
2	VAL DES BOIS	C. McCarron	16–1
3	STAR OF COZZENE	P. Day	19–1
4	DANSEUSE DU SOIR	D. Boeuf	41–1

14 ran (In Excess 22–10 fav)

distances: 1½ lengths, nose
time: 1 min 37.4 secs

Winner owned by A. E. Paulson, trained by R. J. Lundy, bred by J. D. Wimpfheimer

Pari–Mutuel (including $2 stake): win $55.40; places (1-2) $22.00, $15.20; show (1-2-3) $10.60, $7.00, $6.80; exacta (SF) $834.20

Breeders' Cup Juvenile (Grade 1)

2 November 1991

1 mile 110 yards – Dirt (going: fast)

1st: £269,430; **2nd:** £103,627; **3rd:** £62,176; **4th:** £29,016

1	ARAZI	P. Valenzuela	21–10 fav
2	BERTRANDO	A. Solis	5–2
3	SNAPPY LANDING	G. Stevens	61–1
4	OFFBEAT	M. Smith	19–1

14 ran

distances: 4¾ lengths, 3½ lengths
time: 1 min 44.6 secs

Winner owned by A. E. Paulson & Sheikh Mohammed, trained by F. Boutin (France), bred by Ralph Wilson jr

Pari–Mutuel (including $2 stake): win $6.20; places (1-2) $4.80, $4.40; show (1-2-3) $4.80, $4.20, $14.40; exacta (SF) $22.60

Breeders' Cup Turf (Grade 1)

2 November 1991

1 mile 4 furlongs – Turf (going: firm)

1st: £538,860; **2nd:** £207,254; **3rd:** £124,352; **4th:** £58,031

1	MISS ALLEGED	E. Legrix	421–10
2	ITSALLGREEKTOME	J. Velasquez	47–10
3	QUEST FOR FAME	Pat Eddery	58–1
4	SKY CLASSIC	P. Day	33–10

13 ran (Pistolet Bleu 28–10 fav)

distances: ½ length, 2 lengths
time: 2 mins 30.8 secs

Winner owned by Fares Farm, trained by P. Bary (France), bred by Carl M. Freeman

Pari–Mutuel (including $2 stake): win $86.20; places (1-2) $23.60, $6.20; show (1-2-3) $8.40, $4.60, $16.60; exacta (SF) $556.80

Breeders' Cup Classic (Grade 1)

2 November 1991

1 mile 2 furlongs – Dirt (going: fast)

1st: £808,290; **2nd:** £310,881; **3rd:** £186,528; **4th:** £87,047

1	BLACK TIE AFFAIR	J. Bailey	4–1
2	TWILIGHT AGENDA	C. McCarron	14–1
3	UNBRIDLED	C. Perret	43–10
4	FLY SO FREE	J. A. Santos	28–1

11 ran (Festin 31–10 fav)

distances: 1¼ lengths, 2½ lengths
time: 2 mins 02.8 secs

Winner owned by Jeffrey Sullivan, trained by E. T. Poulos, bred by Stephen Peskoff, Ireland

Pari–Mutuel (including $2 stake): win $10.00; places (1-2) $5.40, $12.20; show (1-2-3) $4.20, $7.80, $4.60; exacta (SF) $146.60

RACING POLITICS IN 1991

John Oaksey

Racing is full of optimists and would not last long without them. But you did not need abnormally rose-tinted spectacles last May to see, in the report of Sir John Wheeler's Home Affairs Committee, some surprisingly hopeful signposts to the future.

Sadly, from that moment on things seem to have gone relentlessly downhill. It was all too good to be true, I suppose – and when, at the end of October, the bookmakers and Levy Board finally failed to agree a scheme for the 31st Levy, all our high hopes landed with a discouraging squelch, back on the Home Secretary's desk.

After hearing evidence from all sides of the racing and betting industries, the Home Affairs Committee did not mince words. They firmly proposed a 31st Levy of 'not less than £50 million at today's prices' and also specifically recommended that, 'If the bookmakers do not come forward with proposals of this nature and the Scheme has to be referred to the Home Secretary, 'He should determine it to this effect'.

No independent enquiry has ever taken such a clear, firm line – or proposed anywhere near such a hefty increase in the price bookmakers pay for the raw material of their trade.

A little earlier, in 1989, the Jockey Club had taken what seemed to many a long overdue step towards the twenty-first century by appointing a salaried Chief Executive with business expertise from outside racing. Christopher Haines, the man selected, had made his name by successfully reorganising the sugar industry.

Although an owner on a small scale he had no other connection with racing, none whatever with Messrs Weatherby, the Jockey Club's private (but profit-making) civil servants – and none with any other part of the racing Establishment.

A charming and extremely articulate man, Mr Haines made an immediate good impression on the racing press. He explained, at his first conference, that, in the nature of things, it would take him some time to identify racing's problems. He then hoped to devise a strategy for solving them and, most difficult of all, to get it implemented. If there was any reluctance to welcome this new broom in Portman Square, it seems to have been quickly overcome and Mr Haines set to work.

The Jockey Club has often, with good reason, been accused of failing to put racing's case with sufficient force – and the Home Affairs Committee echoed that complaint in their report.

'Jockey Club/HAC evidence is not as clear as it might have been' they said – and went on, even more crushingly – 'We do not believe that the racing industry at present has the commercial skills or unity and clarity of purpose to take on the big bookmakers in the open market.' When that verdict was delivered Mr Haines had not been long on the job. He has since engaged new Parliamentary consultants and with the help and advice of London Economics, a computerised model of the racing industry ('Racemod') has been constructed.

'It enables us accurately to foresee the effect of any changed circumstance on any section of racing' he claims. 'We know the answer to more "What if?" questions than ever before.'

But it was on those answers that racing, represented by a Jockey Club/HAC Liaison Group, assisted by London Economics and making use of Racemod, produced its submission for the 31st Levy Scheme discussions. The only result, so far, has been disagreement and reference to the Home Secretary. Somehow, racing had still failed to make a convincing case.

Some critics of the Jockey Club have wondered whether, when eagerly welcoming some of the Committee's proposals, the Stewards should not have taken more public and active notice of others – especially those which concerned their own control of racing.

Among those recommendations, for instance was 'A body which represents all sections of the racing industry and combines the functions presently exercised by the Jockey Club and the Horserace Advisory Council.' It is not, of course, the first time such a representative 'Turf Board' has been suggested – but the Jockey Club has still made no overt move in that direction.

Obviously the *right* solution is

essential – a Board designed to work and go on working. But clear proof that the Club is prepared actually to give up some of its power in search of that solution would, to say the least, be welcome.

In the meanwhile, unless a miracle happens, the whole game is still to play for.

The volume and shape of the 31st Levy – the economic oxygen without which racing cannot exist, let alone keep running at a satisfactory rate – must now be decided by Mr Kenneth Baker.

As both he and his predecessors have repeatedly made clear, the present Home Secretary wanted as little as possible to do with what he quite reasonably regards as a domestic squabble between the racing and betting industries. But when Parliament legalised betting shops and set up the Levy Board in 1961 this, in their now questionable wisdom, was how they wrote the law.

So, very reluctantly (probably not until March, if then), Mr Baker and his civil servants will try very hard to look interested as they read or listen to yet another set of submissions from all the interested parties.

Regrettably, and despite a clear recommendation from the Select Committee, these will not include any representation of the punter, from whose pocket comes every penny of both the Levy and the Betting Tax.

The Levy Board's Chairman Sir John Sparrow has promised that he and the other two Government-appointed Levy Board members will make a submission 'distinctive' from those of the other interested parties.

In my dictionary 'distinctive' is defined as 'characteristic' so, by looking up the past form of Sir John and his colleagues, Sir Patrick Meaney and Mrs Anna McCurley, we should be able to predict the line their submission is likely to take. But as bad luck would have it these are not the most fully exposed performers in the book.

This is the first time since Sir John succeeded the late and much lamented Sir Ian Trethowan that he has been involved in a Home Office Determination. Both his colleagues did, in fact, share with Sir Ian a submission to the Home Office three years ago – one which Douglas Hurd chose to ignore. But if you could look Sir Patrick Meaney and Mrs McCurley up in *Timeform* both their names would have to be followed by a question mark.

That is a pity because we and the Home Secretary both know roughly what racing and the bookmakers are going to say about the Levy – 'We need more' on one side and 'You can't have it without upsetting the punters so much they won't bet' on the other. So it seems a fair guess that a comparatively impartial submission from the Government-appointed members may be the one which carries most weight with Mr Baker and the Whitehall boffins.

The last Home Secretary called on to settle a dispute of this kind was Douglas Hurd who, like Mr Baker, had always made it perfectly clear that he wanted as little as possible to do with either the control or finances of racing. In keeping with that attitude Mr Hurd left well alone three years ago – playing a straight 'no change' dead bat to all suggestions of an increase in the 28th Levy scheme for 1989-90.

Two of Douglas Hurd's predecessors, Willie Whitelaw and Leon Brittain, did, it is true, order small percentage increases but Whitelaw's 11 per cent (on a very much smaller turnover than today's) had to be reduced the following year. No Home Secretary has ever gone anywhere near the sort of £50m 'Quantum Leap' which racing now claims it needs to stay afloat.

Mr Baker has not, so far, looked or behaved like a particularly bold or imaginative leader in other fields so, on the face of it, the overwhelming probability must be that he, like Hurd, will wash his hands and leave the existing Levy scheme well alone.

But surely, this time there is, or ought to be, a difference. No previous Home Secretary has ever had such clear advice on his determination from an independent and impartial Parliamentary Committee for which he should, at least in theory, have considerable respect.

Like almost everyone else, the Home Affairs Committee reckons that Mr Baker or, for that matter any other holder of his office, is the wrong man to ask about the Levy. One of the Committee's first recommendations was that the law requiring the determination of disputed Levy schemes by Home Secretaries should be repealed as soon as possible. 'The Home Office' they note rather cattily, 'keeps no track of racing's problems until it is forced to gird up its loins to advise the Home Secretary on a determination.'

Since, unfortunately for all concerned, the law in question has not yet been changed, those loins are presumably now, however reluctantly, being girded up. But surely Mr Baker and his officials will, first of all, study the carefully researched and well-thought-out recommendations of the Home Affairs Committee.

History, alas, is littered with the shelf-bound, dust-covered reports of past Select Committees, Royal Commissions and other well-intentioned enquiries. If all or even some of the Benson and Rothschild recommendations on racing had been followed, the sport would look very different now. So, if they still existed, would the Jockey Club and Levy Board.

Nevertheless Sir John Wheeler and his committee will surely be entitled to feel more than a little hard done by if *all* their work is similarly brushed aside and ignored. The racing world can only cross its collective fingers that Mr Baker will prefer the conclusions of impartial politicians to the perfectly understandable self-interest of the bookies.

HORSES FOR 1992

TONY STAFFORD considers the best prospects.

Unearthing potential winners, especially of the top races, for the following season, is an inexact occupation, and recent history suggests that average two-year-olds can develop over the winter to such an extent that Classic success is not beyond them.

A study of the juvenile form of the 1991 Classic winners offers evidence that such horses can come from unlikely sources.

Mystiko (Two Thousand Guineas) won once in three starts as a juvenile; Generous, a Group One winner as a 50–1 Dewhurst Stakes winner, had been well beaten in the Prix Morny behind Hector Protector; Toulon won a maiden race in France by a neck on his only appearance; Shadayid, unbeaten, won the Group One Prix Marcel Boussac; and Jet Ski Lady, winner of two of her four races, was fifth behind Shadayid in the Longchamp fillies' test.

If there is any link to this quintet, though, it has to be that all five were trained by top professionals and all five boast top pedigrees. Mystiko's sire Secreto won the Derby; Generous is a son of Irish Derby winner Caerleon; Toulon is by the French Derby winner Top Ville; Shadayid's sire Shadeed won the Two Thousand Guineas, and Jet Ski Lady is a daughter of Vaguely Noble, whose ineligibility in the Classic races was forgotten when he beat Derby winner Sir Ivor in the Prix de l'Arc de Triomphe.

The 1991 Classic-winning quintet all clearly showed ability as juveniles and it certainly seems as though the gathering of racing experience in a horse's first season is a help rather than a hindrance to future prospects.

Quest For Fame, the 1990 Derby winner, had just one (placed) run as a juvenile before landing the Derby the following year, but his subsequent record has been slightly disappointing, largely because of training difficulties.

Because the Guineas races come so early into the new season – horses of the requisite class seldom reappear before the Newmarket Craven meeting two weeks earlier – there will be little public form to alter pre-Christmas opinions. But, of course, long-held views can be shattered by a disappointing prep race result in the weeks before the big day.

THREE-YEAR-OLDS OF 1992

ARAZI, bay colt, Blushing Groom–Danseur Fabuleux (Northern Dancer)

When Arazi demolished the best juveniles that America could offer at Churchill Downs in November, he confirmed that he was the outstanding two-year-old in the world.

Horses in the multiple million class are a rarity nowadays, but when before the Juvenile Sheikh Mohammed took an interest in acquiring a share in the colt from owner Allen Paulson, all thoughts of the recession were ignored. The prospect of being able to stand at stud a horse of Arazi's speed and class, coupled with his excellent pedigree and the imminent chance of Classic success, was too much to ignore.

The sale to Japan of Dancing Brave, one of the stallions at Sheikh Mohammed's Dalham Hall Stud, leaves a vacancy at the Newmarket nursery, and should Arazi become the Sheikh's first English Classic-winning colt, he will have been well worth the expense. It came as a shock to recall that Arazi was not unbeaten in Europe. He was beaten over five furlongs on his debut, but after winning a Listed and then a minor Group race, he went through France's four top juvenile races without a worry. The Prix Robert Papin, Morny, de la Salamandre and Grand Criterium are regarded as France's four top races for juvenile colts, and in winning all four, he bettered the achievement of his stable-companion Hector Protector, who won only the last three in an unbeaten six-race campaign the previous year. The interesting thing about Arazi's 1992 prospects is that he could be sent for the Kentucky Derby. But Sheikh Mohammed has that colts' Classic void to fill, and his advisors may well be pressing Mr Paulson to run him at Newmarket on the first Saturday in May. Whatever happens, he is the horse they all have to fear.

Arazi

Rodrigo De Triano

RODRIGO DE TRIANO, chestnut colt, El Gran Senor–Hot Princess (Hot Spark)

Imagine you were the world's leading racehorse owner, but then found you were forced into the background by the spending power and sheer love of the game that the Maktoum family have brought to English racing. You are the owner of a superb training establishment, developed with no thought of expense, but find (a) that the tax laws forbid you, a tax exile, to stay there, and (b) that your principal trainer enjoys rather more success there for his other owners than he does for you. You try to sell it, but nobody wants to pay the market price. What do you do?

No, this is not a test paper for the Young Businessman of the Year, it is precisely the problem that faced Robert Sangster in the autumn of 1990 as Barry Hills' era at Manton was drawing to a close. Luckily, Hills still owned the Lambourn stable in which his son John had been training, and with some hasty organising, was back there for 1991. Sangster's solution, to promote Peter Chapple-Hyam, son-in-law of his second wife Susan, was greeted with scepticism, but, as they say, the rest is history.

The continuing strength of the Sangster operation is the availability of high class stallions on either side of the Atlantic for the strong band of mares owned by Coolmore Stud, which he shares with Vincent O'Brien and John Magnier, and those of Swettenham Stud, which he owns himself.

In the States, El Gran Senor and Woodman are his leading stallions, while Sadler's Wells, Caerleon and Lomond are among his best European sires. El Gran Senor has done well despite fertility problems, and Rodrigo De Triano is probably his best son. This colt went unbeaten through the season, impressing particularly in the Middle Park Stakes over an inadequate six furlongs, beating subsequent Horris Hill winner Lion Cavern with a little to spare. Rodrigo De Triano looks certain to challenge for the mile classic races.

DR DEVIOUS, chestnut colt, Ahonoora–Rose of Jericho (Alleged)

With four wins in six races, Dr Devious was a superb foil for Rodrigo De Triano, and while in terms of performance it may not have been his best run, his second and £200,000 bonus in the Tattersalls Tiffany Highflyer Stakes missed the £500,000 bonanza by just a neck. He easily turned the tables on the winner Young Senor over the same course and distance in the Group One Dewhurst Stakes a fortnight later, by which time he was running for a new owner, the Italian, Mr Gaucci. Like Rodrigo De Triano, this tough colt has been brought along with great skill by Chapple-Hyam, and should continue to pay his way.

SEATTLE RHYME, chestnut colt, Seattle Dancer–Golden Rhyme (Dom Racine)

In the early 1980s the rivalry between the Sangster and Maktoum teams was nowhere more heated than in the Keeneland Sales ring. One July, I saw Sangster see off the Arabs by paying $13.1 million for a Northern Dancer colt, who ran only a few times, never living up to the price. But he is proving to be a promising young sire, and in Seatle Rhyme, Seattle Dancer has a live Classic hope, with the Ever Ready Derby as his principal objective. Seattle Rhyme demolished a class field in the Group One Racing Post Trophy at Doncaster in late October, maintaining the good impression of his earlier third behind Arazi in Paris. Improving with his races, Seattle Rhyme is a serious big-race challenger for 1992.

ST JOVITE, bay colt, Pleasant Colony–Northern Sunset (Northfields)

Jim Bolger has been gradually usurping Vincent O'Brien and Dermot Weld as the leading Irish trainer, and after setting a record number of winners in 1990, in 1991 he gained his first trainer's title in terms of money won. He also collected a first English Classic with Jet Ski Lady in the Gold Seal Oaks, and St Jovite will be a strong challenger to give the Irish their first Derby win since Secreto beat El Gran Senor in 1984.

St Jovite is owned and was bred by Virginia Kraft Payson, who has an exceptional record as a breeder, considering her broodmare band is only around twenty and she tends to go below the top echelon of stallions. The mare Northern Sunset had already produced a trio of high-class colts, Lac Ouimet and Salem Drive, both of whom stand at her Payson Stud in Lexington, and Norberto, who died soon after leaving France to continue a top-class career (he was placed in the French Derby behind Old Vic) in the United States. St Jovite, the only horse to lower El Prado's colours in Ireland, took an unbeaten record to the Grand Criterium in France in early October, and after making the running, dropped back before rallying to finish a close fourth, just behind Seattle Rhyme. The manner in which he battled on under pressure offers great encouragement for his future, and at this stage, I rate him my principal Derby hope. European racegoers may find his pedigree a little obscure, but Pleasant Colony won the Kentucky Derby and invariably gets good runners, while there is Northern Dancer (sire of Northfields) on the dam's side.

ASSESSOR, bay colt, Niniski–Dingle Bay (Habitat)

The New York-based commodity broker Bjorn Nielsen has made a serious inroad into racehorse ownership, with horses in the care of Richard Hannon and James Fanshawe. He had the unenviable distinction of having perhaps the unluckiest loser of 1991 when his filly Hamanaka unseated Walter Swinburn in the last five strides of a maiden race at Redcar when the saddle slipped. Assessor was also unlucky to an extent, in that when Bjorn supplemented him at £16,000 for the Racing Post Trophy he was hopeful of the soft ground which suits Assessor so well, and on which he had proved much too good for Young Senor at Ascot. But the rain kept away and Assessor could do not better than third, albeit a strong-running third to Seattle Rhyme. On that showing, Assessor looks an ideal St Leger type for 1992, but should the ground come up soft at Epsom or The Curragh in the middle of summer, then a far from forlorn case will be made for this good stayer whom Hannon should exploit with his customary skill.

MUSICALE, chestnut filly, The Minstrel–Gossiping (Chati)

Robert Sangster's successes in the 1991 season were not confined to horses trained at Manton or by Vincent O'Brien. Henry Cecil, John Gosden, Michael Stoute and Barry Hills all joined in the fun and Cecil guided Musicale to five wins from as many starts. The daughter of The Minstrel showed tremendous battling qualities, especially in the Rockfel Stakes, a performance which makes her a live One Thousand Guineas hope. Her stamina, speed and courage will be most useful as she meets less-experienced rivals early in the year, and whether or not she wins a Classic, more races should be within her grasp.

FAIR COP, bay colt, Al Nasr–Exclusive Life (Exclusive Native)

In early summer, it looked as though juveniles owned by Fahd Salman would sweep all before them for the rest of the year. Dilum, in beating Dr Devious in the Coventry Stakes, laid claims to being the leading two-year-old, a status which sadly he could not maintain. Magic Ring and Fair Cop also won at the Royal Meeting, and of the trio, Fair Cop did not run again. That could prove a blessing. He won the Chesham Stakes in good style and as long as he is not campaigned over-ambitiously, he should pay his way this year.

MYSTERY PLAY, bay filly, Sadler's Wells–Kereolle (Riverman)

Barry Hills has a good team for 1992, and Mystery Play, lightly raced at two, is a prime big-race candidate. She won her maiden in good style from Midnight Air at Newmarket and that filly's exhilarating win at Doncaster, followed by an unlucky disqualification as Ascot in favour of Culture Vulture, makes Midnight Air a top prospect. The one snag for Mystery Play's fans was that Sheikh Mohammed's filly also competed in the Ascot race and probably found the soft ground against her. She was almost three lengths behind the 'winner' but had the consolation of being promoted a place. Stamina will be her forte, and her main Classic interest could come in the Gold Seal Oaks at Epsom.

HATOOF, chestnut filly, Irish River–Cadeaux d'Amie (Lyphard)

The French invariably pose a bigger threat in the One Thousand Guineas than in the colts' mile classic, so it is usually wise to pursue the likely challengers for the fillies' Classic from that side of the Channel. No horse appeals more obviously from France than Hatoof, whose short-head defeat by Culture Vulture in the Prix Marcel Boussac was most unfortunate. She was hindered when one of her opponents broke a leg during the race, but rallied to such effect that she got on terms close home, only to lose the verdict on the nod. Hatoof has raced only at a mile so far, but has a fine turn of speed which would make her a threat to all at Newmarket in the spring.

KING OLAF, bay gelding, Thatching–Regiura (High Top)

As a gelding, King Olaf cannot be a Classic hope, and with his workmanlike pedigree, will probably be campaigned as a handicapper. But there was plenty to like about his single run in a Newmarket back-end maiden, when he was run out of it in the final stride by Youseffia. The verdict went against him there, but in 1992 King Olaf can maintain the high strike rate of trainer Peter Chapple-Hyam and owner Robert Sangster.

Musicale

OLDER HORSES

Mystiko

MYSTIKO, 4 years, grey colt, Secreto–Caracciola

It is rare enough for Classic winners to stay in training. But Mystiko is not back just to try to make a stud niche for himself. His owner Lady Beaverbrook has her horses to race and Mystiko proved that point when bouncing back to win the Challenge Stakes in the autumn after a midsummer slump. Clive Brittain guided the grey's career with skill and attack, and those qualities should ensure some more big pay-days in 1992.

SUAVE DANCER, 4 years, bay colt, Green Dancer–Suavite (Alleged)

With wins in the Arc and French Derby, Suave Dancer deserved a share of the 1991 honours with Generous, with whom he shared a one-all score, losing only in the Irish Derby. For a mile-and-a-half horse, he had blinding acceleration, and with a highly respectable Classic pedigree, could well be the type to attract breeders back to France. Cash Asmussen has skilfully handled the colt's career with trainer John Hammond, and further success looks guaranteed.

DESERT SUN, 4 years, bay colt, Green Desert–Solar (Hotfoot)

After coming through the winter as the top hope for the Two Thousand Guineas, Desert Sun fell away on the track, finishing only sixth in the Classic and even losing a small race at Yarmouth. But he came back in the autumn with an emphatic effort at Doncaster, beating Ristna, who later showed the worth of that effort when fourth in the Champion Stakes. At distances up to a mile, Desert Sun will be hard to beat in 1992 and races such as the Sussex Stakes look tailor-made for him.

Suave Dancer

CORRUPT, 4 years, bay colt, Lear Fan–
Nirvanita (Right Royal V)

The big races eluded Corrupt, who
failed when hopes were high both in
the Derby and St Leger. But wins at
Kempton, Lingfield (Derby Trial) and
York (Great Voltigeur) showed him a
class act on his day, which is generally
when he gets some give in the ground.
Granted such conditions, Corrupt will
be a force in top races at around a mile
and a half.

Corrupt

CRUACHAN, 4 years, bay colt, Lear Fan–Sugar Hollow (Val de l'Orne)

Guy Harwood must have been boiling when his impressive Glasgow Stakes winner Cruachan was injured just before the Ever Ready Derby, a race for which he and Corrupt, also by Lear Fan, would have been fierce rivals. But Cruachan came back later in the year and in running a good second to the French colt Tel Quel, proved his potential for the coming year. Cruachan got the mile and a quarter well enough, but his inadequate preparation made him a sitting duck when Tel Quel launched his final challenge. When they meet again it could be a different story.

Cruachan

1991 STATISTICS

The 1991 Flat season officially ends on 31 December to allow for all-weather racing until that date. The following statistics cover the year to 11 November, the date on which the Flat turf season came to a close at Folkestone.

JOCKEYS

	NAME	WINS	RIDES	%	2ND	3RD	£1 LEVEL STAKE
1	Pat Eddery	165	807	20	130	76	−£137.58
2	W. Carson	155	890	17	130	93	−£181.35
3	M. Roberts	118	864	14	109	96	− £13.71
4	A. Munro	109	780	14	91	78	− £69.06
5	S. Cauthen	107	472	23	79	57	− £15.41
6	R. Cochrane	102	718	14	103	84	− £28.08
7	L. Dettori	94	707	13	94	85	−£203.89
8	T. Quinn	93	661	14	78	78	−£422.28
9	J. Carroll	87	580	15	75	66	−£184.61
10	D. Holland	83	556	15	68	61	− £2.15
11	G. Duffield	81	618	13	44	61	−£107.13
12	J. Reid	80	676	12	94	74	− £94.55
13	G. Carter	74	595	12	59	58	−£172.68
14	Paul Eddery	72	666	11	62	62	−£141.78
15	B. Raymond	71	665	11	66	77	−£201.94
16	W.R. Swinburn	68	499	14	66	66	− £98.06
17	Dean McKeown	68	682	10	78	88	−£356.51
18	W. Ryan	67	467	14	67	43	−£227.61
19	K. Darley	66	576	11	63	66	−£253.81
20	R. Hills	63	465	14	59	58	+ **£48.60**
21	M. Hills	62	432	14	60	51	− £87.99
22	J. Williams	58	757	8	53	70	−£177.41
23	M. Birch	54	519	10	53	73	−£154.34
24	J. Lowe	54	641	8	60	57	−£286.92
25	L. Piggott	48	320	15	41	44	− £55.11
26	A.S. Cruz	43	370	12	40	48	− £54.56
27	J.K. Fanning	39	488	8	44	43	− £51.52
28	F. Norton	37	353	10	35	21	− £61.11
29	R. Perham	36	258	14	25	24	− £11.94
30	Alex Greaves	33	265	12	33	41	− £19.42

TRAINERS

	NAME	WIN & PLACE PRIZE MONEY	WIN PRIZE MONEY	WINS	RUNS	%	2ND	3RD	£1 LEVEL STAKE
1	P.F.I. Cole	£1,510,929	£1,264,071	70	376	19	55	43	− £25.43
2	R. Hannon	£1,342,392	£872,906	126	951	13	121	103	−£142.52
3	M.R. Stoute	£1,282,833	£825,838	83	412	20	57	44	− £56.70
4	C.E. Brittain	£1,164,499	£732,442	53	543	10	53	55	−£115.41
5	J.L. Dunlop	£1,040,654	£616,648	58	366	16	48	47	− £64.14
6	L.M. Cumani	£1,009,207	£574,600	72	334	22	60	42	− £63.43
7	H.R.A. Cecil	£980,647	£666,974	118	378	31	80	59	+ £15.10
8	B.W. Hills	£916,104	£606,221	98	481	20	87	57	+ £15.43
9	J. Berry	£872,625	£602,490	143	834	17	112	110	−£181.88
10	D.R.C. Elsworth	£792,256	£519,934	38	349	11	40	37	− £97.66
11	J.H.M. Gosden	£657,094	£452,273	84	376	22	57	43	− £5.12
12	I.A. Balding	£638,839	£449,794	53	362	15	49	43	− £46.92
13	A. Fabre	£634,708	£507,492	5	12	42	3	0	+ £15.94
14	G. Harwood	£621,994	£371,865	55	325	17	47	41	− £46.76
15	G. Wragg	£550,207	£400,278	50	215	23	38	20	+ £26.18
16	Lord Huntingdon	£502,886	£427,232	36	250	14	33	27	+ £95.26
17	M.H. Easterby	£489,812	£328,882	58	531	11	58	68	−£187.04
18	P.W. Chapple-Hyam	£434,777	£385,024	27	112	24	11	12	+ £20.35
19	J.R. Fanshawe	£399,799	£350,911	22	152	14	13	15	+ £7.14
20	R. Akehurst	£389,765	£272,086	41	293	14	35	25	+ £30.71
21	R. Charlton	£367,939	£103,892	26	178	15	31	18	− £55.48
22	M. Moubarak	£363,873	£294,546	18	128	14	18	16	− £10.67
23	M.H. Tompkins	£313,457	£229,422	41	394	10	35	43	−£111.54
24	W.R. Hern	£310,236	£139,134	23	138	17	25	14	− £27.87
25	J.S. Bolger	£295,625	£163,030	2	20	10	2	1	+ £40.00
26	A.A. Scott	£294,679	£194,381	22	222	10	23	29	−£114.18
27	P.T. Walwyn	£265,776	£134,205	24	254	9	26	21	− £93.99
28	P.J. Makin	£264,388	£188,948	22	184	12	34	19	− £41.46
29	M. Bell	£251,430	£181,727	43	278	15	36	27	+ £13.14
30	G. Lewis	£245,779	£166,521	41	354	12	45	35	− £41.71

OWNERS

	NAME	1ST	2ND	3RD	WIN & PLACE PRIZE MONEY
1	Sheikh Mohammed	139	129	104	£1,834,590
2	Hamdan Al Maktoum	92	87	69	£1,338,766
3	Fahd Salman	47	28	27	£1,156,945
4	K. Abdullah	71	46	24	£801,650
5	Maktoum Al Maktoum	33	24	21	£643,532
6	R.E. Sangster	54	34	32	£570,606
7	Lady Beaverbrook	18	11	5	£498,262
8	David Thompson	17	10	13	£374,085
9	A.F. Budge Ltd	25	22	24	£373,534
10	George Strawbridge	10	5	6	£356,212
11	Ecurie Fustok	16	14	15	£353,308
12	Lord Weinstock	18	16	13	£276,762
13	Luciano Gaucci	6	6	7	£240,851
14	W.J. Gredley	5	2	5	£235,447
15	Richard L. Duchossois	10	4	2	£222,801
16	Brian Cooper	3	1	2	£203,611
17	Mitsuo Haga	1	1	0	£202,183
18	P.D. Savill	33	29	31	£197,214
19	Christopher Wright	12	7	9	£193,733
20	C.A.B. St George	13	8	7	£191,059
21	R.A. Kirstein	3	0	0	£170,732
22	D.F. Cock	7	1	2	£164,409
23	H.J. Senn	3	1	0	£163,656
24	Lord White of Hull	12	13	6	£159,689
25	Paul Mellon	14	18	19	£158,725
26	Hilal Salem	3	2	1	£156,761
27	E.J. Loder	4	1	1	£146,933
28	Brian Brackpool	3	1	1	£145,519
29	P.E.T. Chandler	6	2	0	£139,753
30	S. Harper	3	4	1	£136,429